CHILDREN LIVING IN TRANSITION

Children Living in Transition

*HELPING HOMELESS AND FOSTER
CARE CHILDREN AND FAMILIES*

Cheryl Zlotnick

EDITOR

 COLUMBIA UNIVERSITY PRESS   NEW YORK

COLUMBIA UNIVERSITY PRESS
Publishers Since 1893
New York   Chichester, West Sussex

cup.columbia.edu

Library of Congress Cataloging-in-Publication Data

Children living in transition : helping homeless and foster care children and families /
edited by Cheryl Zlotnick.
    pages cm
  Includes bibliographical references and index.
  ISBN 978-0-231-16096-4 (cloth : alk. paper) — ISBN 978-0-231-16097-1 (pbk. : alk. paper) —
ISBN 978-0-231-53600-4 (ebook)
  1. Foster children. 2. Foster parents. 3. Foster home care. 4. Homeless children.
  I. Zlotnick, Cheryl, editor of compilation.

HV873.C48 2014
362.73'3—dc23

2013034468

Cover design: Julia Kushnirsky
Cover illustration: Claire Lazarus

We write this book in honor of the strength, courage, and resilience of families living in transition, whether they are temporarily residing in homeless shelters, foster care, doubled-up situations, or a series of different locations with friends or family.

We wish to dedicate this book:

- to the frontline workers, including medical, nursing, mental health, case management, outreach, and social service professionals, who are committed to helping families in transition to obtain greater stability and improved living situations;
- to the administrators and office workers who support the programs' operation, without whom the work to support transitional families would not be possible; and
- to the memory of Mohini Singh and Ellen Eve Seligman, our beloved colleagues at the Center for the Vulnerable Child (CVC), who worked tirelessly to support families in transition.

CONTENTS

IN THE UNITED STATES, an increasing number of children are being shuffled from one transitional and temporary situation to another: living with family or friends, staying in homeless shelters, residing in other kinds of out-of-home placements (away from birth parents) such as foster care or group homes. Why are children and families living in these transitional situations? Many researchers and administrators believe there are two major contributing factors: (1) intergenerational poverty, combined with a shortage of affordable permanent housing, transitional housing, and long-term family shelters; and (2) parents suffering from trauma, mental illness, and substance abuse problems.

For adults who are in the transitional living situation of homelessness, day-to-day life is a struggle, but when the family unit includes children, the challenges are multiplied. Children are still growing and developing. Living in unsafe environments inflicts not only physical harm but also psychological harm on children. Both have potentially permanent deleterious ramifications. For some children, the psychological stress of living in transition is compounded by growing up with parents who are suffering from trauma, mental illness, and/or substance abuse. Families who live in shelters or who have had contact with the child welfare system are exposed to the scrutiny of representatives from shelters, police and criminal justice departments, substance abuse or mental health treatment centers, and schools. If the representatives of these entities believe that the children are living in potentially dangerous situations, they can begin procedures to have them removed from their birth parents and placed in foster care.

Although homeless shelters and other tenuous living situations are far from ideal, children placed with friends/family or in foster care may experience this change as even more isolating and scary than the homeless shelters where they have been living. After all, placement in foster homes or with friends/family separates them from the one constant in their lives—their birth parent(s). Disconnection from parents coupled with yet another change in residence results in anxiety and trauma, which different children express in different ways. While some children exhibit aggressive and angry behaviors, others appear to be completely withdrawn, docile, or even willing to approach and embrace utter strangers. It is not easy to provide care for children who are exhibiting difficult behaviors as a result of trauma. Unfortunately, in some situations the difficult behaviors, which may be linked to instability, may precipitate further instability. For example, a child who has lived in a series of homeless shelters with his or her birth parents and then, due to family circumstances, is placed in foster care, may begin exhibiting aggressive and hostile behaviors as a result of the accumulating stress and trauma. Not all foster parents are able to cope with these difficult behaviors. Some may request that the child be removed from their home and placed in another foster home. This scenario is not uncommon. Sadly, the children who exhibit the behaviors that are most difficult to deal with are often the very children who are suffering most from trauma and who will be further destabilized and traumatized by cycling through a series of foster care placements.

Perhaps the one advantage for children who are "in the system" is that they are known to the child welfare, health, or social services agencies, and therefore have access to resources. Conversely, children who have no stable residence but constantly move from place to place, rather than staying in homeless shelters, are unlikely to be in the system, and because they are unknown, they are unlikely to be offered assistance. This situation is common among undocumented and poor immigrant families who live in unstable accommodations. The heads of households, new to the United States, are unfamiliar with available services and how to obtain them. Moreover, neither the families nor the children are known to the public systems. Since they are invisible to those systems, their needs go unnoticed and they are more likely to fall through the cracks. This population of children is hard to find, and much less is known about them than about the children who are living in transitional situations such as homeless shelters or foster care.

Children in the latter category are more likely to experience high rates of school absenteeism, learning difficulties, grade failures, school suspensions, risky sexual behaviors, and contact with the juvenile justice system. An alarmingly high number of youths who age out of the foster care system enter the ranks of the homeless adult population. Targeted, early interventions can reduce the stress that such transition imposes on families and children, and may reduce the likelihood that foster placement will become necessary, or at least reduce the number of placement changes necessary if foster care is required. Interventions with children/youth earlier in life may have a lasting impact that may reduce the cycle of homelessness in which a formerly homeless child becomes a currently homeless adult. Collaborations among service agencies and systems are essential for all children living in transition, whether they are part of new immigrant families living in unstable situations, families living in homeless shelters, or families who are part of the foster care system.

This book addresses these issues. It represents the culmination of more than two decades of experience among staff of the Center for the Vulnerable Child (CVC), who provide community-based mental health and intensive case management services to more than 3,000 children and families living in transient and impoverished situations. The services described here are unique and emanate from a multidisciplinary, community-based, social justice approach along with the philosophy that although we may provide guidance and assistance, family members bring their own wisdom and have their own culture that must be embraced and incorporated into any plan of care.

In keeping with our philosophy, we discuss here the journey that individual staff members, programs, and the department undertook so that all staff, but particularly clinicians, became more aware of the influences that power, privilege, and beliefs have had on their own upbringing and education, and the impact that these factors ultimately have had on their approach and their ability to provide effective treatment. This issue is particularly important since many U.S. children who currently live in impoverished homeless shelters, unstable residences, or foster care family situations are children of color, from families that have multigenerational histories of living in poverty, and often lack education. In contrast, the helping professionals whom they encounter are usually white, middle class, and college-educated.

As you read this book, you will explore with us the challenges that different families confront, and join the clinicians who hear about the histories of trauma, and the struggles of the parents and children. You will read about how the clinicians assess the situational context and the cultural issues, and will learn about approaches that are being used to engage families who all too often feel either disrespected by the assistance meted out by the helping professionals or betrayed by their forgotten promises. This book does not shy away from discussing both the successes and the failures of working with families living in transition, but it also offers hope for an evolving multidisciplinary, community-outreach approach that maintains the core value of respecting family, culture, strength, and wisdom.

Please note that names of family members described in the vignettes and cases presented in the text have been changed.

CHILDREN LIVING IN TRANSITION

PART 1

Theories of Practice with Transitional Families

Many families living in transitional situations are stressed, in crisis, and have histories of multigenerational trauma. A disproportionate number of them are from diverse ethnic and racial groups that have historically suffered from racism and oppression. Usually they have encountered more than one "helping professional." The families' investment of time, emotion, and effort has been burdensome but often yields no results.

You want to make a difference. Where do you start?

Chapter 1 offers theoretical frameworks from the perspectives of public health, social justice, and child development. Chapters 2 and 3 use these approaches and demonstrate the vital importance that cultures and history play in client responses. Surprisingly, there is unity in these perspectives that can guide clinicians in practice, administrators in creating programs, and researchers in focusing their studies.

CHAPTER 1

Transitional Families

WHERE DO I BEGIN?

▸ *CHERYL ZLOTNICK AND LUANN DEVOSS*

TRANSITIONAL FAMILIES—WHO ARE THEY?

TRANSITIONAL FAMILIES ARE A UNIQUE and growing population. "Transitional" means that some aspect of the family is in flux. It can be the family structure, the living situation, or both. There is no single type of transitional family. An example of a transitional living situation is homelessness, which is most apparent when families are living in shelters. According to the U.S. Department of Housing and Urban Development (2010), 1.56 million people used homeless shelters and emergency homeless centers between October 1, 2008, and September 30, 2009, and a third of them were families. Some homeless individuals and families are constantly on the move, looking for a place to spend the night. One day they may stay with friends, the next day at a shelter, and the day after that they may be living under a bridge, in a car, or in an abandoned building. Some individuals and families who have no residence avoid going to shelters, choosing to rely on family and friends for a place to stay. This "doubled-up" family lifestyle is common among immigrant families and families with histories of intergenerational poverty. The number of families staying in doubled-up situations—defined as staying temporarily in the homes of others rather than entering homeless shelters—is increasing (U.S. Department of Housing and Urban Development—Office of Community Planning and Development, 2010). Understandably, enumeration of this subgroup is difficult. Whether families are temporarily residing in homeless shelters or staying with family/friends, their situation is virtually the same. They have no stable residence, and no secure place to call home.

"Transitional" can also mean an unstable family unit or a change in the family members. For example, if the parents become incapacitated or incarcerated or unable to care for their children, they may decide it is in the best interest of the child for him or her to live in a more stable residence with family or friends. As with the doubled-up family situations described above, there is no clear methodology to tabulate the numbers of children living in these temporary informal arrangements. Another example is involuntary child placement, in which the parents are charged with neglect or abuse and the government-supported child welfare system takes custody of their children. In this situation, the child usually is placed in foster care or a group home. In 2008, almost half a million children were in foster care at any given time (Children's Bureau, 2009). Parental substance abuse is among the leading causes of children's entering the foster care system (U.S. General Accounting Office, 1997).

Although children living in homeless situations and children entering foster care appear to constitute very different populations, an increasing number of studies have helped to elucidate the overlap. In fact, the overlap or cycle of homelessness and foster care occurs at several junctures throughout childhood. The cycle begins with mothers (of children under age 18) who live in homeless situations. Several studies have demonstrated that the majority of children under age 18 who are in homeless situations are living with someone besides their parents. In fact, as many as 24% of homeless mothers have children in the foster care system (Burt, Aron, & Lee, 2001; Zlotnick, Tam, & Bradley, 2007). One study found that almost half of the young children entering foster care had been removed from homeless families (Zlotnick, Kronstadt, & Klee, 1998). In adolescence, the overlap is even more striking, as large numbers of homeless or runaway adolescents report histories of being in foster care or group homes; and conversely, large numbers of foster care or group home youth report histories of running away or being homeless (Greene, Ennett, & Ringwalt, 1997; Kushel, Yen, Gee, & Courtney, 2007). This pattern of overlap continues as foster care youth "graduates" experience episodes of homelessness in adulthood at astonishingly high rates within 18 months of exiting the foster care system (Courtney & Dworsky, 2006; Kushel et al., 2007).

The children living in transitional families, whether in homeless, doubled-up, or foster care situations, have three characteristics in common. The first is that these population subgroups have a history of living in poverty. In fact, many have lived in poverty for generations. Homelessness is a manifestation of extreme poverty, and many of those who are heads of homeless households have grown up in poverty and on welfare (Weitzman, Knickman, & Shinn, 1990). Children and families living in doubled-up situations as a result of unstable residence find themselves relying on family and friends who themselves have very low incomes and live in impoverished circumstances (Bolland & McCallum, 2002). Likewise, children entering the foster care system are more likely to have been removed from very low-income or poor families, rather than from middle- or upper-class homes (Nelson, 1992).

The second common characteristic in the population of transitional families is the disproportionality of children of color. African American or black individuals constitute 12.6% of the U.S. population, while Latino or Hispanic individuals account for 16.3% (U.S. Census Bureau, 2011). Yet, in the homeless population, almost half the homeless families are African American or black, and another quarter are Latino or Hispanic (U.S. Department of Housing and Urban Development—Office of Community Planning and Development, 2010). Similarly, in foster care almost 30% of the children are African American or black and about 20% are Latino/Hispanic (Children's Bureau, 2009). Historically the foster care population was composed of children from new immigrant families, many of whom were economically disadvantaged, socially isolated, and lacking in the resources that had been available to most others in the general population (Rosner & Markowitz, 1997). Rosner and Markowitz noted that in 1942, the state of New York had an influx of black children who were in need of foster care, but the agencies of that period refused to admit the children because of their skin color. Sadly, by 1955, the vast majority of children being placed in foster care in New York were black children. Similarly, children "of color" still account for the majority of children in foster care today.

The third common characteristic is the insidiousness of parental trauma and comorbidity of substance abuse or mental illness. Although not all heads of household of homeless families suffer from one or both of these morbidities, there is evidence that the incidence of these problems is higher among parents in homeless families than among those in poor but stably housed families (Shinn et al., 1998). Linked to these morbidities is the presence of childhood and adulthood trauma. That is, mothers—the vast majority of homeless families are headed by single women (Burt, Aron, & Lee, 2001)—with long histories of substance abuse or mental health problems are more likely to have experienced the trauma of childhood physical abuse or sexual abuse, and to have histories of living in childhood foster care themselves (Zlotnick, Tam, & Bradley, 2010).

A PUBLIC HEALTH ISSUE . . .

What perspective or stance will help clinicians, administrators, and policy-makers better understand transitional families? First, the proliferation of transitional families is a serious public health issue. A public health issue is one that suggests that an increased risk of morbidity or mortality is being experienced by either part or all of the population. Poverty, which once was viewed as solely an economic issue, qualifies as a public health issue. Socioeconomic status is the single greatest predictor of health status, and overwhelming evidence demonstrates that prevalence rates of acute and chronic illness are higher among children living in poor families than children living in middle- or higher-income families; and compared to poor stably housed children, homeless children exhibit even higher rates of morbidity (Bassuk & Rosenberg, 1990; Shinn, Rog, & Culhane, 2005; Woolf, Johnson, & Geiger, 2006; Wood, Valdez, Hayashi, & Shen, 1990; Zima, Wells, Benjamin, & Duan, 1996).

Second, although homeless families and families living in poverty share the characteristic of impoverishment, there is clear evidence that children and their parents who have been identified as homeless are *different* from housed families who live in poverty. Their levels of morbidity are different; and their histories are different. Homeless mothers, compared to poor stably housed mothers, are more likely to have experienced childhood traumas such as foster care and to have been the victims of rape or physical attack as adults (Bassuk et al., 1996; Shinn, Knickman, & Weitzman, 1991).

Like children who have lived in homelessness, children in foster care experience higher rates of acute disease, chronic physical illnesses, and behavioral and mental health problems than other children do (Halfon, Mendonca, & Berkowitz, 1995; McMillen et al., 2004; Schorr, 1982). Often these problems are linked to school-related problems. Festering and untreated issues among young school-age children lead to more serious social consequences later, in adolescence. Unfortunately, an unstable family life adds yet another layer of difficulty to requesting or receiving health or social service interventions. The adolescence of many youth in transitional living situations is punctuated by difficulties in school, risky sexual behaviors, and contact with the criminal justice system (Kushel et al., 2007). Are the differences in health status related to transiency and the inability to gain access to or obtain needed health services? Does the answer lie with the environmental conditions found in homeless shelters; or with the stress and problems preceding and perhaps even increasing as a result of being separated from birth parents and being placed in foster care? Or are these differences attributable to intergenerational poverty mixed with the parents' morbidity and accumulation of daily stresses and crises? No clear answers have been found to these questions.

What is the impact of such difficult beginnings for children when they reach adulthood? Studies have just begun investigating this issue. The rather static public health perspective of assessing inequities in health status outcomes among population subgroups has been expanded by an interesting framework called Life Course Epidemiology. Life Course Epidemiology is the multidisciplinary study of the dynamic and long-term effects of a physical or social exposure that occurs during gestation, childhood, or adolescence (Kuh, Ben-Shlomo, Lynch, Hallqvist, & Power, 2003). Few doubt that a permanently physically disabling condition suffered as an infant will have long-term ramifications, even throughout adulthood. Yet it is only recently that mainstream epidemiology has accepted the idea that long-term effects in adulthood may result from psychosocial traumas sustained in childhood. The Life Course framework suggests that psychosocial and physical exposures in childhood and even in utero may have an impact later, in adulthood. Furthermore, the Life Course framework suggests that effects from the initial exposure may have cumulative effects due to the damage from added illness, injury, environmental conditions, and health behaviors. Studies employing this framework have found surprising results. For example, in one recent study a history of childhood foster care was associated with worse physical and mental health, and higher rates of chronic disability later in life, even after adjusting for age (Zlotnick, Tam, & Soman, 2012). This study was unable to adjust for the duration of childhood foster care (i.e., longer versus shorter periods of being in foster care) or to determine whether the most detrimental exposure was foster care or the *events* that led to foster care placement. Still, the study indicates that whether the traumatic episode was entering foster care or the situation that necessitated foster care, the traumatic episode was associated with later morbidity. This same finding was noted in a British study with a longitudinal cohort of adults who had histories of being in the child welfare system (Viner & Taylor, 2005). In fact, one study found that the childhood exposure of being raised in poverty appeared to be linked to morbidity and even cardiovascular mortality (Kuh, Hardy, Langenberg, Richards, & Wadsworth, 2002). An increasing number of studies are examining the Life Course framework, but more investigation is needed to assess whether there is a particular point in childhood that is more vulnerable to change than others, and which specific interventions are most effective for ameliorating or reducing the long-term adulthood ramifications of childhood trauma. Still, existing evidence supports the need for health officials, researchers, and practitioners first to determine which type of early intervention program would be most effective and then to implement that program in order to stabilize children who are living in transitional conditions.

. . . AND A SOCIAL JUSTICE ISSUE

Equally important, the disparities between the treatment received by families in transition and the treatment received by other families make it a social justice issue. A social justice issue is one in which there is evidence of disparities in treatment and those disparities are promoted by existing institutional practices, procedures, policies, or laws. Living in the transitional situations of homelessness and foster care or group homes is disproportionately prevalent among very low-income families. Among low-income families, disproportionately more families of color, particularly in the African American community, have children entering the foster care system or residing in homeless shelters or transitional housing.

These inequities are reported by the U.S. government in the *2009 Annual Homeless Assessment Report to Congress (AHAR)* (U.S. Department of Housing and Urban Development—Office of Community Planning and Development, 2010). The report, which attempts to count and describe the characteristics of the U.S. homeless population, notes that poverty is the primary reason that individuals and families have no stable place to live. Moreover, the existing shelter system and bed capacity are inadequate, which requires use of overflow beds and other means to address the shortage. Utilization rates of the existing system average over 80%. *AHAR* notes that communities have been encouraged to create more permanent, low-cost housing for poor individuals and families. Meanwhile, impoverished transitional families have less access to housing than other families do.

Poverty is not the only social justice issue found among transitional families. Ethnic/racial disparities were also noted. *AHAR* 2009 demonstrated that white, non-Hispanic individuals were disproportionately less likely to live in poverty or to live in a homeless shelter than were Latinos/ Hispanics and African Americans or blacks. The same report also found that of the approximately 16% of the U.S. population who were categorized as Hispanic/Latino, 25% had lived in poverty and 20% had lived in homeless shelters. Similarly, of the more than 12% of the U.S. population who were categorized as African American or black, 22% had lived in poverty and 39% had lived in homeless shelters (U.S. Department of Housing and Urban Development, 2010).

These ethnic/racial disparities also are found among children entering the foster care system. While approximately 12% of the U.S. population is African American or black, 31% of foster children are African American or black (Children's Bureau, 2009). Furthermore, this inequity appears to be perpetuated by the low numbers of African American or black children who are reunified with birth parents compared to the numbers of white and Latino children who are reunified (Children's Bureau, 2005; Westat, Inc., & Chapin Hall Center for Children, 2001), as well as in the disproportionate allocation of services available to children and families in foster care (Garland et al., 2000).

Another social justice concern is the overrepresentation of lesbian, gay, bisexual, transgendered, and queer (LGBTQ) youth in the child welfare system and living on the streets. Between 20% and 40% of all homeless youth identify as LGBTQ, yet they account for only between 3% and 5% of the entire U.S. population (Ray, 2006). Even more troubling is the finding of one study, that 65% of the LGBTQ youth reported having been in a child welfare placement at some point in their life (Berberet, 2006). The disparity between youth in the general population and LGBTQ youth in homeless and child welfare populations suggests the contribution of family or societal rejection based on sexual orientation, affection, or gender identity.

The public health perspective indicates long-term impact among population subgroups and the social justice perspective describes long-term inequities among impoverished, disenfranchised population subgroups. Together they indicate (1) the breadth of the risk factors that are produced or magnified by inequities, whether biological, physical, social, or psychological, and (2) the lifelong impact of these risk factors. Even worse, when considered together, these two perspectives illustrate a very troubling picture of compounding inequities and risk factors that are not bound within a single generation, but perpetuate the trauma that has affected the mother, passing on the effects that will shape the life course of the unborn child.

A FRAMEWORK

How do these inequities influence families living in transition and the health and social service professionals who are providing interventions? Urie Bronfenbrenner's bioecological theory describes them. He envisions the world as a series of concentric onion-like layers, with the child or the microsystem at the center (Bronfenbrenner, 1979, 1986, 1988, 2005) (fig. 1.1). Each successive environmental layer influences the others, but the layers closest to the center (and to the child) are the ones that have the greatest influence (called the mesosystem). Usually the parents occupy this closest layer and are therefore the most influential teachers and role models for the child. Influence is reciprocal: the child has an impact on the parents and the parents have an impact on the child. Later, as the child grows and develops, the mesosystem expands to include schools and peers, and the influences that result from interactions with these systems. Another layer of influence positioned even further from the child (or microsystem) than the mesosystem is the exosystem. The exosystem comprises structures and systems that have less-frequent contact with the child, and sometimes indirect contact through the parents. Components of the exosystem include health, social services, and other helping professionals. The amount of influence is generally directly proportional to the amount of contact; consequently, it is important that we remind ourselves that we have less contact with the child than other individuals and systems do, and therefore they may have a greater effect than we do. Finally, even more distal to exosystem is the macrosystem of culture, government policies, community influences that may

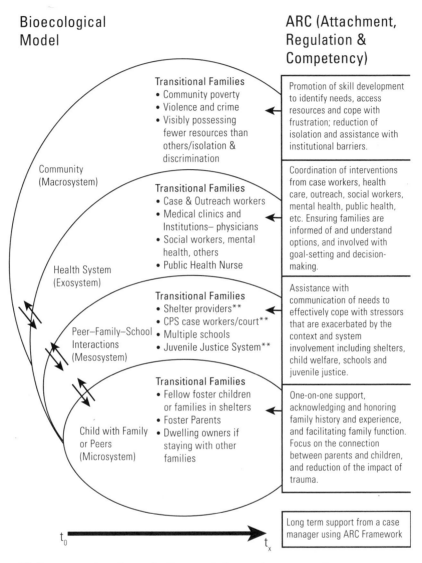

Bioecological Model

ARC (Attachment, Regulation & Competency)

Transitional Families
- Community poverty
- Violence and crime
- Visibly possessing fewer resources than others/isolation & discrimination

Promotion of skill development to identify needs, access resources and cope with frustration; reduction of isolation and assistance with institutional barriers.

Community (Macrosystem)

Transitional Families
- Case & Outreach workers
- Medical clinics and Institutions– physicians
- Social workers, mental health, others
- Public Health Nurse

Coordination of interventions from case workers, health care, outreach, social workers, mental health, public health, etc. Ensuring families are informed of and understand options, and involved with goal-setting and decision-making.

Health System (Exosystem)

Transitional Families
- Shelter providers**
- CPS case workers/court**
- Multiple schools
- Juvenile Justice System**

Assistance with communication of needs to effectively cope with stressors that are exacerbated by the context and system involvement including shelters, child welfare, schools and juvenile justice.

Peer–Family–School Interactions (Mesosystem)

Transitional Families
- Fellow foster children or families in shelters
- Foster Parents
- Dwelling owners if staying with other families

One-on-one support, acknowledging and honoring family history and experience, and facilitating family function. Focus on the connection between parents and children, and reduction of the impact of trauma.

Child with Family or Peers (Microsystem)

Long term support from a case manager using ARC Framework

t_0 ⟶ t_x

**Influences vary depending on situation – may be in exosystem or mesosystem

FIGURE 1.1 Bioecological Model (Bronfenbrenner, 1979) and ARC Framework (Blaustein & Kinniburgh, 2010. Copyright Guilford Press. Information reprinted graphically with permission of Guilford Press. Guide Trauma-Informed, Case-Management and Mental Health Services for Families Living in Transition. Note: This graphic has been adapted by the author from information in the above sources, but not directly reprinted.

include high crime and unemployment, and other structures that influence everyday life in a much less tangible but very real way.

A final structure of this model, which is *not* included in the concentric layers but is nevertheless very important, is time. As a child learns, develops, and gains experiences, the knowledge and perspectives are reinforced and become more and more entrenched.

The bioecological theory and its layers of influences clearly illustrate that children and families living in poverty and struggling with transitional situations including foster care and homelessness will be influenced by those struggles; by the health and social service organizations with which they come in contact; by the neighborhood residents who also may feel hopeless, frustrated, distrustful, and angry; and by the environment itself. Consistent with the Life Course framework, the bioecological theory acknowledges that the influences of these many layers on the child may increase or decrease, as will the resulting attitudes or behaviors, with the total impact accumulating over time.

This model shows the layers of influences on children who are growing up in transitional families. They feel the strongest influences from their parents; they absorb their parents' stresses, tension, and anguish (microsystem). Often, in precarious doubled-up situations, homeless shelters, or foster care homes, there are other individuals and families (mesosystem), who also are experiencing stressful life circumstances, sometimes compounded by substance abuse or mental health problems and histories of intergenerational poverty and inequity. The lives of children and families living in transition are complicated, and crowded. Caseworkers, the juvenile justice system, and even case managers or public health nurses may be involved. In some situations, these figures may exert a powerful, intrusive, and authoritative influence that equals the influence of foster parents or shelter providers (mesosystem), while in other cases the involvement may be infrequent and less strong (exosystem). The environment (macrosystem) has both tangible and intangible components. From a distance, children living in transition observe the treatment of others and compare it to the treatment that they and their families receive. They observe their own living situation and compare it to that of others around them. They quickly understand what it means to live in poverty, to be vigilant of daily threats of violence and crime, and to realize that others living in nontransitional situations do not have the same stressors that they do. As both Bronfenbrenner's bioecological theory and the Life Course framework indicate, the impact of these influences does not abruptly change, even if the child moves to a more stable situation. Instead, it becomes a part of the complicated, intricate history of the developing child.

THE ROLE OF PARENTS AND HEALTH/SOCIAL SERVICE PROFESSIONALS IN TRANSITIONAL FAMILIES

Still, at the core of the bioecological theory is the nature of the parent-child relationship, and transiency can interfere with this relationship. Parents in homeless families are distracted by their daily struggle for basic needs, and obtaining food, clothing, education, child care, employment, legal aid, and public assistance is prioritized over parent-child time. Moreover, because of the instability of living conditions, the parents usually are unable to institute a routine. Routine adds the comfort of structure and establishes a clear understanding of family members' roles and relationships. Within this structure, the child has the ability to learn about the environment. Moreover, it affords parents time with their children. For homeless families, times of waking up or going to bed, attending school, or even having regular meals may fluctuate daily. Equally problematic are the parents' stress, worry, and frustration, all of which may be absorbed by the child.

Given the nature of the child's contact with caseworkers or social workers in the child welfare system, or case managers who work daily with families in homeless shelters, it may be argued that the influence and the invasiveness of these people are so strong that their impact on the child is best described as being at the level of the mesosystem or even the microsystem. The individuals working in these systems have a great deal of power with respect to the parents or caregivers, and have both direct and indirect influences on how the children are treated. For example, in homeless shelters, case managers and shelter providers may enforce rules that govern allowable and prohibited behaviors. They have the power to evict a family if a child (or a parent) exhibits one of the prohibited behaviors. A foster care family has a similar situation. Child welfare workers have the authority to overrule a foster parent's decisions on parenting. For example, if a foster parent searched the child's room because of suspicion of drug use, the child welfare caseworker may insist that the foster parent cease this activity because it can be viewed as an invasion of privacy.

The impact of these authority figures can increase the stress of the transitional living situation. To make matters worse, other crises are often ongoing as well. For homeless families, it may be the daily struggle of securing housing, finding food, and obtaining transportation to take children to school. For foster families, it may be the struggle of engaging newly placed children who have been traumatized by events preceding foster care. To add to the stresses, intrusions and demands made by authority figures external to the family, such as the child welfare system or the criminal justice system, may play a role. These entities have the power to dictate to the family what they can and cannot do, which not only can diminish the integrity and function of the family unit but also can in some cases make the heads of households feel that their authority is subjugated and undermined (Zlotnick, Wright, Sanchez, Murga-Kusnir, & Te'o-Bennett, 2010).

PRIORITIES AND TRAUMA

The needs of the homeless family or the family in transition can be overwhelming for the provider. There are some consistencies regardless of the variation in presenting problem and developmental stage of the child(ren), and there are also some significant differences in treatment approach and priorities. The first step for health professionals is building alliances, beginning to establish a relationship with the caregivers in the family. However, the parents may not rank either mental health services or building a relationship with a clinician as high a priority as seeking the basic needs of food/shelter and safety. As Maslow's (1954) hierarchy of needs theory suggests, the most basic physiological and safety needs must be met before more-complex needs such as love and belonging, self-esteem, and self-actualization can be addressed. The clinician will want to assess the family's situation, and the possibility that the family may be struggling to meet the most basic needs. The parents may want assistance with health or mental health services, but the basic needs *must* take priority.

Providers working in the community speak of "meeting clients where they are." The expression means that the providers recognize the importance of the clients' perspective and the social and physical environment in which they live. Moreover, it indicates that the provider will assess the clients' goals, priorities, and the context of their living situations before deciding on the treatment and services that the clients need. This approach is crucial, since many clients will be seeking assistance with basic needs such as food, housing, or transportation. Although it may seem untraditional to expect mental health workers, therapists, and psychologists, whose role is providing mental health services, to assess the living situation and consider helping the family with basic needs, it often is an essential prerequisite to the goal of alliance building or establishing a relationship. In the context of the families' circumstances, this approach is a well-established practice among agencies working with homeless families and children (Zlotnick & Marks, 2002). It serves two purposes: it demonstrates that the provider is listening to the client and responding to some of the family's needs, and it marks the first step in building a relationship on which therapy is based.

Although this is an important first step, it is just a beginning. It is difficult to persuade transitional families not only to acknowledge that they need mental health services but also to accept them. Children and families living in homeless, doubled-up, or foster care situations have long histories of trauma. The trauma may result from an acute event such as a car accident, or it may be the result of a series of chronic, recurring, and accumulating events such as living in impoverished conditions without sufficient safety, food, or shelter; experiencing daily victimization, violence, and death; feeling increasingly helpless and hopeless; and becoming convinced that the situation will *never* improve. Often families in such dire situations have sought help from professionals and have been disappointed. Such encounters merely reinforce the families' belief that no one can or will help, and therefore further contribute to the families' trauma. As a result, it is rare for families who live in these difficult situations to seek assistance. More likely, the health professional or clinician will need to take the initiative and meet the family at the location where they are staying. An important issue that is not often addressed in such situations is the necessity of considering the safety of everyone: the caregivers, the children, and the health professional. The presence of substance abuse or domestic violence may compromise the safety of all those involved, and it is vital to address these problems first, before the health professional attempts to initiate a relationship with the family.

Trauma manifests itself differently in adults and in children. In fact, even fetuses are affected by trauma. For example, pregnant women with post-traumatic stress disorder (PTSD), a condition associated with suffering from a past trauma, are more likely to experience ectopic pregnancies, spontaneous abortions, hyperemesis, and other prenatal complications (Seng et al., 2001). Studies suggest that strong emotion increases the production of maternal prenatal cortisol, a substance that not only has an impact on the pregnant woman but also crosses the placenta and affects fetal development (Field & Diego, 2008).

For families with histories of trauma—and most transitional families have such histories—the Attachment, Self-Regulation, and Competency (ARC) model provides a structure for thinking about this stage of treatment (Blaustein & Kinniburgh, 2010) (see fig. 1.1). The first step is to examine the relationship between the caregiver and the child. Many times the caregivers do not have a secure **attachment** (the **A** in the ARC model) to their own primary caregivers; if that is the case, they may need specific guidance on how to build positive relationships with their own children and how to develop the most secure attachment possible under the circumstances.

Attachment is extremely important for growth and development of infants and toddlers. Very young children, from birth to three years, depend on a single, consistent, stable caregiver for a secure attachment, and in order to develop the ability to explore and understand the world through the relationship to a caregiver (Ainsworth, 1978). For infants growing up in a transitional family, attachment to the parents is a grave concern, as trauma can interfere with this bond. If the parents' attention must necessarily be focused on obtaining basic needs of food, housing, and safety, establishing a bond with their young child often takes second place. Parents in such tenuous living situations feel isolated and alone in their struggles. This level of stress can impose a barrier to building a relationship with one's child. If the caregiver has difficulty relating to the child, if there is a lack of consistency in primary caregivers (e.g., if the infant is placed in foster care and has multiple placements), or if there is interference with the process of attachment, children may have difficulties with attachment and exhibit developmental problems. Current studies suggest that only if problems with attachment are addressed early in life can the interventions repair or help the child "catch up developmentally" (Dozier & Bernard, 2009). If these problems go unnoticed when the child is a toddler and remain untreated until the child starts school, it can be much more difficult or even impossible to help the child "catch up" on the developmental delays. Attachment is essential for a child's development, and therefore it is the essential starting place in the treatment of trauma.

Another common manifestation of problematic primary relationships between child and parent, and unstable home environments, is a lack of **self-regulation** (the **R** in ARC), or the ability to learn to tolerate frustration and to avoid erratic mood swings. Many caregivers instinctually succumb to the fight-or-flight impulses that have been absolutely necessary for survival in their lives. Clinicians will be working hard to help the caregiver recognize this instinct and guide them in developing their individual self-regulatory abilities. This first step is crucial before the clinician, with the aid of the caregiver, can proceed to the second step—fostering self-regulatory abilities in their child(ren).

As the child reaches preschool age (3–5 years), he or she is expected to learn how to relate to peers and to begin participating appropriately in the classroom setting. This social skill reflects **regulation**. The skills and competencies needed to succeed in kindergarten are rarely taught or encouraged in a transitional living environment. In shelters, in cars, in hotels, and sleeping on the couch of another family, the rules change frequently, the child is often over- or understimulated, and there is very little opportunity for caregivers to help children develop their attention span, frustration tolerance, or even the ability to play with others in a nondestructive fashion. The number of children in such living situations who are expelled from preschool is more than three times the number among their peers (Gilliam, 2005). The inability to regulate one's own behavior can affect school performance—and even work or career prospects years later; consequently, for children living in precarious situations, a preschool setting in which they can begin working on self-regulation is essential. It teaches the skills and behaviors that will be needed to succeed in kindergarten. The likelihood of expulsion decreases significantly for children with behavioral problems when they have access to classroom-based behavioral consultation (Domitrovich, Cortes, & Greenberg, 2007; Gilliam, 2005). Many of these children will need individualized in-class guidance and intervention to build the school-readiness competencies that did not develop naturally in their homeless environments.

Finally, **competency** (the **C** in ARC) refers to the fact that many skills and abilities of the caregiver and the child(ren) may have remained undeveloped while the family was dealing with the unmet basic needs. As the survival needs are addressed and satisfied, they can retreat into the background, allowing the emotional, social, and cognitive development of every family member to move into the foreground.

Usually, children are expected to learn competency in grade school (5–18 years). Competency includes the ability to learn from successes and failures, to build a sense of self, to integrate past experiences, and to plan for the future. Children in transitional and unstable living environments experience multiple moves and are more likely to have school absences and school failures. All too often, these events have a negative impact on school behavior and school performance (Morales & Guerra, 2006). To address the accumulation of the problems resulting from instability, effective treatment is often multi-pronged and involves multiple stages. It can include any one or a combination of family therapy, individual therapy, parental guidance and support, school-based observations and interventions, and interventions involving the child within his or her peer group.

Children who grow up in transitional living situations may be at a disadvantage. They may have had difficulties with all three of the vitally important stages of the ARC model (Attachment, Self-Regulation, and Competency). Infants with insecure attachment to a parent figure have difficulties building relationships later. Children who have difficulties with self-regulation have difficulties participating in school and socializing. Adolescents and young adults who have difficulties with competency may have difficulty, learning from disappointments and successes, and integrating experiences that are vital for holding jobs and sustaining long-term relationships. Using the ARC model, the interventionist must help build awareness that there are choices and options that can pull the child, adolescent, or young adult out of the life of daily trauma into a life with positive relationships and with attainable goals.

A FLEXIBLE PERSPECTIVE—INDIVIDUAL, FAMILY, COMMUNITY, SOCIETY

While it goes without saying that transitional families have a daily struggle, it also is true that the health and social service professionals who choose to work in partnership with transitional families are joining their struggle. It can be overwhelming. The dictates and boundaries of the roles are less rigid, the methods are more variable, and the place to start services is less clear. The approach must be engaging, multimodal, and multilayered. Often the first step for the health and social service professionals is to focus narrowly on the child. From that point, they can gradually change and expand the perspective, by widening the lens to examine the family, then the community, and finally the society.

REFERENCES

Ainsworth, M. (1978). The development of infant-mother attachment. *Review of Infant Development, 3*, 1–89.

Bassuk, E. L., & Rosenberg, L. (1990). Psychosocial characteristics of homeless children and children with homes. *Pediatrics, 85*, 257–261.

Bassuk, E. L., Weinreb, L. F., Buckner, J. C., Browne, A., Salomon, A., & Bassuk, S. S. (1996). The characteristics and needs of sheltered homeless and low-income housed mothers. *Journal of the American Medical Association, 276*(8), 640–646.

Berberet, H. (2006). Putting the pieces together for queer youth: A model of integrated assessment of need and program planning. *Child Welfare Journal, 85*(2), 361–384.

Blaustein, M., & Kinniburgh, K. (2010). *Treating traumatic stress in children and adolescents.* New York: Guilford Press.

Bolland, J. M., & McCallum, M. (2002). Touched by homelessness: An examination of hospitality for the down and out. *American Journal of Public Health, 92*(1), 116–118.

Bronfenbrenner, U. (1979). *The ecology of human development.* Cambridge, MA: Harvard University Press.

——. (1986). Ecology of the family as a context for human development: Research perspectives. *Developmental Psychology, 22*(6), 723–742.

——. (1988). Strengthening family systems. In E. F. Zigler & M. Frank (Eds.), *The parental leave crisis: Toward a national policy* (pp. 143–160). New Haven, CT: Yale University Press.

——. (2005). *Making human beings human: Bioecological perspectives on human development.* Thousand Oaks, CA: Sage Publications.

Burt, M. R., Aron, L. Y., & Lee, E. (2001). *Helping America's homeless: Emergency shelter or affordable housing?* Washington, DC: Urban Institute Press.

Children's Bureau. (2005). The AFCARS (Adoption and Foster Care Analysis and Reporting System) Report. Retrieved September 25, 2008, from http://www.acf.hhs.gov/programs/cb/publications/afcars/report9.pdf.

——. (2009). The AFCARS (Adoption and Foster Care Analysis and Reporting System) Report. Retrieved June 2, 2011, from http://www.acf.hhs.gov/programs/cb/stats_research/afcars/tar/report16.htm.

Courtney, M. E., & Dworsky, A. (2006). Early outcomes for young adults transitioning from out-of-home care in the USA. *Child and Family Social Work, 11,* 209–219.

Domitrovich, C. E., Cortes, R. C., & Greenberg, M. T. (2007). Improving young children's social and emotional competence: A randomized trial of preschool "PATHS" curriculum. *Journal of Primary Prevention, 28*(2), 67–91.

Dozier, M., & Bernard, K. (2009). The impact of attachment-based interventions on the quality of attachment among infants and young children. In R. Tremblay, R. Barr, & R. Peters (Eds.), *Encyclopedia on early childhood development* [online]. Montreal, Quebec: Centre of Excellence for Early Child Development. Retrieved August 30, 2011, from www.child-encyclopedia.com/documents/Dozier-BernardANGxp_rev.pdf.

Field, T., & Diego, M. (2008). Cortisol: The culprit prenatal stress variable. *International Journal of Neuroscience, 118*(8), 1181–1205.

Garland, A. F., Hough, R. L., Landsverk, J. A., McCabe, K. M., Yeh, M., Ganger, W. C., et al. (2000). Racial and ethnic variations in mental health care utilization among children in foster care. *Children's Services: Social Policy, Research, and Practice, 3*(3), 133–146.

Gilliam, W. S. (May 2005). Prekindergarteners left behind: Expulsion rates in state prekindergarten programs. *Foundation for Child Development,* Policy Brief Series No. 3. Retrieved August 30, 2011, from http://www.challengingbehavior.org/explore/policy_docs/prek_expulsion.pdf.

Greene, J. M., Ennett, S. T., & Ringwalt, C. L. (1997). Substance use among runaway and homeless youth in three national samples. *American Journal of Public Health, 87*(2), 229–235.

Halfon, N., Mendonca, A., & Berkowitz, G. (1995). Health status of children in foster care. *Archive of Pediatric and Adolescent Medicine, 149,* 386–392.

Kuh, D., Ben-Shlomo, Y., Lynch, J., Hallqvist, J., & Power, C. (2003). Life Course Epidemiology. *Journal of Epidemiology and Community Health, 57*(10), 778–783.

Kuh, D., Hardy, R., Langenberg, C., Richards, M., & Wadsworth, M. E. (2002). Mortality in adults aged 26–54 years related to socioeconomic conditions in childhood and adulthood: Postwar birth cohort study. *British Medical Journal, 325,* 1076–1080.

Kushel, M. B., Yen, I. H., Gee, L., & Courtney, M. E. (2007). Homelessness and health care access after emancipation: Results from the Midwest Evaluation of Adult Functioning of Former Foster Youth. *Archives of Pediatrics and Adolescent Medicine, 161*(10), 986–993.

Maslow, A. (1954). *Motivation and personality* (3rd ed.). New York: Harper and Row Publishers.

McMillen, J. C., Scott, L. D., Zima, B. T., Ollie, M. T., Munson, M. R., & Spitznagel, E. (2004). Use of mental health services among older youths in foster care. *Psychiatric Services, 55*(7), 811–817.

Morales, J. R., & Guerra, N. G. (2006). Effects of multiple context and cumulative stress on urban children's adjustment in elementary school. *Child Development, 77*(4), 907–923.

Nelson, K. M. (1992). Fostering homeless children and their parents too: The emergence of whole-family foster care. *Child Welfare League of America, 71*(6), 575–584.

Ray, N. (2006). *Lesbian, gay, bisexual, and transgendered youth: An epidemic of homelessness.* New York: National Gay and Lesbian Task Force Policy Institute and the National Coalition for the Homeless.

Rosner, D., & Markowitz, G. (1997). Race, foster care, and the politics of abandonment in New York City. *American Journal of Public Health, 87*(11), 1844–1849.

Schorr, E. L. (1982). The foster care system and health status of foster children. *Pediatrics, 69*(5), 521–528.

Seng, J. S., Oakley, D. J., Sampselle, C. M., Killion, C., Graham-Bermann, S., & Liberzon, I. (2001). Posttraumatic stress disorder and pregnancy complications. *Obstetrics and Gynecology, 97*, 17–22.

Shinn, M., Knickman, J. R., & Weitzman, B. C. (1991). Social relationships and vulnerability to becoming homeless among poor families. *American Psychologist, 46*(11), 1180–1187.

Shinn, M. B., Rog, D. J., & Culhane, D. P. (2005). *Family homelessness: Background research findings and policy options.* University of Pennsylvania, School of Social Policy and Practice. Retrieved May 22, 2012, from http://repository.upenn.edu/cgi/viewcontent.cgi?article=1085&context=spp_papers.

Shinn, M., Weitzman, B. C., Stojanovic, D., Knickman, J. R., Jimenez, L., Duchon, L., et al. (1998). Predictors of homelessness among families in New York City: From shelter request to housing stability. *American Journal of Public Health, 88*(11), 1651–1657.

U.S. Census Bureau. (2011). *2010 Census shows America's diversity.* Retrieved May 22, 2012, from http://2010.census.gov/news/releases/operations/cb11-cn125.html.

U.S. Department of Housing and Urban Development—Office of Community Planning and Development. (2010). *The 2009 annual homeless assessment report (AHAR).* Washington, DC: Author.

U.S. General Accounting Office. (1997). *Parental substance abuse: Implications for children, the child welfare system, and foster care outcomes* (No. GAO/T-HEHS-98-40). Washington, DC: Subcommittee on Human Resources, Committee on Ways and Means, House of Representatives.

Viner, R. M., & Taylor, B. (2005). Adult health and social outcomes of children who have been in public care: Population-based study. *Pediatrics, 115*(4), 894–899.

Weitzman, B. C., Knickman, J. R., & Shinn, M. (1990). Pathways to homelessness among New York City families. *Journal of Social Issues, 46*(4), 125–140.

Westat, Inc., and Chapin Hall Center for Children (2001). The role of race in parental reunification. In *Assessing the context of permanency and reunification in the foster care system* (pp. 6.1–6.15). Washington, DC: Department of Health and Human Services, Assistant Secretary for Planning and Evaluation. http://aspe.hhs.gov/hsp/fostercare-reunif01/.

Wood, D., Valdez, R. B., Hayashi, T., & Shen, A. (1990). Health of homeless children and housed, poor children. *Pediatrics, 86*(6), 858–866.

Woolf, S. H., Johnson, R. E., & Geiger, J. (2006). The rising prevalence of poverty in America: A growing threat to public health. *American Journal of Preventive Medicine, 31*(4), 332–341.

Zima, B. T., Wells, K. B., Benjamin, B., & Duan, N. (1996). Mental health problems among homeless mothers: Relationship to service use and child mental health problems. *Archives of General Psychiatry, 53*(4), 332–338.

Zlotnick, C., Kronstadt, D., & Klee, L. (1998). Foster care children and family homelessness. *American Journal of Public Health, 88*(9), 1368–1370.

Zlotnick, C., & Marks, L. (2002). Case management services at ten federally funded sites targeting homeless children and their families. *Children's Services: Social Policy, Research, and Practice, 5*(2), 113–122.

Zlotnick, C., Tam, T., & Bradley, K. (2007). Adulthood trauma, separation from one's children, and homeless mothers. *Community Mental Health Journal, 43*(1), 20–33.

———. (2010). Long-term and chronic homelessness in homeless women and women with children. *Journal of Social Work in Public Health, 25*(4), 470–485.

Zlotnick, C., Tam, T., & Soman, L. A. (2012). Life course outcomes on mental and physical health: The impact of foster care on adulthood. *American Journal of Public Health, 102*(3), 534–540.

Zlotnick, C., Wright, M., Sanchez, R. M., Murga-Kusnir, R., & Te'o-Bennett, I. (2010). Adaptation of community-based participatory research methods to gain community input on identifying indicators of successful parenting. *Child Welfare, 89*(4), 9–27.

CHAPTER 2

"We Don't Get Whuppings Here Anymore"

TOWARD A COLLABORATIVE, ECOLOGICAL MODEL OF PARENTING

▸ MARGUERITE A. WRIGHT

THE BESIEGED MOTHER, LENA, seemed hassled, frantic, and overwhelmed. She entered my office with her rambunctious 9-year-old boy, Aaron, trailing grudgingly behind her. "Do you want another whupping? Get your [expletive] behind in here," she yelled. He looked scared as he scampered into the room. To me, she said, "Excuse my language but this boy is driving me nuts. If I have to go up to this brat's school one more time to get him, I might lose my job." Aaron had received several suspensions from his school for his aggressive, defiant, and disruptive behaviors. This last infraction was "too much"; he had physically "attacked" a classmate who teased him. The school was on the verge of "throwing him out," according to his mom.

Lena and her three kids resided in a transitional home. Although she relished the support that she received from the staff, she did not "appreciate how they keep messing in my business . . . telling me how to discipline my kids . . . Who gives them the right to tell me I can't whup my child? If I stayed on his behind, he wouldn't keep acting up in school . . . The only thing he understands is a good butt whupping."

OVERVIEW

Traditional approaches, anchored in individual therapy, family therapy, and parent education programs, are limited to addressing the socioemotional and educational problems of an increasing number of low-income black children, particularly boys, who are typically saddled with stigmatizing diagnoses like oppositional defiant disorder (ODD), conduct disorder, attention deficit disorder/attention deficit hyperactivity disorder (ADD/ADHD), or the current flavor of contemporary times, bipolar disorder. Yet the traditional approaches for the child who has externalizing symptoms, like aggression and defiance, are inadequate not only in diagnosing but also in treating these symptoms. Sometimes the child is placed on medications that do little to alleviate his symptoms and may actually harm his development. Such approaches fall short of addressing the complexities that socioeconomic status, particularly the impact of living in transitional situations such as homelessness, contributes to the child's behaviors and social context.

There is a burgeoning literature indicating that harsh discipline, specifically corporal punishment (i.e., spanking, hitting, beating, whipping) and psychological aggression (i.e., yelling, screaming, scolding, swearing, threatening to spank without doing so), is detrimental to a child's development (Gershoff, 2002; Hashina & Amato, 1994; Smith & Brooks-Gunn, 1997; Straus, Sugarman, & Giles-Sims, 1997; Taylor, Manganello, Lee, & Rice, 2010).

This chapter begins by briefly examining the impact of punitive discipline on different aspects of the child's development, and then exploring the reasons why many black parents and other caregivers in at-risk communities tend to rely on harsh discipline to manage their children's unacceptable behaviors. Finally, it revisits the opening client-based vignette, as an introduction to a collaborative, ecological approach for working with caregivers, particularly those residing in transitional housing, to nurture the child's development by supporting positive parenting beliefs and practices.

CORPORAL DISCIPLINE

Corporal punishment is used by the majority of American parents at some time in their children's growing years; it is arguably a normative disciplinary practice in our society (Wauchope & Straus, 1990). There are conflicting findings, and a vibrant debate continues among researchers, but the preponderance of the evidence shows that corporal discipline has a detrimental effect on the child's brain development, socioemotional functioning, intelligence, behavior, and school performance (Gershoff, 2002; Horn, Cheng, & Joseph, 2004; Horn, Joseph, & Cheng, 2004; McCord, 1996; Straus, 1994; Straus, Sugarman, & Giles-Sims,1997; Socolar, Amaya-Jackson, Eron, et al., 1997; Taylor, Hinton, & Wilson, 1995).

The most robust of these findings suggest that children who are spanked are more likely than others to manifest externalizing symptoms, including oppositional defiant and conduct disorders, but primarily aggression. Spanking is a strong predictor of aggressive and violent behaviors (Taylor et al., 2010). Black children, particularly black boys, relative to their white peers, receive a disproportionate number of school suspensions (Lewin, 2012). A pattern of chronic suspensions along with the high risk that children will internalize labels like "aggressive," "angry," "defiant," "oppositional," "destructive," or "incorrigible," used by school personnel to describe them, place these children at a higher risk for socioemotional problems and school failure.

Transitional living situations contribute to this negative spiral. Frequent school changes and high absentee rates increase the likelihood that children and youth will be ill-prepared to fully participate at their grade level. The trauma of their living situation also compounds the problems children have at school. As a result, children and youth struggle with both the academic and the socialization challenges they encounter in school. Compared to other children, homeless and foster children have disproportionately higher rates of mental health and school problems (Nabors et al., 2004).

Children living in shelters and other transitional housing have to cope with strict restrictions on their behavior. Caregivers struggling to manage their children's behavior so that they can conform to the behavioral expectations of their hosts may be inclined to resort to learned punitive parenting. However, many shelters and other transitional housing have strict rules against punitive discipline, and so parents feel stripped of their strongest tool to manage their children's behavior.

FACTORS ASSOCIATED WITH THE USE OF CORPORAL DISCIPLINE

Research has identified several factors that are associated with parental use of corporal discipline, among them mother's mental health (e.g., depressed mothers are more likely to use corporal punishment) (Jackson, Gyanifi, Brooks-Gunn, & Blake, 1998), mother's age (e.g., younger mothers are more inclined to use physical discipline) (Kelley, Sanchez-Hueles, & Walker, 1993), socioeconomic status (lower-income parents tend to rely more on spanking) (Regalado, Sareen, Inkelas, Wissow, & Halfon,

2004), and religion (studies suggest that a fundamentalist/conservative lifestyle is associated with the use of corporal discipline) (Horn, Cheng, & Joseph, 2004).

Findings on the effect of race are conflicting, but the majority suggest that black parents have more "authoritarian" (high level of control, low level of warmth) disciplinary beliefs (Abell & Clawson, 1996; Baumrind, 1978) and are more likely to use corporal discipline (Giles-Sims, Straus, & Sugarman, 1995; Gunnoe & Mariner, 1997; Kelley, Power, & Winbush, 1992; Pinderhughes, Dodge, Bates, Pettit, & Zelli, 2000; Regalado et al., 2004; Socolar & Stein, 1995; Straus & Stewart, 1999; Wissow, 2002).

Psychological Aggression

There is only a small body of research discussing the impact of psychological aggression on a child's development. Most studies suggest that psychological aggression has an adverse impact on the child's behavioral and socio-emotional functioning (Straus & Field, 2003). Given the paucity of studies, the impact of race/ethnicity on psychological aggression is unclear (Sedlak, Broadhurst, & Thomas, 1997). Straus and Field (2003) found that only the parent's age influenced the use of psychological aggression (i.e., younger parents are more likely to use this type of discipline).

Stereotype of Black Parenting

A negative stereotype found in black parenting has emerged in the literature, indicating a "tendency to use harsh and aversive disciplinary practices" (McLoyd, 1990, p. 335). Several scholars have pointed to the methodological limitations of many of these studies, primarily the tendency of some researchers to conflate race and social class, leading them to compare the parenting styles of middle-class whites with those of low-income blacks (Bradley, 1998; Horn, Cheng, & Joseph, 2004; Kelley, Power, & Winbush, 1992; McLoyd, 1990; Socolar & Stein, 1996). Indeed, the studies that disaggregated these variables have shown an interaction between race and social class, indicating that black parents with lower versus higher incomes are more likely to use corporal discipline. Similarly, low-income (versus higher-income) white parents also are more likely to spank their children (Straus & Stewart, 1999).

The stereotype of the punitive black parent has been increasingly chal-lenged, but like other racial/ethnic stereotypes, it is difficult to uproot. Some researchers have shown that there is more variability among black parenting styles (Brady & Flor, 1998; Kelley, Sanchez-Hueles, & Walker, 1993) and have argued for the importance of taking an ecological perspec-tive in doing research on black families (Kelley, Power, & Winbush, 1992; McLoyd, 1990; Peters & Massey, 1983). By considering contextual factors (e.g., parents' marital status, co-parenting support, parents' employment, parents' experience of poverty and economic loss, adequacy of housing, quality of schools, neighborhood safety), some scholars have convinc-ingly argued that harsh parenting is associated more strongly with hav-ing to struggle against adverse life events than with the color of one's skin (McLoyd, 1990). For example, parents who are impoverished and living in homeless shelters tend to have limited co-parenting support and meager social support, reside in dangerous neighborhoods, have limited employ-ment opportunities, face a revolving door of shelter locations and other life stressors, and are more likely to use punitive disciplinary practices to ensure that their children survive their neighborhoods.

Corporal discipline is a deeply ingrained parenting practice in many cultures worldwide. Some black clients, child care workers, other mental health professionals, and educators believe it is a uniquely black "cultural" parenting style (Wright, 2000). As long as their examination of the child does not indicate physical signs (e.g., bruises, contusions) consistent with the legal definition of abuse, some practitioners minimize the child's report of having been spanked or "whupped" with remarks like "I don't want to be judgmental . . . that's the way those people discipline their kids." Mis-guided efforts to be "culturally sensitive" can leave the maltreated child emotionally stranded. Some black caregivers themselves, including parents, grandparents, foster parents, and adoptive parents, maintain a vigorous defense that physical punishment is "cultural." Referencing a white boy's tantrum in a supermarket while his mother tried unsuccessfully to talk him into calming down, a black grandmother observed: "Those white people let their children get away with everything but if he were a black child, he would have gotten his butt whipped." Oprah Winfrey, the renowned Afri-can American talk show host, remembered that as a child she "wanted to be a white kid because they didn't get whippings . . . They got talked to" (Richman, 1987).

The seemingly societal assumption that blacks deserve harsher discipline—"excessive force"—(e.g., black public school students' higher rate of school suspensions; black men's higher rates of arrests and incarceration) has its roots in the historical subjugation of blacks in the period of slavery (Wright, 1982). Ample documentation survives (e.g., slave narratives) to suggest that slaves were harshly disciplined (i.e., whipped, and even killed) for minor infractions. Slave children and their parents were under total control, and completely at the mercy of the slave owners' whim. Harsh standards of disciplining blacks, who were regarded as inferior, were arguably established during this period. Later, although emancipated to live as "free" people, blacks were still regarded and treated as inferior and deserving of harsher discipline by authorities.

The atrocities that blacks endured across several generations of racial segregation compelled parents to keep tight reins on their children. Black parents relied on corporal punishment to force their children to follow society's rules, which allowed them to navigate an inhospitable racial landscape and survive. Parents' reliance on corporal punishment to manage their children's behaviors was, therefore, adaptive (Kelley, Power, & Winbush, 1992; Murry, Bynum, Brody, Willert, & Stephens, 2001; Parke & Buriel, 1998). It is distressing that in the 21st century the legacy of this harsh parenting style, corporal discipline as well as the psychological aggression that invariably accompanies it, endures and continues to plague many black children struggling to adapt to a society that they still experience as perilous. Given their more vulnerable status in society, they are placed at higher risk than their white peers when they are punitively disciplined. One has only to examine the data on school referrals, suspensions, and failure, as well incarceration in the juvenile justice system to appreciate the troubling dimensions of this impact (Dillon, 2010; Eckholm, 2010; Losen & Skiba, 2010). Although punitive parenting is only one contributor to these children's problematic functioning, those who are regularly maltreated experience a profound impact on their psychological development.

Reasons for the Enduring Reliance on Punitive Discipline

The literature, as well as anecdotal evidence gathered from personal conversations and interviews with black parents and other caregivers, suggests at least three explanations for many low-income black caregivers' reliance on harsh discipline in managing their children's behavior.

First, as briefly discussed above, many black caregivers in at-risk communities view corporal discipline as a manifestation of their "cultural" parenting practices. As noted, recent studies find that blacks do employ diverse parenting practices, but that many economically disadvantaged blacks believe corporal punishment is unique to their culture. Black culture is inextricably intertwined with the black church, widely recognized as the foundation of black society (Blank, Mahmood, Fox, & Gutenbock, 2002). Adherents to religious fundamentalism, even those no longer affiliated with a church, embrace the oft-misattributed biblical exhortation "spare the rod, spoil the child" as fundamental to their parenting. Informed by mental health professionals of the deleterious effects of harsh discipline, some caregivers respond by quoting some version of this scripture in defense of their deeply held belief that they are spiritually compelled to use corporal punishment to discipline their disobedient children; otherwise they will be regarded as unfit parents and thereby will betray their faith.

Clinicians working with these caregivers need extensive knowledge of their clients' faith and should be well versed in the scriptures so they will be able to engage in meaningful, respectful dialogue with caregivers about their interpretation of the "spare the rod . . ." scripture and be able to challenge that interpretation. The mother in the opening vignette once confided in a therapy session that she felt faith-bound to adhere to that biblical admonition when her son misbehaved. She became argumentative when informed that the "scripture" she quoted was not actually from the Bible but excerpted from the 16th-century poem "Hudibras," by Samuel Butler. (The closest scripture in the King James version of the Bible, which she used, was found in Proverbs 13:24: "He that spareth his rod hateth his son: but he that loveth him chasteneth him betimes.") In challenging the mother's disciplinary approach, it was helpful to engage her in a discussion of biblical scriptures in which the punishment of adult "sinners" was extremely disproportionate to their offense (such as the proposed stoning of an adulterous woman) and reflect on the reason that people in our society do not reference these scriptures as often as they do the one they perceive to endorse the physical punishment of children. It is also important to highlight biblical scriptures that emphasize providing care and guidance to children and examine the reason these scriptures are seldom invoked.

Caregivers who become fully engaged in this process may challenge their pastors and other church members to examine their beliefs about the role of punitive discipline in raising their child to be a healthy functioning adult. This process can be wrenching for caregivers, who often must decide whether to continue following the teachings of their church, which they may realize could be harming their child, or to renounce their beliefs about the centrality of corporal discipline in parenting their child. In abandoning their belief in corporal punishment and other harsh discipline, caregivers risk the judgment of church members who may view them negatively. Since the church is a primary source of support for some caregivers, it is important that they have an alternate support system in place (e.g., a parenting group) to compensate if they are denied their church's support.

Caregivers who do not attend church but nevertheless adhere to the "spare the rod" dictum may be just as difficult to convince of the risks of punitive parenting as devout caregivers are. Often the use of corporal punishment is so deeply entrenched in a family's culture that it requires extensive efforts and resources to uproot. Research consistently shows that people tend to parent like they themselves were parented. Most parents will say, "I got spanked or I got whupped. Look at me; I turned out all right, so it's right for my child." Often the parents have psychological issues that suggest that they are not as "all right" as they claim. That is, on the surface they may be functioning well enough, but a deeper examination of their lives often reveals interpersonal issues or other problems that diminish their satisfaction. Their self-awareness about the impact of the harsh discipline that they endured as children is generally lacking. Others realize a need to "break the cycle," but the steps between the motivation to change and making an actual change are very steep and challenging. Community-based interventions, which rely primarily on caregivers who have already successfully transitioned from using punitive parenting practices to positive ones, are arguably the most effective allies in changing their parenting style.

Second, many black caregivers rely on punitive discipline to instill in their children unquestioning obedience to a shelter or society's rules. In a homeless shelter, behavioral problems among either the parents or the children can result in being ejected. In society, obedience to laws can prevent them from falling into the clutches of the criminal justice system. These caregivers have a deep and understandable fear and mistrust of the police, manifested by the expectation that their children will be inevitably harmed, perhaps fatally, if they don't obey authority figures. As the mother in the opening vignette bemoaned during one of our many counseling sessions, "If I don't whup some sense into him, the man will get him." She believed that "the man" (white authority) "will get" (hurt/imprison) her son if she fails to instill obedience to authority figures, and for children this begins with obedience to parents and teachers. Caregivers' fears are not irrational, especially if one considers that blacks, as a demographic group, are more likely to be arrested and incarcerated than are whites (Pettit & Western, 2004; Stewart, Baumer, Brunson, & Simons, 2009).

Third, McLoyd (1990) maintained that exposure to a higher level of stressful life events (poverty, homeless shelters, poor housing, unsafe neighborhoods, etc.) results in psychological distress for low-income black parents, who, in turn, are more likely to use punitive discipline to manage their child's misbehaviors. These caregivers seek to instill in their children respect for authority and to protect their children from being victimized by the predators in their community who may entice or recruit them to prey on their own communities. They feel the need to toughen their children to prepare them to deal with the multiple chronic stresses that they will encounter throughout their childhood and into their later years. Too often, however, rather than toughening their children, harsh punishments actually weaken them, making them more susceptible to the negative influences (like substance use, gangs, and violence) in their environment.

LIMITATIONS OF TRADITIONAL APPROACHES TO PARENTING GUIDANCE FOR CAREGIVERS IN AT-RISK COMMUNITIES

For many caregivers in at-risk communities, the lone therapist may be a good starting point, but proves insufficient for enacting enduring change in caregivers' renunciation of punitive disciplinary beliefs and behaviors and adoption of more-effective disciplinary practices. Nor are parenting workshops and classes, lasting anywhere from a few weeks to several months, sufficient to bring about fundamental changes in parenting beliefs and practices. Caregivers often emerge with good intentions from parenting classes and workshops, where some of them tearfully renounced physical punishment and other harsh discipline as they grasped the harm that it inflicts on their children, only to return to their former habits of harsh discipline when they again confront the realities of raising their children in a dangerous environment. These caregivers are highly motivated to adopt new and positive parenting strategies after taking the workshops and classes. Some are even successful in doing so for a while, but eventually many of them, faced with the stark reality of raising children in a high-risk environment, succumb to the pressures of relatives and friends who tell them, when their child "mouths off" to them for the umpteenth time or doesn't do something that the parent asks: "You better whup him. Talking is for white people." Parenting instructors and clinicians can easily underestimate the pressure that the community exerts on parenting beliefs and practices in its effort to maintain the status quo. A caregiver who is one of the few members of his social circle to rely on noncorporal discipline bears a tremendous burden that threatens his standing in his social circle, since he no longer conforms to his community's norms of disciplining children. Anecdotal evidence shows that parents' most difficult challenge, other than managing their own temper, in eschewing corporal punishment and relying on non-punitive strategies to discipline their child is dealing with relatives and friends who "bad-mouth" and pressure the parents to use corporal punishment when they observe their children misbehaving.

A large proportion of parents who reside in shelters and other transitional housing arrangements were mistreated if not abused when they themselves were children. Given the traumas endured from their own families as well as those inherent in growing up in a culture that condones such mistreatment, they find it difficult to overcome this punitive mindset. Culturally sensitive parenting guidance from the transitional housing staff and ongoing support when these parents are reintegrated into their community can help them to learn new ways of disciplining their children.

Like substance abusers, punitive caregivers need a comprehensive, transformational, and long-term treatment approach to "break the cycle"—to challenge, renounce, and replace dysfunctional parenting beliefs and practices with effective ones. Just as the addict is engaged in a lifelong recovery process, so should parents become involved in an ongoing recovery process while they are raising their children. Like recovering substance abusers, recovering punitive parents need regular support to raise their children.

TOWARD A COLLABORATIVE, ECOLOGICAL
MODEL OF PARENTING

The limitations of traditional approaches to parenting education and counseling (short-term parenting workshops and classes, as well as counseling approaches that are not informed by the community's child-raising beliefs and challenges) create an urgent need to develop a culturally informed model of effective parenting that will guide parents and other caregivers to examine their beliefs and parenting behaviors and adopt practices that will optimize their children's healthy socioemotional development.

Regalado et al. (2004) recognized the need for a "conceptual framework that emphasizes the importance of parenting style (the social and emotional context for effective teaching) and specific parenting practices to guide children towards socialization goals" (p. 1952).

Informed by the pioneering work of Ogbu (1981) and Bronfenbrenner (1989), the proposed collaborative, ecological model emphasizes the contextual nature of parenting beliefs and practices and uses a multifaceted, community-based approach to address children's psychosocial and behavioral problems that are assessed to be primarily related to parenting issues. This model indicates that children's development and functioning are fundamentally grounded in their relationships with their parents (or other primary caregivers), their families, and their social circle, as well as in relationships that they develop with people in their community (such as the school faculty, church members, staff members of after-school programs, police officers, etc.) (fig. 2.1). Consistent with this formulation, "interventions" with the goal of improving children's functioning address not only their own and their caregivers' needs, but also those of the community where they are being raised.

The model supports the implementation of a community-based program (housed in schools) that is spearheaded by parents and other caregivers in collaboration with mental health professionals, school faculty representatives, child care workers, clergy members, staff members (including coaches) of after-school recreational/athletic programs, and, when indicated (for example, in high crime communities), law enforcement. Each participant in the community collaboration is expected to endorse and send a consistent message that punitive discipline and excessive force (whether at home, school, church, after-school centers, or on the street by

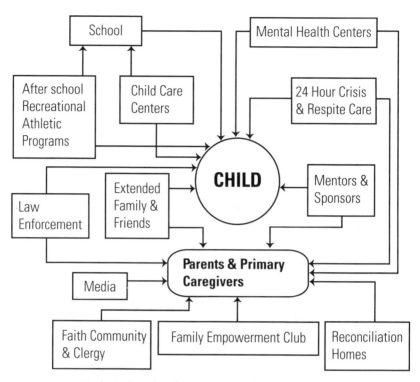

FIGURE 2.1   Ecological model of support network to promote and sustain positive discipline.

the police) are harmful to children's development and will not be tolerated by the community. Educational workshops to train participants in the collaborative about relationship building and positive disciplinary strategies will be offered. In addition, an ongoing awareness-raising campaign (with media assistance) is necessary to publicize the message of positive discipline to the community. The aim of this approach is to provide comprehensive support mainly to parents and other caregivers, but also to other adults who regularly interact with children, to enable them to use positive disciplinary strategies to manage children's behaviors and to develop caring relationships with them.

To illustrate, consider this chapter's opening vignette about the overwhelmed and exhausted mother of the 9-year-old boy who resided in transitional housing. School expulsion had been threatened unless his mother obtained professional counseling to address his defiant and aggressive behaviors in school. She disclosed that she had previously obtained counseling for her son, who had been expelled from his preschool program, as well as attended several parenting workshops and classes over the years in order to address not only his behavioral problems but also those of his older siblings, at various times in their childhood. Lena believed that the transitional house's strict rule of no spanking tied her hands and contributed to her son's behavioral problems despite complaints from staff at both the transitional house and her son's school about her punitive parenting (which she eventually acknowledged was a primary contributor to her son's problematic behaviors). The traditional remedies available to her proved to be temporary fixes that quickly lost their effectiveness under the multiple stresses of raising children in a community besieged by violence and poverty.

In formulating a care plan with the goal of improving the child's classroom behavior, the staff incorporated the relevant aspects of a traditional "intervention" approach into a more comprehensive, collaborative, ecological approach tailored to the family's unique strengths and needs, and relying heavily on community resources. The mother believed that her primary parenting goal was to keep her son and his siblings safe from the perils of the street—a daily, unrelenting, and scary task. To ensure his safety, his mother had demanded absolute "obedience." She felt an almost sacred obligation to ensure that her children obey and respect her and their elders, including family and friends, as well as those in their faith and school communities. Although the mother used other disciplinary methods (talking, time-outs, "bribing") to implement her goals, she felt that "tough" parenting (spanking, yelling, demeaning—"putting children in their place") proved most effective, although admittedly short term. After refraining, sometimes for weeks at a time, from hitting her son (and his sibling), and decreasing her yelling, her son would do something (e.g., "mess up in school," "hit his brother," "sass me") "that would make me lose it. . . . Children are so hardheaded. It's the only thing they really understand." When the transitional house staff learned that she had spanked her son, there were the inevitable arguments, sometimes accompanied by threats of eviction. The staff were unaware that Aaron was struggling to keep a secret that he was occasionally spanked by his mother when he was away from the transitional house— on weekend visits to his grandmother's house. His mother received little support from her family for using the parenting strategies that were repeatedly explained and modeled for her by the staff at the transitional house. Indeed, her family viewed her as a "bad" parent if she did not use punitive discipline to control her child's behavior.

The assessment of 9-year-old Aaron's socioemotional functioning revealed, among other concerns, an insecure attachment to his mother. Although there are several factors that contribute to an insecure parent-child relationship, a primary factor, along with the child's experiencing or witnessing domestic violence, is punitive discipline. Research suggests that spanking is associated with attachment insecurity (Coyl, Newland, & Freeman, 2008). Lena blamed the transitional house's staff for alienating her son's affection—he was conflicted—was she the "bad mom," who whupped him (and he needed to run to the staff for protection), or the good mom, who kissed him and tucked him in at night? Aaron expressed confusion about his mother's love for him. In his artwork, he painted a self-portrait punctured with red gashes depicting the blows his body sustained from being spanked. In the same sentence, he alternately spoke of his love and his hate for his mom. His conversation and play revealed that he feared her as much as he craved her love and attention. Aaron's revelations were typical of many children who are punitively disciplined, and he showed similar symptoms, including anxiety, depression, anger, hostility, impulsivity, defiance, inattention, hyperactivity, and aggression. Many such children display affect-regulation problems, which are often first identified by schools when the children, disproportionately black males like Aaron, are regarded most often as bullies (and, to a lesser extent, as victims). Schools tend to overreact to these children's behavioral problems, which are typically disruptive, aggressive, defiant disorders, by suspending them. A recent study (Losen & Skiba, 2010) found that middle-school black boys were "nearly three times as likely to be suspended as white boys." Black girls were "suspended [at] four times the rate of white girls."

After several sessions, Lena grudgingly accepted my observation that her harsh parenting style was having a deleterious effect not only on Aaron's functioning but on their relationship. When she made it strikingly clear that I was not the first therapist to bring this to her attention, I had a sinking feeling that unless she had a breakthrough, I would not be the last.

Bowlby's seminal work (1969) places the mother-child attachment at the foundation of a child's psychological health. Punitive discipline imperils this bond. Not only did punitive discipline present a stumbling block in Lena's relationship with her son, but her discomfort in expressing affection to him and his siblings additionally contributed to his insecurity. Her own history of trauma (abuse, neglect, abandonment) contributed to her problems with connecting emotionally to her children. Although she had obtained some benefits from a couple of years of individual therapy, it did not enable her to bridge the emotional chasm that was widening between her and her children.

The collaborative, ecological approach to this case was multi-layered. First, Aaron received weekly play therapy. The principal collaborative work, however, was engaging with Lena to shore up her strengths and improve her knowledge of child development and, just as important, working with the staff of the transitional house to use a culturally sensitive approach to engage Lena in adopting a non-punitive disciplinary style. As she prepared to transition back into her own home, the staff recruited community allies (i.e., sponsor/mentor) to support Lena in her use of non-punitive disciplinary strategies.

Similar to most other well-meaning parents who seek to raise well-adjusted children, Lena subscribed to satisfactory parenting goals. The primary issue for her was her punitive parenting style. Challenging these strategies and the beliefs that accompanied them, which had been sanctioned for generations by members of her own family and her community, proved daunting.

When she transitioned to her own home, Lena attended the weekly Family Empowerment Club, a group of parents and other relative caregivers that provided emotional, informational, and parenting support (Zlotnick, Wright, Cox, Te'o, & Stewart-Felix, 2000). The members of the group, who were at various stages of "recovery" from punitive parenting, became Lena's allies in transforming her parenting style by examining her parenting beliefs and adopting positive disciplinary strategies. These caregivers, from neighborhoods similar to Lena's, understood the perils and benefits of raising children in those communities.

At various times, other caregivers confronted Lena when she offered weak excuses for "backsliding" (reverting to punitive discipline), commended her when she deftly managed a stressful parenting problem, and supported her when her own family members verbally attacked her for "going soft" (not using punitive discipline) on her children and predicted horrible futures (e.g., prison) for them. In this group, she found a camaraderie that gave affection and support for her own interests, which previously had been absent in her life. She became increasingly more comfortable in expressing affection to her own children. Researchers using an ecological perspective have shown the importance of parenting support in children's psychological health (Petit, Bates, & Dodge, 1997). McLoyd (1990), in her review of the literature, points to "compelling evidence" that parents' social networks "lessen[ ] erratic and harsh discipline among black and white parents . . . and indirectly enhance socioemotional functioning among poor black children" (p. 336).

Consultation with Lena's pastor on his parenting advice led to a vigorous debate about the "true" interpretation of the "spare the rod, spoil the child" scripture. Although he remained convinced that the scripture endorsed corporal punishment, he no longer insisted in his sermons that parents spank their children to be "right with God." He supported Lena's efforts to tailor her parenting to her son's needs, thereby removing a psychological and spiritual obstacle that was interfering with her adopting positive parenting strategies.

Finally, as a result of my collaboration with the school, Aaron's teacher and other members of the faculty developed an understanding of Aaron's and his family's unique challenges and the assets they provided to the school. Their awareness led them to reject Aaron previous diagnosis as an "ODD child" and view him as a child who was dealing with overwhelming stresses and managing them as well as he could. In managing his behaviors, his teachers no longer relied on punitive strategies (e.g., yelling, humiliating, sending him out of the classroom, giving him suspensions) but turned to supportive strategies that sought to improve his ability to regulate his own behaviors. Aaron, no longer stigmatized as the "problem" student, gradually improved. The effectiveness of this treatment approach is best observed in Aaron's remarkable long-run progress, in both his socioemotional development and his school functioning. It was almost two years before Aaron believed that his mother had finally renounced corporal punishment, as she had broken so many promises over the years that she would not spank him. One day when his usually absent father visited and threatened to slap Aaron for something he told him not to do, Aaron firmly held up his hand to block him and said, "We don't get whuppings here anymore."

•   •   •

Research on punitive discipline, particularly corporal discipline, has shown that it has a detrimental effect on children's development, socioemotional functioning, and school functioning. Black children, growing up in at-risk circumstances such as transitional living situations, are particularly vulnerable to the risks of punitive discipline. Obviously, punitive discipline is only one among a host of life stressors that place black children at increased risk for socioemotional and other problems. Specifically, there are stubborn systematic racial disparities that contribute to and, some may argue, are the principal source of the problems of black children and their families. Along with advocating for these macro systematic changes, there is an urgent need to attend to micro changes that are within the control of parents and other caregivers. The evidence is compelling that positive parenting leads to significant improvement in a child's development and functioning. Given the alarming rates of inequity between white and black children with regard to mental health issues, school failure, and involvement in the juvenile justice system, as well as the high level of community violence in their neighborhoods, there is an urgent need to adopt strategies that will mitigate the racial disparities that are frequently publicized. To provide meaningful support that will increase parents' motivation to use positive discipline, it is essential to expand innovative community-based supports (e.g., 24-hour parent support groups, 24-hour crisis respite care, "reconciliation homes" for children and parents who are experiencing unmanageable conflicts that increase the risk of family violence). The collaborative, ecological model offers a promising approach to harnessing community support to reduce children's vulnerabilities related to growing up in at-risk communities and to developing protective factors that will allow them to thrive.

REFERENCES

Abell, E., & Clawson, M. (1996). Parenting values, attitudes, behaviors, and goals of African American mothers from a low-income community. *Journal of Family Issues, 17,* 593–614.

Baumrind, D. (1978). Parental disciplinary patterns and social competence. *Youth and Society, 9,* 239–276.

Blank, M., Mahmood, M., Fox, J., & Gutenbock, T. (2002). Alternative mental health services: The role of the black church in the South. *American Journal of Public Health, 92*(17), 1668–1672.

Bowlby, John. (1969). *Attachment* (1st ed.) (pp. 177–209). New York: Basic Books.

Bradley, C. (1998). Child rearing in African American families: A study of the disciplinary practices of African American parents. *Journal of Multicultural Counseling Development, 26,* 273–281.

Brady, G., & Flor, D. (1998). Maternal resources, parenting practices, and child competence in rural, single-parent African American families. *Child Development, 69,* 803–816.

Bronfenbrenner, U. (1989). Ecological systems theory. In R. Vasta (Ed.), *Annals of Child Development* (Vol. 6, pp. 198–249). Greenwich, CT: JAI Press.

Coyl, D., Newland, L., & Freeman, H. (2008). Predicting preschoolers' attachment security from parenting behaviors, parents' attachment relationships, and their use of social support. *Early Child Development and Care, 180*(4), 499–512.

Dillon, S. (2010, December 10). What works in the classroom? Ask students. *New York Times,* p. A15.

Eckholm, E. (2010, March 19). School suspensions lead to legal challenge. *New York Times,* p. A14.

Gershoff, E. (2002). Corporal punishment by parents and associated child behaviors and experiences: A meta-analytic and theoretical review. *Psychological Bulletin, 128,* 539–579.

Giles-Sims, J., Straus, M., & Sugarman, D. (1995). Child, maternal, and family characteristics associated with spanking. *Family Relations, 44,* 170–176.

Gunnoe, M., & Mariner, C. (1997). Toward a developmental-contextual model of the effects of parental spanking on children's aggression. *Archives of Pediatrics and Adolescence Medicine, 151,* 768–775.

Hashina, P., & Amato, P. (1994). Poverty, social support, and parental behavior. *Child Development, 65,* 394–403.

Horn, I., Cheng, T., & Joseph, J. (2004). Discipline in the African American community: The impact of socioeconomic status beliefs and practices. *Pediatrics 113*(5), 1236–1241.

Horn, I., Joseph, J., & Cheng, T. (2004). Nonabusive physical punishment and child behavior among African-American children: A systematic review. *Journal of the National Medical Association, 96*(9), 1162–1168.

Jackson, H., Gyanifi, P., Brooks-Gunn, J., & Blake, M. (1998). Employment status, psychological well being, social support, and physical discipline practices of single black mothers. *Journal of Marriage and the Family, 60,* 894–902.

Kelley, M., Power, T., & Winbush, D. (1992). Determinants of disciplinary practices in low-income black mothers. *Child Development, 63,* 573–582.

Kelley, M., Sanchez-Hueles, J., & Walker, R. (1993). Correlates of the disciplinary practices in working- to middle-class African American mothers. *Merrill Palmer Quarterly, 39*, 252–264.

Lewin, Tamar. (2012, March 6). Black students punished more, data suggests. *New York Times*, A11.

Losen, D., & Skiba, R. (2010). *Suspended education: Urban middle schools in crisis.* Montgomery, AL: Southern Poverty Law Center.

McCord, J. (1996). Unintended consequences of punishment *Pediatrics, 98*, 832–834

McLoyd, V. (1990). The impact of economic hardship on black families and children: Psychological distress, parenting, and socioemotional development. *Child Development, 61*, 311–346.

Murry, V., Bynum, M., Brody, G., Willert, A., & Stephens, D. (2001). African American single mothers and children in context: A review of studies on risk and resilience. *Clinical Child and Family Psychology Review, 4*(2), 133–155.

Nabors, L. A., Weist, M. D., Shugarman, R., Woeste, M. J., Mullet, E., & Rosner, L. (2004). Assessment, prevention, and intervention activities in a school-based program for children experiencing homelessness. *Behavior Modification, 28*(4), 565–578.

Ogbu, J. (1981). Origins of human competence: A cultural ecological perspective. *Child Development, 52*, 413–429.

Parke, R., & Buriel, R. (1998). Socialization in the family: Ethnic and ecological perspectives. In Damon, W., & Ersenberg, N. (Eds.), *Handbook of child psychology: Social, emotional, and personality development: Vol. 3* (5th ed., pp. 463–552). New York: John Wiley,

Peters. M., & Massey, G. (1983). Mundane extreme environmental stress in family stress theories: The case of black families in white America. *Marriage and Family Review, 6*, 193–218.

Petit, G., Bates, J., & Dodge, K. (1997). Supportive parenting, ecological context, and children's adjustment: A seven-year longitudinal study. *Child Development, 68*, 908–923.

Pettit, B., & Western, B. (2004), Mass imprisonment and the life course: Race and class inequality in U.S. incarceration. *American Sociological Review, 69*, 151–169.

Pinderhughes, E., Dodge, K., Bates, J., Pettit, G., & Zelli, A. (2000). Discipline responses: Influences of parents' socioeconomic status, ethnicity, beliefs about parenting, stress, and cognitive-emotional processes. *Journal of Family Psychology, 14*, 380–400.

Regalado, M., Sareen, H., Inkelas, M., Wissow, L., & Halfon, N. (2004). Parents' discipline of young children: Results from the National Survey of Early Childhood Health. *Pediatrics, 113*(6), 1952–1958.

Richman, A. (1987). "Oprah." *People, 27*(2), 49–55.

Sedlak, A., Broadhurst, D., & Thomas, C. (1997). *Third national incidence study of child abuse and neglect* (Data Collective Report No. NIS-3). Washington, DC: U.S. Department of Health and Human Services.

Smith, J., & Brooks-Gunn, J. (1997). Correlate and consequences of harsh discipline in children. *Archives of Pediatric Adolescence Medicine, 151*, 777–786.

Socolar, R., Amaya-Jackson, L., Eron, L., Howard, B., Landsverk, J., & Evans, J. (1997). Research on discipline. *Archives of Pediatric and Adolescent Medicine, 151*, 758–760.

Socolar, R., & Stein, R. (1995). Spanking infants and toddlers: Maternal beliefs and practices. *Pediatrics, 95*, 105–111.

——. (1996). Maternal discipline of young children: Context, belief, and practice. *Journal of Developmental and Behavioral Pediatrics, 17*, 1–8.

Stewart, E., Baumer, E., Brunson, R., & Simons, R. (2009). Neighborhood racial context and perception of police-based racial discrimination. *Criminology, 47*(3), 847–887.

Straus, M. A. (1994). *Beating the devil out of them: Corporal punishment in American families*. San Francisco: Jossey-Bass/Lexington.

Straus, M., & Field, C. (2003). Psychological aggression by American parents: National data on prevalence, chronicity, and severity. *Journal of Marriage and the Family, 65*, 795–808.

Straus, M., & Stewart, J. (1999). Corporal punishment by American parents: National data on prevalence, chronicity, severity, and duration, in relation to child and family characteristics. *Clinical Child and Family Psychological Review, 2*, 55–70.

Straus, M., Sugarman, D., & Giles-Sims, J. (1997). Spanking by parents and subsequent antisocial behavior in children. *Archives of Pediatric and Adolescent Medicine, 151*, 761–767.

Taylor, C., Manganello, J., Lee, S., & Rice, J. (2010). Mothers' spanking of 3-year-old children and subsequent risk of children's aggressive behavior. *Pediatrics, 125*(5), 1057–1065.

Taylor, L., Hinton, I., & Wilson, M. (1995). Parental influence on academic performance in African American students. *Journal of Child and Family Studies, 4*(3), 293–302.

Wauchope, B., & Straus, M. (1990). Physical punishment and physical abuse of American children: Incidence rates by age, gender, and occupational class. In M. Straus & R. Gelles (Eds.), *Physical violence in American families* (pp. 133–148). New Brunswick, NJ: Transaction Publishers,

Wissow, L. (2002). Child discipline in the first three years of life. In N. Halfon, K. McLaren, & M. Schuster (Eds.), *Child rearing in America: Challenges facing parents with young children* (pp. 146–147). New York: Cambridge University Press.

Wright, K. (1982). Sociocultural factors in child abuse. In B. A. Bass. G. Wyatt, & G. Powell (Eds.), *The Afro-American family: Assessment, treatment and research issues* (pp. 237–261). New York: Grune & Stratton.

Wright, M. (2000). *I'm chocolate, you're vanilla: Raising healthy black and biracial children in a race-conscious world.* San Francisco: Jossey-Bass.

Zlotnick, C., Wright, M., Cox, K., Te'o, I., & Stewart-Felix, P. (2000). The family empowerment club: Parent support and education for related caregivers. *Child and Youth Care Forum, 29*(2).

CHAPTER | 3

Giving Voice

AN EXPLORATION OF THE INTEGRATION OF
SOCIAL JUSTICE AND INFANT MENTAL HEALTH

▸ *ERICA TORRES AND KATHRYN ORFIRER*

STELLA'S STORY

STELLA MARTINEZ, A 10-MONTH-OLD biracial (African American and Latina) girl, was cold, hungry, and terrified. Wearing nothing but her diaper and swaddled in a thin blanket, she was lying on the sidewalk of a busy street. The ground was hard and uncomfortable, and Stella did not know how long she had been lying there. She watched in terror as her parents yelled, shoved, and hit each other. Her parents, high on methamphetamines, were loud and unpredictable. She had a deep desire to be held and comforted by someone; anyone would do at this point, but she had given up on crying a long time ago. She also had given up on expecting that someone would meet her needs on a predictable basis. All she could hope for was to get something to eat before she fell asleep. She was becoming accustomed to this experience. After all, it had practically been her daily routine since the day she was born.

Unbeknownst to Stella, today was a different day. Late on this particular afternoon, when she had finally lost the strength to stay awake and was dozing off, she was jostled awake by a stranger in a dark uniform. She was confused as she witnessed her parents get taken away by other strangers in uniforms. Stella then found herself in a car with these unknown adults, and she spent the evening in a foreign but warm and comfortable room. The next day, she awoke to smiling strangers, her foster parents. She was cleaned, clothed, and fed. For the first time in a long while, Stella's body did not long for food or warmth. She did, however, long for the love and familiarity of her parents.

The first few months in her foster home were difficult. The shock of losing her parents and the world to which she had become accustomed was immense, and Stella struggled. Where were her parents? Who were these strangers? Everything that her five senses registered was foreign—from touch to the smells to the tastes, to what she saw and heard. None of it seemed familiar. Stella was overwhelmed and confused. Her whole system wrestled with the yearning for familiarity along with the desire to be loved and cared for in this new way.

Over the next several months, Stella seemed to be adjusting. She even began to cry to communicate, gesturing and using words to indicate what she wanted or needed. She learned to seek out her foster mother for comfort and security. She laughed easily but also hid behind her foster mother when she felt scared or unsure. All of these were behaviors that we would expect to see in a child Stella's age. The foster mother was pleased. Despite her difficult and traumatic start, Stella seemed to be settling into a stable and secure relationship with her caregivers.

Meanwhile, Stella's birth mother was working to regain custody of Stella. This was an uphill battle, as this mother had lost legal custody of her three older children. Still struggling to remain clean and sober, Stella's mother worked on her case plan and visited with Stella on a weekly basis. The visits were satisfying to neither Stella nor her mother. Stella was confused and terrified and made every attempt to steer clear of her mother. Her mother, appearing annoyed, responded by saying things like, "Don't you love me?" "You're evil," and "I'm your mother, don't you ever forget that, little girl." These visits continued to be very stressful for Stella and her mother. Intervention was necessary if the visits were to continue.

THE STORY DEEPENS

In the story of Stella, we have given voice to Stella's experience through the knowledge gained in the study of infant mental health, and attachment theory in particular. Giving voice to Stella is somewhat revolutionary; the voices of young children have been pervasively quieted throughout our society as well as over generations. In their voices, the deep and long-lasting importance of early relationships becomes clear, as does the impact of early traumatic experiences on the very young child. Upon deeper exploration, however, we find that the story becomes more complex as we learn the histories of Stella's parents. After all, "a story is a map that extends through time" (Freedman & Combs, 1996, p. 15).

It appears that Stella's parents may never have been given a chance. Stella's mother, Lisa, was neglected and sexually abused as a young child herself. She remembers trying crack cocaine with her own mother when she was only 6 years old. She was moved from foster home to foster home throughout her childhood. She never really knew what it meant to have a stable primary caregiver and definitely never felt loved and claimed by anyone. Now she was grappling with a helpless yet demanding baby of her own who was needing and wanting what Lisa had never received, and possibly faced with the huge chasm between the type of mother she longed to be and the mother that she was.

Stella's father, Luis, was the only boy of five children. Luis was raised by a single mother in homeless shelters and transitional housing complexes. He resorted to methamphetamine and cocaine use at a very young age, not for recreation but to stay awake and alert, and protect his family while on the streets. Unfortunately, the substance he once used to protect his family was now destroying him.

The complexity is evident. Lisa and Luis are most certainly failing to provide what Stella needs, but one suspects that they are parenting from a place of pain and ambivalence. If they had been given a voice as infants, their own earliest months and years would tell a story very similar to Stella's story. What's more, Stella's parents have a personal history of being disadvantaged and marginalized, a pattern that has been present in their family for generations. Their current behaviors and responses cannot be separated from their experiences of being parented themselves and their subsequent internalized representations of parenting and parenting behavior.

Furthermore Lisa and Luis cannot be considered separate from their cultural backgrounds and the historical injustices of those backgrounds. Both Lisa and Luis have cultural identities that have been framed by the negative attitudes, behaviors, and responses of the dominant culture, and then imprinted with the indelible stamp of unique experiences. This cultural legacy has been passed down through the generations. Now we must imagine the impact on Luis and Lisa as they find themselves dealing with child protective services (CPS), a system that current studies have found not only has disproportionately higher rates of placing children of color in foster care, but also has disproportionately lower rates of reuniting children of color with their birth parents (Westat, Inc., and Chapin Hall Center for Children, 2001). Such practices demonstrate a dominant system's ideology and ability to perpetuate institutional racism that can affect generations of families.

The Martinez family has been referred to the Services to Enhance Early Development (SEED) program, a program that specializes in providing infant mental health interventions and culturally accountable services to infants, toddlers, and their families. The SEED program, located in Oakland, California, is a collaboration between the Alameda County Social Services Agency Department of Children and Family Services, the Alameda County Public Health Department, and Children's Hospital & Research Center Oakland. The goal of this collaboration is for specially trained therapists and child welfare workers to meet the parents in a relationship-based manner. While safety and protection mandates are held primarily by child welfare, that agency also partners with the clinical and medical staff to meet the overall health, mental health, and developmental needs of the infant, and always in the context of his or her primary relationships. Given that the disproportionate representation of families of color is evident in the SEED program and the vast majority of the clients come from marginalized communities, it is a mission of the SEED program to provide clinical practice not only from an infant mental health framework but also from a social justice theoretical framework. This chapter reviews infant mental health and social justice concepts, and discusses the complexities involved in interconnecting and applying these concepts within a mental health collaboration with the child welfare system.

UNDERSTANDING DISPROPORTIONALITY

The plight of children of color in the foster care system is distressing. Although several national incidence studies have found that there are no statistically significant differences in overall maltreatment rates between African American and Caucasian families (Hill, 2006), children of color continue to be disproportionately represented in the child welfare system (Westat, Inc., and Chapin Hall Center for Children, 2001). In fact, at least one research study has found race to be an important factor in making reports to child protective services hotlines (Albert, 1994). Additionally, both public and private hospitals have been found to overreport abuse and neglect among African Americans, while underreporting maltreatment among Caucasians (Sedlak & Schultz, 2005). Once in foster care, families of color, in comparison to Caucasian families, have less contact with child welfare workers, receive fewer services, and are less likely to receive in-home services (Roberts, 2002). Finally, an analysis of national data found not only that race continues to be a strong predictor of reunification, but more specifically that Caucasian children are four times more likely than African American children to be reunified with their families (Hill, 2005).

These are daunting findings, and theories of possible causes are equally disturbing. It has been stated that racial overrepresentation results from the decision-making processes of child protective services agencies, cultural insensitivities and biases of workers, and institutional racism (National Association of Public Child Welfare Administrators, 2006). These findings have propelled the SEED program from providing culturally sensitive therapeutic interventions to providing ones that are culturally accountable and socially just. The difference between the two may not be immediately obvious; striving toward culturally accountable care and socially just interventions means actively working to eradicate disproportionality in the child welfare system. Integrating social justice and infant mental health is not merely an important part of providing sensitive and compassionate care to transitional families; it is essential. As illustrated earlier, transitional families are quite vulnerable. In order to address the various vulnerabilities that transitional families with infants experience and provide the best possible treatment, we must not only hold in mind our knowledge base of infant mental health, but also incorporate historical contexts and social justice.

From an infant mental health perspective, the SEED program's goal is to reduce or eradicate symptoms related to early traumatic experiences within the caregiving environment and to promote and support primary attachments. From a social justice perspective, this means understanding ways in which power, privilege, and oppression have affected parents' lives, along with ways in which providers' own places of privilege perpetuate that cycle of oppression. Given the disproportionate representation of families of color in the child welfare system, it is strongly indicated that the work be viewed through both an infant mental health lens and a social justice lens. To conceptualize the importance of integrating both perspectives, we often use the metaphor of a vision examination, in which you are sitting in the ophthalmologist's chair and you are looking into the apparatus with the multiple lenses. The ophthalmologist asks you again and again which lens is clearer. We strongly believe that both infant mental health and social justice lenses need to always be in place when working with young children in the foster care system. Otherwise, the picture will be blurry.

The SEED program works within a close collaborative relationship with the child welfare system to bring to light the need for developmentally sensitive child welfare for the youngest children as well as relationship-based work with parents and caregivers. The unique way this program is structured results in both advantages and challenging impasses or crossroads. Sometimes an understanding of the needs of the child (attachment and developmental theory) and an understanding of the needs of the parent in social and historical context (social justice theory) seem to come into direct conflict, particularly when recommendations and decision making are at hand.

AN INFANT MENTAL HEALTH PERSPECTIVE

Nationally, infants and toddlers are disproportionately represented in all areas of the child welfare system. Young children consistently make up the largest proportion of abuse and neglect reports. In federal fiscal year 2008, for example, infants and toddlers, while making up 34% of the overall population, accounted for 40% of the children reported for maltreatment. Further, of the population of children screened for child abuse or neglect, 45% were five years old or younger. Infants and toddlers are also more likely to be placed in out-of-home care, making up 31% of the children who entered foster care in 2009, the largest single age group entering care. The risk for re-reporting is highest for the youngest children—infants and toddlers in particular. Most ominously, 87% of all maltreatment fatalities occurred among children from birth to five years old (DeVooght, McCoy-Roth, & Freundlich, 2011). Studies have shown that infants and toddlers experience longer placements (especially those who enter at less than three months of age) and higher rates of reentry into foster care, with statistics approaching nearly one in three of reunified infants and toddlers reentering foster care (Wulczyn, Chen, Collins, & Ernst, 2011).

Infant research has clearly shown that birth to three years is a critical developmental period. Through positive, nurturing, consistent interactions with loving adults, babies develop attachments that allow for the experiences that support positive and optimal development in all areas (Lieberman & Zeanah, 1995; Sroufe, 1983). The actual growth and development of the infant's brain occurs as a result of the interaction over time, or transaction (Sameroff & Chandler, 1975), of the infant's inborn biology and experience in the world (Perry & Pollard, 1997; Shonkoff & Phillips, 2000; Shore, 1997). The infant's experience is characterized by day-to-day and minute-to-minute interaction with the primary caregiver. The quality of this infant-caregiver interpersonal experience is paramount. What's more, an ecological model of infant mental health holds that this relationship lives within the wider contexts of family, community, society, and culture. The field of infant mental health has allowed us to better understand infants and toddlers, giving voice to an age group that has often been misunderstood. In the field of child welfare, it has the potential to inform policy, practice, and treatment of infants, families, and caregivers. The SEED program seeks to bring these concepts to the multidisciplinary collaborative effort and integrate this information into the system through education, consultation, and treatment.

Treatment of families in this program has used and adapted infant-parent psychotherapy, which was originated by Selma Fraiberg and her colleagues in Ann Arbor, Michigan, in the 1970s (Fraiberg, Adelson, & Shapiro, 1975). Groundbreaking and unique in so many ways, this therapeutic model integrated knowledge and approaches from the fields of developmental psychology, education, social work, nursing, psychiatry, and psychoanalysis. Therapists regularly did their work in the families' homes, knowing that this approach, nicknamed "kitchen table therapy," would reach families who otherwise would not receive the benefits of it.

Integrated into the therapy are concrete assistance and clinical case management that allow therapists the freedom to recognize real-life needs of clients, such as housing, food, and health care. The treatment plan may also include non-didactic developmental guidance along with psychodynamically informed therapy, with the target of intervention being the disturbance in the relationship between the child and the caregiver. Therapy of this sort provided an opportunity for parents to have therapists who explored such questions as: "What about the baby?" "What about the parent who cannot provide consistent nurturing care?" "How can we offer a clinical intervention to protect both?"

The field of infant mental health has expanded over the succeeding decades. Attachment theory and the results of numerous scientific attachment studies provide a knowledge base for our consultation (Ainsworth, 1978; Bowlby, 1979). New technology allowing brain imaging has provided the opportunity to glean scientific evidence of not only the emotional but also the physiological effects of neglectful and abusive care and the witnessing of domestic violence and trauma in general. Two areas of theoretical significance will be highlighted here, as they have particular relevance to our work in SEED: Bronfenbrenner's Ecological Model (Bronfenbrenner, 1986) and the concept of intergenerational transmission of trauma (Albert, 1994).

Bronfenbrenner's Ecological Model acknowledges that the infant and parent or caregiver are intrinsically embedded in their environment (Bronfenbrenner, 1986). They are a part of many interacting systems and exist only in relation to the wider cultural context. They are in constant two-way reciprocal interaction with their cultural environment. From this perspective, an infant or parent cannot be understood separate from the social-cultural-historical context. This is basic to an infant mental health approach that encourages and supports an infant and parents within the cultural context of their early developing, social, and emotional relationships. Culture is broadly defined and includes those relationships, past and present, that shape each emerging connection, contribute to shared understanding, and effect change.

An understanding of intergenerational transmission also is key to implementing a socially just infant mental health program in a child welfare context. In sociological terms and psychological learning theory, behaviors or characteristics are passed on through the experience of witnessing behaviors of parents over time and identifying with these behaviors (Bandura, 1996). In infant mental health, a more complex means of transmission is hypothesized. A highly influential idea conceptualized by Selma Fraiberg was that of "ghosts in the nursery" (Fraiberg, Adelson, & Shapiro, 1975). This image expresses the lingering, invisible, unconscious traces of the parent's own early experiences of being parented as those experiences insidiously take up residence inside the parent, silently affecting feelings about caregiving, interpretations of experiences, and subsequent behaviors. Interactions with the parent's own baby ignite visceral and immediate feelings. Some parents might have memories of tender, loving, and soft interactive moments that recall their own experiences of the world being a safe, predictable, and loving place, thereby transmitting positive parenting and a sense of self intergenerationally. For adults who did not experience the nurturing and responsiveness they needed in these critical years, the ghosts may return as unconscious feelings of pain, jealousy, resentment, disinterest, numbness, or even hate in relation to their own babies. Such unconscious feelings may create a lack of attunement or worse—neglect and abuse. This lack of attunement has been described as an inability to "hear the baby's cries" (Fraiberg, Adelson, & Shapiro, 1975) and as a distortion of the attachment system. The result is that this vulnerable parent then lacks the capacity to help the child feel held, safe and secure, and loved and lovable, and may even become neglectful or abusive.

A multitude of studies of adults using the Adult Attachment Interview (George, Kaplan, & Main, 1985; Main & Solomon, 1986) have found that unless the adult integrates those broken-off preverbal painful memories and is able to form a coherent narrative (often within a later secure relationship with a partner or other significant figure), the experiences that he or she had as an infant are painfully reenacted and emerge within the parent-infant relationship (IJzendoorn, 1995). Intergenerational transmission occurs because of the intense emotional bond and the durability of the experiences and influence of that early relationship.

Despite the information from highly studied areas of infant mental health such as brain research and attachment theory, it is not uncommon for other systems to be slow in recognizing psychological research in policy and practice. This is true of the juvenile dependency and child welfare system. Despite scientific information to the contrary, there is a ubiquitous tendency in the child welfare system to believe babies are "resilient," will be or are "fine," and will bounce back. "I was fine and I was raised like that." "She won't remember." "Babies don't feel pain the same way adults do." However, the passage of the Adoption and Safe Families Act (ASFA) of 1997 has spurred an increased emphasis on the need for permanency for young children, birth to three years old, in the child welfare/dependency system. For example, legal timelines have been shortened to acknowledge the immediacy of the needs for young children to form and maintain attachments. Concurrent planning has also been enacted with the intent of establishing permanency and decreasing the number of placements for young children.

How do we hold the voices of the generations—the babies as well as the lingering child ghosts of the past in the parents with whom we work? Both are crying out for nurturing in a world where they are reminded minute to minute of their powerlessness through racism, oppression, marginalization, sexism, and perhaps drug addiction and violence. In SEED, we think in terms of opportunity: opportunity for the babies to be heard and have their needs met, and opportunity for parents to care for their children in ways that they never had available to them as infants, and opportunity to demonstrate a capacity to nurture that they might not have known they possessed. We advocate for the babies of today by giving them a voice in therapy and in the courtroom. We advocate for parents by allowing the ghosts of babies past to speak out loud in therapy and by bringing to life in child welfare and the courts, the obstacles that parents must overcome in a real-world context. However, in order to acknowledge the wider picture that includes the complexity of culture, layers of historical trauma in marginalized and oppressed groups (Brave Heart & DeBruyn, 1998; DeGruy-Leary, 2005), and a lack of attention to the voices and psychology of families of color, we are cautioned to reflect on our theory and practice for ways in which we are consciously and/or unconsciously supporting and maintaining racism, oppression, and the marginalization of groups of people. Accordingly, we must be ever watchful of the ways in which our own culture, position of privilege, and role within the system affect our therapeutic relationships and practices. For this reason, a specific focus on social justice is essential to our work. The following section outlines this theory and its application to the work at SEED.

A SOCIAL JUSTICE PERSPECTIVE

The multicultural movement in psychology can be traced back to the late 1960s and early 1970s, when a small group of black counselors and psychologists began to bring attention to the ineffective and often harmful psychological interventions among diverse client populations (D'Andrea & Daniels, 2010). Theoretical concepts of that time tended to view everyone through the same cultural lens, assuming that everyone held the same cultural values and that all therapeutic approaches could be applied equally across different cultures. Some of the pioneers of multicultural psychology noted the uphill struggle of incorporating "multicultural awareness and sensitivity" into the dominant discourse (Ponterotto, Suzuki, Casas, & Alexander, 2010). The efforts of the early proponents of multiculturalism in psychology have borne fruit in more-inclusionary practices and cultural competence in the mental health professions (D'Andrea & Daniels, 2010). In particular, they can be credited with the development and implementation of multicultural training practices (Grieger & Tolliver, 2001), culturally sensitive research methods (Sue & Sue, 2008), and multicultural competencies and standards in the psychology profession (Sue, Arredondo, & McDavis, 1992). While the incorporation of multiculturalism has been a critical advancement in the mental health field, there is recognition of the need for mental health professionals to embrace new professional roles that promote a greater level of justice in our society.

Even though Sue et al. (1998) stated that "multiculturalism is about social justice, cultural democracy, and equity" (p. 5), there has been less of an emphasis on social justice and more of an emphasis on diversity and cultural competence in the field of psychology. While the field of infant mental health has roots in social work ideologies, the emphasis has been on providing concrete assistance via acquisition of resources when the family is in need. Otherwise, consideration of ways in which power, privilege, and oppression affect the client's and family's quality of life appears to be absent in the infant mental health literature.

Psychologists, for the most part, have been trained to understand and conceptualize human behavior from a Eurocentric perspective. In addition, we have created Eurocentric models of treatment without always adequately considering how these interventions work for clients of color. McGoldrick and Hardy (2008) state, "Racial, sexist, cultural, classist, and heterosexist power hierarchies constrain our clients' lives and determine what gets defined as a problem and what services our society will set up to respond to these problems" (pp. 4–5). For therapists to adopt a socially just approach, while having previous training in historically oppressive ideologies and collaborating with a historically oppressive system, they must acquire "a consciousness that will permit [them] to go beyond the limits imposed by [their] socialization and the boundaries set by [their] professional fields" (Martín-Baró, 1994, p. 6). Martín-Baró further argues that psychologists are actually perpetuating injustice by being overly fixated on individual factors to explain social behaviors, which extracts the person from the sociohistorical context. These points explain that in order for us to use psychological knowledge to promote human welfare, we must consider larger-scale interventions. Humphreys (1996) stated, "Psychologists can more effectively benefit society by making long-term commitments to improving social institutions and social policy than they can by doing psychotherapy" (p. 195). Therein lies the mission of the SEED program, to serve as advocates for social justice in collaboration with a social institution, while providing services for infants and their families.

Taking on a social justice perspective means going beyond the traditional stance of multicultural competency, which has been limited to a focus on the therapist's ability to effectively incorporate cultural diversity into his or her therapeutic work (Arredondo, 1998; Pope-Davis, Breaux, & Liu, 1997). Social justice has more to do with critiques of power and the inequitable distribution of power. Therefore, one approach to social justice works to "rectify fractures and ills that may be attributable to the inequitable distribution of power" (Hardy, 2008). Another approach to social justice, called deliberative justice or deliberative democracy, focuses on exploring practices of power and oppression, and scrutinizing and transforming the processes that initially facilitated unequal outcomes (Young, 1990). This latter approach then turns to the process of decision making and interactions that occur at the individual and systemic levels, as opposed to suggesting the redistribution of resources. Psychologist Martín-Baró (1994) describes a socially just psychologist as one who focuses "not on what has been done but what needs to be done" (p. 6).

Goodman et al. (2004) identified six principles to define ways of utilizing social justice theory in the practice of psychology today. The purpose of these principles, which come from multicultural and feminist perspectives, is to provide a social justice lens for the conceptualization and implementation of psychotherapy. First, Goodman and colleagues identify the importance of examining the assumptions and values that we hold as psychologists, and understanding how power dynamics affect interactions with clients and communities. As SEED therapists working collaboratively with child welfare workers, we are aware that our therapeutic role is a very sensitive one, complicated by the various institutional powers that we hold. We are conscious of the power that we are afforded as agents of care. We are more critically aware of the power we maintain as a collaborator with a very powerful system in the parents' lives: child protective services. Because of our collaboration, we are privy to a considerable amount of information before meeting the family. At the outset, we must be aware of our assumptions and biases, and be reminded that the information we are receiving comes from a scrutinizing system. Therefore, we must create space for an alternate story to emerge, keeping in mind that the impact of oppression has not been factored into the "presenting problem." To our clients, this unearned power with which we enter their lives is blatant and can be threatening. We are often initially met with rightful suspicion and guardedness. Questions like, "What is your role?" and "Will you be weighing in on whether I get my baby back?" are common. As we begin establishing a relationship and building rapport, we seek to be transparent about our role as clinicians.

The second principle describes the importance of shared power. The idea behind shared power is that the therapist does not assume that he or she holds the absolute answer to the problems (Goodman et al., 2004). In this context, the psychologist is a co-learner, and can expect to learn culturally relevant ways in which the client may deal with the problem. As SEED therapists, we apply this principle by making explicit the notion that we are entering the therapeutic relationship with a specific lens. First, that lens includes the beliefs and worldviews that we bring from our own cultural background and experiences. The lens also includes our theoretical orientation of attachment theory and concepts of infant mental health. Finally, it includes social justice concepts and practices. Together, these lenses allow us to see our clients holistically, and as a result, more clearly.

The principle of shared power would also include the promotion of community empowerment. Seeking solutions within the community itself and working in partnerships to support community empowerment are key elements of social justice.

Goodman et al. (2004) describe the third principle as the importance of "giving voice" or, rather, amplifying the voices of the oppressed. In particular, this includes considering the cultural context in which the person has developed his or her identity and worldview. The application of this concept to developmentally sensitive child welfare practice is a complicated matter for therapists working with families during their journey through the child welfare system, for therapists are holding interests of both parents and children when they can be in most opposition with each other. How do we weigh the voices and the needs? The parent, whose history of oppression and marginalization must be heard and validated before healing can occur? The infant-parent dyad in all of its psychological complexity? Or the infant, whose experiences are rarely given voice, and for whom the foundation of the sense of self and the world is being constructed and set in place in the very structure of the infant brain? Is it possible to give voice to both parent and infant? Infant-parent psychotherapy principles lay the groundwork for that, yet how does one take it further, to examination through the social justice lens? Is the dedication to maintaining both the attachment lens and the social justice lens too immense? The SEED program grapples with all of these questions and strives to keep them in its conscious awareness while working with every family.

The fourth and fifth principles described by Goodman et al. (2004) involve the facilitation of consciousness raising and building on strengths—specifically, helping clients understand the context in which they live and how societal institutions (e.g., child protective services and educational systems) contribute to community oppression and individual difficulties. A focus on individual and community strengths is also an aspect of these two principles, which are ever present in our work at SEED. Our clients come into therapy already struggling against various powerful systems. Often, the impact of oppression is so apparent to them that our work is not so much in helping our clients understand this oppression as it is in acknowledging and validating the existence of institutional oppression in their lives. In terms of building on strengths, we ask clients what community resources have assisted them in the past and are assisting them now. We then work toward incorporating these resources into our collaborative approach. Goodman et al. (2004) state the sixth principle as follows: "The aim . . . is not to develop a one-sided or hierarchical dependency that may render communities or systems helpless once we leave, but rather to support strengths that will continue to thrive beyond our explicit involvement" (p. 807). Helping families become aware of personal and community strengths is a critical aspect of our work. We strive to empower families and assist them in understanding ways in which their physical and emotional needs can continually be met. We believe in the idea of leaving clients with the tools for social change because we know that this can be an integral component of supporting our clients in their efforts to maintain reunification and avoid reentry into the child welfare system.

In this collaboration within large and powerful systems, SEED mental health therapists, child welfare workers, and public health nurses understand the importance of combining social justice concepts and practices with infant mental health knowledge. Our practice utilizes an infant mental health evidence-based framework with integration of applied social justice research and theories. Our struggles to simultaneously hold both affect us on a daily basis, with every new client and life circumstance. However, we continue to strive toward strategies that empower oppressed and marginalized communities. Our work with some of the most vulnerable populations requires us to constantly look at our clients' needs and concerns from an individual level, a community level, and a societal level. As we could not know Stella without knowing Lisa and Luis, we could not know Lisa and Luis without knowing their histories and without viewing those histories within the context of their culture and communities, including both present-day and historic oppression. Furthermore, if we are to authentically engage with Luis and Lisa, we must be aware of and acknowledge our own position within institutions of power and within our own cultural contexts. We cannot afford to fail to take up the task of integrating social justice with infant mental health practice.

REFERENCES

Ainsworth, M. (1978). The development of infant-mother attachment. *Review of Infant Development, 3*, 1–89.

Albert, V. (1994). From child abuse report to child welfare services. In R. Barth, M. Courtney, J. Berrick, & V. Albert (Eds.), From child abuse to permanency planning: Child welfare services pathways and placements (pp. 55–75). New York: Aldine de Gruyter.

Arredondo, P. (1998). Integrating multicultural counseling competencies and universal helping conditions in culture-specific contexts. *Counseling Psychologist, 26*, 592–601.

Bandura, A. (1996). Social cognitive theory of human development. In T. Husen & T. N. Postlethwaite (Eds.), *International encyclopedia of education* (2nd ed. , pp. 5513–5518). Oxford: Pergamon Press.

Bowlby, J. (1979). *The making and breaking of affectional bonds* (2nd ed.). London: Tavistock Publications.

Brave Heart, M. Y. H., & DeBruyn, L. M. (1998). The American Indian holocaust: Healing historical unresolved grief. *American Indian and Alaskan Native Mental Health Research, 8*(2), 56–78.

Bronfenbrenner, U. (1986). Ecology of the family as a context for human development: Research perspectives. *Developmental Psychology, 22*(6), 723–742.

D'Andrea, M., & Daniels, J. (2010). Promoting multiculturalism, democracy, and social justice in organizational settings: A case study. In J. G. Ponterotto, J. M. Casas, L. A. Suzuki, & C. M. Alexander (Eds.), *Handbook of multicultural counseling* (pp. 591–602). Thousand Oaks, CA: Sage.

DeGruy-Leary, J. (2005). *Post traumatic slave syndrome: America's legacy of enduring injury and healing.* Oakland, CA: Uptone Press.

DeVooght, K., McCoy-Roth, M., & Freundlich, M. (2011). Young and vulnerable: Children five and under experience high maltreatment rates. *Child Trends: Early Childhood Highlights, 2*(March), 1–20.

Fraiberg, S. Adelson, E., & Shapiro, V. (1975). Ghosts in the nursery: A psychoanalytic approach to the problems of impaired infant-mother relationships. *Journal of the American Academy of Child and Adolescent Psychiatry, 14*(3), 387–421.

Freedman, J., & Combs, G. (1996). *Narrative therapy: The social construction of preferred realities.* New York: W. W. Norton.

George, C., Kaplan, N., & Main, M. (1985). *Adult attachment interview.* Unpublished manuscript, University of California, Berkeley.

Goodman, L. A., Liang, B., Helms, J. E., Latta, R. E., Sparks, E., & Weintraub, S. R. (2004). Training counseling psychologists as social justice agents: Feminist and multicultural principles in action. *Counseling Psychologist, 32*, 793–837.

Grieger, I., & Tolliver, S. (2001). Multiculturalism on predominantly white campuses: Multiple roles and functions for the counselor. In J. G. Ponterotto, J. M. Casas, L. A. Suzuki, & C. M. Alexander (Eds.), *Handbook of multicultural counseling* (2nd ed., pp. 825–848). Thousand Oaks, CA: Sage.

Hardy, K. (2008). Interview with Ken Hardy by Randall C. Wyatt. Retrieved November 4, 2011, from https://psychotherapy.net/interview/kenneth-hardy.

Hill, R. B. (2005). The role of race in parental reunification. In D. Derezotes, M. F. Testa, and J. Poertner (Eds.), *Race matters in child welfare: The overrepresentation of African American children in the system.* Washington, DC: Child Welfare League of America.

——. (2006). *Synthesis of research on disproportionality in child welfare: An update.* Draft prepared in May 2006 for the Casey Center for the Study of Social Policy Alliance for Racial Equity. Retrieved November 1, 2011, from http://www.cssp.org/reform/child-welfare/other-resources/synthesis-of-research-on-disproportionality-robert-hill.pdf.

Humphreys, K. (1996). Clinical psychologists as psychotherapists. *American Psychologist, 51*, 190–197.

IJzendoorn, M. H. (1995). Adult attachment representations, parental responsiveness, and infant attachment: A meta-analysis on the predictive validity of the adult attachment inventory. *Psychological Bulletin, 117*(3), 387–403.

Lieberman, A. F., & Zeanah, H. (1995). Disorders of attachment in infancy. *Infant Psychiatry, 4*, 571–587.

Main, M., & Solomon, J. (1986). Discovery of an insecure disorganized/disoriented attachment pattern: Procedures, findings, and implications for the classification of behavior. In T. B. Brazelton and M. Yogman (Eds.), *Affective development in infancy* (pp. 95–124). Norwood, NJ: Ablex.

Martín-Baró, I. (1994). *Writings for a liberation psychology* (Adrianne Aron & Shawn Corne, Eds.). Cambridge, MA: Harvard University Press.

McGoldrick, M., & Hardy, K. (Eds.). (2008). *Re-visioning family therapy: Race, culture, and gender in clinical practice*. New York: Guilford.

National Association of Public Child Welfare Administrators. (2006). *Disproportionate representation in the child welfare system: Emerging promising practices survey*. Washington, DC: Author. Retrieved November 4, 2011, from http://www.napcwa.org/Home/docs/Disproportionate-Representation.pdf.

Perry, B. D., & Pollard, R. (1997). Altered brain development following global neglect in early childhood. *Proceedings of the Annual Meeting of the Society for Neuroscience, New Orleans*.

Ponterotto, J. G., Suzuki, L., Casas, M., & Alexander, C. M. (2010). *Handbook of multicultural counseling*. Thousand Oaks, CA: Sage.

Pope–Davis, D. B., Breaux, C., & Liu, W. M. (1997*). A multicultural immersion experience: Filling a void in multicultural training*. Thousand Oaks, CA: Sage.

Roberts, D. E. (2002). *Racial disproportionality in the U.S. child welfare system: Documentation, research on causes, and promising practices* (Working Paper No. 4). Baltimore, MD: Annie E. Casey Foundation.

Sameroff, A. J., & Chandler, M. J. (1975). Reproductive risk and the continuum of caretaker casualty. In F. D. Horowitz (Ed.), *Review of child development research* (Vol. 4). Chicago: University of Chicago Press.

Sedlak, A., & Schultz, D. (2005). Race differences in risk of maltreatment in the general child population. In D. M. Derezotes, J. Poertner, & M. F. Testa (Eds.), *Race matters in child welfare: The overrepresentation of African American children in the system* (pp. 97–115). Washington, DC: CWLA Press.

Shonkoff, J. P., & Phillips, D. (2000). *From neurons to neighborhoods: The science of early childhood development.* Washington, DC: National Academy Press.

Shore, R. (1997). *Rethinking the brain.* New York: Families and Work Institute.

Sroufe, L. A. (1983). Infant-caregiver attachment and patterns of adaptation in pre-school: The roots of maladaptation and competence. In M. Perlmutter (Ed.), *Minnesota symposium in child psychology* (Vol. 16). Hillsdale, NJ: Erlbaum.

Sue, D. W., Arredondo, P., & McDavis, R. J. (1992). Multicultural counseling competencies and standards: A call to the profession. *Journal of Counseling and Development, 70,* 477–483.

Sue, D. W., Carter, R. T., Casas, J. M., Fouad, N. A., Ivey, A. E., Jensen, M., et al. (1998). *Multicultural counseling competencies: Individual and organizational development.* Thousand Oaks, CA: Sage.

Sue, D. W., & Sue, D. (2008). *Counseling the culturally diverse: Theory and practice* (5th ed.). New York: John Wiley.

Westat, Inc., & Chapin Hall Center for Children. (2001). The role of race in parental reunification. In *Assessing the context of permanency and reunification in the foster care system* (pp. 6.1–6.15). Washington, DC: Department of Health and Human Services, Assistant Secretary for Planning and Evaluation. http://aspe.hhs.gov/hsp/fostercare-reunif01/.

Wulczyn, F., Chen, L., Collins, L., & Ernst, E. (2011). The foster care baby boom revisited: What do the numbers tell us. *Zero to Three, 31*(3), 4–10.

Young, I. M. (1990). *Justice and the politics of difference.* Princeton, NJ: Princeton University Press.

PART 2

Preparing the Organization for Its Work with Transitional Families

Organizations striving to make a difference in the lives of transitional families must start with their own staff, but an organization cannot change:

- if its position on culture, power, and privilege is merely management rhetoric;
- if the approach is not uniform in all its programs and at all levels of the organization; and
- if the programs within the agency are unable to implement the philosophy so it is meaningful and usable for all staff.

Chapter 4 describes the macro-level impact, including all the successes and stumbles, of the organization's efforts to promote an atmosphere of cultural awareness, sensitivity, and humility among its staff. Chapter 5 describes how the macro-level organizational change filtered down to make micro-level changes in the individual programs and among individual staff members.

Letting Some Air into the Room

OPENING AGENCY SPACE FOR CONSIDERATIONS OF CULTURE AND POWER

▶ LISA R. BERNDT

How do workers, men and women and people of different cultures in an agency or institution, protect against . . . cultural bias in their work on a day-to-day basis? Furthermore, how do they do this in societies where racist assumptions are an integral part of their upbringing and way of life, as they are in most modern industrial states?
—Tamasese & Waldegrave (1993)

THIS IS A STORY OF ONE AGENCY'S movement to respond to the questions posed above. It is a story of what happened at a time in our history when the status quo became unbearable for enough of us that we were willing to work toward change. It is a story of a process of awakening to the privilege and power that we wield as individuals, as a hospital-based department, and as part of bigger systems; and it is part of an ongoing story of our efforts to use that privilege and power responsibly. It is a story of our efforts to heighten our awareness of the actual effects of our actions and attitudes on the families and communities we serve, and on each other, and our coming to understand how these are not separate constituencies. It is meant to be a part of a wider conversation in the fields of health, mental health, and education about accountability to our mission and to the families who entrust their stories to us.

Because it is an account of attempts to address oppressions, especially racism, between its lines are slow simmers and boiling points, microaggressions (Sue et al., 2007) and gaping schisms, alarm and hope, trust and disappointment, determination and discouragement, stuck places and turning points. Laurin Mayeno (2010) reminds us that breakdowns can be transformed into breakthroughs, and this reminder has played a crucial part in our journey. There is ample frustration in the story, and there are moments of joy. As we have worked to move beyond multiculturalism to antiracist practice (Greene & Suskind, 2006), we find that issues of culture and power that used to be marginalized in our daily work are now at the center of our conversations, our thinking, and our practice. For some of us, this has meant the difference between leaving and staying. For some, it has been experienced as letting "more air into the room, or space to breathe." Some find it more comfortable, others less so. We are trying to let it be a fertile discomfort.

LEANING INTO THE COMPLEXITIES OF CULTURE AND POWER

At this point in our journey, we see culture as multidimensional and central to meaning making. Using Pamela Hays's (2001) ADDRESSING format, we consider such aspects as age and generation, developmental and acquired disabilities, religion, ethnicity, socioeconomic status, sexual and affectional orientation, indigenous heritage, national origin, and gender (table 4.1). We also

TABLE 4.1 Hays's Multicultural Assessment Model

A	Age-related factors. Actual age and age cohort (generation).
D D	Disability/Development. Acquired, visible and invisible developmental disabilities.
R	Religion and spirituality.
E	Ethnic identity. Race, culture (includes people of color as well as Caucasian, white ethnic).
S	Socioeconomic status. Current and former, especially in childhood.
S	Sexual and affectional orientation. Gay, lesbian, bisexual, heterosexual, asexual, kinky, and monogamous or polygygamous.
I	Indigenous heritage. First nation's peoples.
N	National identity. Immigrants, refugees, temporary residents, and their children.
G	Gender. Biological sex, transgender, gender roles, and stereotypes.

Source: P. Hays (2001, pp. 3–16)

recognize the effects of the historical legacies of genocide, slavery, and imperialism on our national consciousness and understand that membership in one group or another can bring protection and privilege, or oppression and danger (Batts, 2002). We try to stay accountable around the power differentials set in place by this history (Tamasese & Waldegrave, 1993). We also try to recognize that given the centuries of oppression and the patterns of racism that have tried to silence acknowledgment of its existence, conscious and continual effort is required to put the values of accountability and respect into practice. What becomes possible when we risk discomfort? How does it improve the quality of treatment when workers are able to bring themselves fully to their relationships with families and coworkers? Here are scenes from recent agency-wide meetings.

A therapist shares her work at a recent all-staff meeting. "I welcome your feedback," she says, "because I'm very close to this." She proceeds to describe the obstacles that an African American teen has faced: poverty, foster care, painful and complicated reunification with mother, intergenerational trauma, and racial discrimination. The therapist describes the teen's resilience, the crisis points where the young woman was able to ask for help, and the ways the therapist has made herself available outside appointed hours. Rage, despair, and grief infuse the young woman's life every day, along with humor and determination. She was on the verge of being expelled from school at least three times, but her therapist advocated with the school and held fast to the student's dreams, even when the young woman herself could not. "I will not let another one of our children become a statistic," the therapist tells us. Listening to her account of this work, many of us are on the edge of our seats. The odds against this young woman's survival and self-esteem have been great. The dropout rate in Oakland, California, is high. The link between foster care and homelessness is high. The risk of sexual exploitation is high. Economic conditions, past trauma, depression, and social conditioning can rob young people of color of any vision for the future (Turner, Finkelhor, & Ormrod, 2006). Yet this young woman has made it to community college.

We reflect together: How had this therapeutic relationship supported her to overcome these odds and claim her right to dream? What did it mean to have this particular therapist available to her? The therapist, an African American psychologist, described herself as being "mother, coach, aunty" to her. She called upon clinical judgment, cultural wisdom, and love—as a mother, as an elder, as a woman, as an African American psychologist, and as a social justice therapist, to meet this young woman and walk with her in new directions. All of these cultural expressions informed the service she provided and the relationship that these two women formed.

Consider this scene as well: At a staff meeting, the clinical director and executive director opened up space for us to talk about preparations the city and our hospital had been making for reactions to a verdict in a very painful court case. A young African American man had been shot in the back by a white police officer, and the reaction in the city had reflected anguish and outrage. City of Oakland officials were taking measures to contain further demonstrations by closing downtown businesses, including one of our clinics. We were invited by our managers to voice our feelings about the policy, and to address its impact on our clients. What would it convey to clients to have the building closed at a time of such pain? How would we convey support for families in their grief and rage, and our own? What did it mean that many of us would have the option to move away from the neighborhoods that were most affected, while the children and families we serve would not? For staff of color, the man who was killed could have been a son or a brother or a father. At the same time, some of us were of dominant ethnic and class backgrounds where we were trained to think of the police as protectors and the African American man who was killed as "Other," someone to fear. "Look at me," said an African American social worker to her white colleague. "Look at my face. What you are talking about is being afraid of me."

There was passion in the room, and grief and rage and despair and bewilderment. Some expressed concern over property and worker safety. We were reminded that for many of our clients and colleagues—men and women of color, lesbian, gay, bisexual, transgendered, Jewish, or Muslim—safety is an illusion. As one Latina worker said with great anguish, "It sounds as if we are talking about protecting ourselves from our clients." Another Latina worker spoke up, her voice quivering: "It seems like we are forgetting that a young man is dead." This helped move us into speaking from the heart.

These conversations are vital to our work if we are to meet homeless families where they are. Having a workplace that nurtures workers' cultural wisdom and healing traditions is vital to quality treatment. We see antiracist, anti-oppression practice as essential to ethical, respectful practice. We aim to build a culture where we can be present with our passions and our pain, with honest reactions and responses. What do we mean by respect? How do we operationalize it? How do we sit, bear witness, and go into the areas where we feel most defensive, on behalf of the families who are entrusting us with their stories? These conversations are painful, but what would be the cost if we couldn't have them?

If racism, sexism, heterosexism, and religious oppression had their way, we would not be speaking and listening in this manner. We don't take any of these moments for granted. There have been, and still are, times when silence and superficiality take over.

WHERE WE COME FROM: A WELL-INTENTIONED SILENCE

The Center for the Vulnerable Child was created in 1986. Currently, we serve young people (0–25 years of age) and their families who are living in high-stress environments, including foster care, homelessness, and poverty. From its inception, the CVC has made an effort to respond to children's needs with flexibility and respect and to assign high priority to the value of meeting people where they are, both psychologically and physically. Consequently, in addition to clinic visits, clinicians make home visits, or go to shelters, coffee shops, or schools to meet with children, teachers, and caregivers. This flexibility, along with the intention to resist pathologizing discourses (Madsen, 2003) and to go to any lengths to give children every chance at health and well-being, has always been part of what has emerged as "the CVC way."

The fact that from early days at the CVC, people were hired who understood this suggests that there has long been an overall vision of respect for families and an honoring of diversity (Waldegrave, Tamasese, Tuhaka, & Campbell, 2003). Having people on staff who understand from experience the effects of racism, sexism, and other kinds of marginalization is one thing; actually creating an environment that allows people from marginalized communities to stay and to thrive is another. How have we welcomed and nurtured workers of color, considering the extra toll it takes on them to watch their own community suffer? We value diversity and stand for respect. But how are we at operationalizing these values?

The fact is that this work affects us differently, and that those differences have to do with life experiences, personality, and location in the matrix of culture and power. Some who are trained in oppressive practices remain oblivious to the effects of these practices on others. Racism, sexism, and

heterosexual dominance keep many of us unaware of our own privilege, and of the historical and institutional obstacles placed in the path of others, even getting us to believe in meritocracy and the superiority of our ways. Systems of oppression lead those of us in positions of privilege and dominance to think it's rude to point out differences (Pinderhughes, 1989). Such a code rubs others raw as they endure microaggressions and systemic assaults to themselves and their communities (Sue et al., 2007). A workplace where unacknowledged racism is operating inflicts injury on staff of color, stifles cooperation for all, and allows other oppressions to thrive (Greene & Siskind, 2006).

Many of the children and families we serve have suffered generations of trauma and marginalization. Legacies of genocide, slavery, and systematic marginalization of immigrants have left scars on victims, perpetrators, bystanders, and their descendants, and continue to inform institutions that many of us take for granted. Compared with white youth, African American, Latino, and Native American youth are more vulnerable to being removed from their families, not graduating from high school, becoming unemployed, becoming homeless, and dying young. Medicine, social science, psychology, and many religious ideologies have been used to justify and support brutal and dehumanizing practices (Jackson, 2002; Leary, 2005). We are serving families who have the least protection, and who feel the legacies of historical trauma most acutely. They have every reason to be suspicious of us. How can those of us protected by "mainstream status" know if we are colluding in dehumanizing, colonizing practices (Waldegrave et al., 2003)? We have had to acknowledge the power that we wield as clinicians—the power to define and label, the power to speak for people without understanding them, the power to impose norms that require families to become like the dominant culture and to leave behind traditions and wisdom that have sustained them through years and generations. We have had to consider that privilege has kept some of us protected from and unaware of the suffering that we very well may have been perpetrating. We have had to start listening to, and being guided by, voices from the margins.

CONFESSIONS OF A WHITE SUPERVISOR

This may go without saying, but because there is limited space, and it is my telling, there will be many details missing from this account of our journey, and my interpretation will be different from those of others. I am a clinical social work supervisor, middle management, of dominant (or white) culture in terms of race, religion, sexual and affectional orientation, and class. Because of these characteristics, I am wrapped in layers of privilege, and that very gauze of "protection" can keep me from seeing things that are all too obvious to others with different levels of insight and life experiences of being marginalized and targeted for oppression (Batts & Brown, 2009).

When I came to work at the CVC in 2002, I felt welcomed and found an environment that was affable and amazingly upbeat, given the pain of the families' experiences. There were laughter and food and good-natured teasing. There were support from management and beautiful examples of workers going to great lengths to meet the needs of families. Yet every so often I would come upon a pocket of silence, a zone of tension that did not fit into these experiences of trust and mutual respect. As best as I could identify it, the dominant discourse of the CVC was this: "We trust one another; we put families first. We know we all have good intentions so we don't question or challenge one another." I wanted to fit in, and to do right by supervisees and right by the children and families who were confiding in me. I wanted to deserve this job, to be part of this remarkable working community.

In my first case presentation, I introduced the question of how to think about the impact of my whiteness on the African American family with whom I was working. My questions fell flat. The consultation team reassured me that the family sounded happy to have me. I wanted to believe this, but I felt uneasy. Instead of recognizing my own participation in cultural racism hiding behind our good intentions, I fell into my own cultural practices of individualizing and self-doubt, and drifted into the familiar fog of niceness. At the time all the supervisors had white-skin privilege, and I timidly asked why we didn't have any supervising therapists of color since we were working primarily with families of color, but I let the issue drop after a few attempts.

CRACKS IN THE SILENCE

What was vaguely unsettling and dissatisfying to me was a source of deep pain, frustration, anger, and stress to my office mate, a young African American woman whose life experience, loved ones, training, and values put her closely in touch with the experiences of many of the families with whom the CVC worked. While I provided her clinical supervision, it was she who oriented me to the spirit of practical, respectful, and culturally accountable case management. She was willing to tell me what it was like for her to sit in the required CVC clinical meetings, and she conveyed her alarm at the apparent disconnect from families' cultural experience, and what that disconnect implied about the quality of care being provided to families. In supervision and at the meetings, she expressed pain at the disrespect with which families were treated in our conversations. She was alone in bringing this to the group's attention, and that was a double injury (Batts, 2002; Constantine & Sue, 2007).

I saw her passion, and then I saw older clinicians respond in what seemed like dismissive and even patronizing ways. It looked like the racism of not naming racism, and the microaggression of invalidation (Batts, 2002; Chisom & Washington, 1997; Sue et al., 2007). It was so easy for those of us from dominant groups, and even those from marginalized groups who had been at the CVC for a long time, to try to reassure her or to imply that she was overreacting or didn't understand the complexities of the situation.

Many of us didn't see what we didn't see. There were predictable responses to the young worker's observations and pleas: "Say it nicely." "Curb your anger." "You're overreacting." "It's not about race; it's about class." "Our job is to protect children." By minimizing their colleague's experience, and ignoring the present-day expressions of historical, interpersonal, and institutional oppression, these attempts at helpfulness were doing damage.

When another young woman of color came to the agency, she reported similar experiences of physical and emotional pain, and frustration in the meetings. If this was the tone and conversation at the meetings, she reflected, what was happening in the clinical work with families? If we could not acknowledge these wounds—in our clients, our society, ourselves—how could we work effectively as helpers and healers (Hardy & Laszloffy, 1995; Leary, 2005; Vasquez & Macgraw, 2005)?

The three of us expressed our concern to the management, who made funds available for us to organize a staff retreat focusing on culture and power and issues of respect. Maybe all we lacked, we thought, was a way to talk to each other.

We consulted with experienced facilitators, experts in communication across power and difference, who surveyed the staff about perceptions and recognized the wide range of awareness. They led the staff through a day of training, but the participants were uncomfortable with some of the techniques taught to raise awareness, and saw them as instigating animosity between white staff and staff of color. "We trust each other here" was the message that met the facilitators, as if they had been attacking "the CVC way." It seemed that the facilitators came ready to name and talk about racism, and many of us were not ready to do that. Discouraged, we did not follow up with the facilitators, who felt baffled by the wall of "niceness."

This had not been the first such attempt. Early in the CVC's history, some of the staff of color identified disrespectfulness in a program director. The institution's administrators were recruited to mediate, and Employee Assistance Program (EAP) services were used to intervene. A few years later a staff retreat was organized to focus on diversity. It raised issues about black-white relations, and left individuals in other groups feeling lost and alienated. The facilitator was blamed, and the subject was not discussed openly afterward (Bradley, Miller, Svingos, & Driscoll, 2008). Some time later, several staff attended trainings by the hospital's diversity committee, which included curricula about cultural humility (Tervalon & Murray-Garcia, 1998). Yet these conversations about privilege and power rarely entered into case consultations, program meetings, or staff meetings at the CVC. There seemed to be many obstacles to real change. Leary (2005) refers to the cognitive dissonance of living in the "land of the free" that was built on stolen land and forced labor. For some of us, terms such as "racism" call forth images of brutal bigotry—and we could separate ourselves from that, while remaining unaware of the real effects of historical and political factors, along with the ways that modern racism and internalized oppression operate on many levels: personal, interpersonal, institutional, systemic, and cultural (Batts, 2002; Chisom & Washington, 1997). We could hold liberal values and still perpetrate oppressive practices and microaggressions (Sue et al., 2007). We did not yet have enough people on hand who could hold the long view and could remind us about breakdowns on the road to breakthroughs, or expose the tricks that modern oppression was playing on us. Some staff at the CVC were raised (as I had been) with the message that naming racial categories was itself racist, and so, out of respect, they did not bring up cultural or ethnic identifiers (Bradley et al., 2008). Many of us felt a call to acknowledge racism or other oppressive or insensitive practices as an injury to a relationship, not seeing that the injury had already occurred and that we had perpetrated it. We interpreted such a call as an end to relationship, instead of as an opportunity to learn, atone, and engage more accountably, and we closed ranks to protect each other from such a risk. In addition, if a conversation went badly, the person already most marginalized was the one who was blamed and targeted, so even allies could be caught in a quagmire of ineffectiveness.

MOMENTUM BUILDS

Despite the obstacles to change, the managers continued to hold the value of providing quality services to vulnerable families, and we were able to hire people of color and white people who were aware of their privilege. They brought fresh eyes, and had a passion for anti-oppression work and respect for families that was based not just on ideology but on shared life experiences and an understanding that those in power need to form accountable relationships with those holding less power. With this reinforcement, an analysis of racism, privilege, power, and oppression gained momentum.

Because of who was now at the agency and the degree of pain that the workers of color were experiencing, there were many hallway conversations about how to deal with the culture of clinical meetings and about how we see and do clinical work at the CVC. More and more frequently in these informal settings, the women of color, who expressed the feeling of vulnerability and the sense of "no room to breathe," were being joined by white staff who wanted to make changes. The women of color were tired of bringing it up and not feeling supported or heard by their supervisors (Lewis, Torres, Orfirer, & DeVoss, 2010). Moreover, they were gravely concerned about the quality of care for families of color that was reflected by this silence, this gap. Yet they continued to name oppression and to invite the staff to see beyond where we had been. They risked speaking of their experience to their white supervisors (Constantine & Sue, 2007). They led lunchtime film series focusing on intuitional racism and its effects on disparities in health, education, and involvement in the child welfare system. Shocked by the absence of talk about culture in case conferences, they continued to raise the issue.

One of the new staff, an African American woman with a doctorate in psychology, introduced us to the ADDRESSING format (Hays, 2001) (see table 4.1). This format offers a structure for building awareness of our location based on demographic characteristics that can give us power and privilege or marginalization. These characteristics include such aspects of culture as age and generation, acquired or developmental disability, religion, ethnicity, socioeconomic status, sexual and affectional orientation, indigenous heritage, and gender. We can use these prompts in coming to know the families we are serving, making room for their values and honoring their worldviews. Even more importantly, the template is intended as a tool for clarifying our own locations in the many dimensions of culture, and becoming aware of our own biases, and the effects of cultural differences and commonalities on our assumptions and relationships. We thought that this template would give us a way to engage more fully and respectfully with the families we were trying to serve, and to reflect more productively on our own position of power and the impact of that position on the families with whom we worked. We thought it would enrich our work by helping us find words for experiences that had been unspoken or made invisible.

THE TIPPING POINT

The first individual who was invited to use the ADDRESSING format at an all-staff case conference was a white case manager with a keen sense of social justice and respect for families. Unfortunately, we had not prepared her adequately, and instead of using ADDRESSING to identify her own location in terms of privilege, she was using the acronym to identify the demographic characteristics of the family. When an African American colleague questioned one of her attributions, the white case manager was caught off guard and some in the group responded as if she had been attacked. They came to her defense, leaving the woman who had raised the concerns alone, targeted as "the angry black woman." What emerged were heat, and pain, and honest talk about the confluence of racism and class. Some of the women of color began to share their own experiences of being seen as "less than." It was being named, but there were complaints from some in the room about the presenter not being "safe." It was as if our quietness and "niceness" had been disrupted, and many of us did not know what to do.

Here we were again, exactly where we had been stymied before. The subject of race had been broached and panic had ensued. Indeed, it seemed we couldn't talk about this. This time, though, people refused to let it go back underground. At the end of this case conference, a small group of individuals asked if others at the CVC would like to change the dynamics of the conversation, and talk about race, privilege, and power. Instead of just a few interested staff, one third of the staff showed up—including supervisors, program directors, and managers. As we discussed our purpose, one of the African American women said, "Let's not be a committee . . . committees don't do anything. Let's form a task force." With this distinction, she called us to come together for action, not just to conduct academic-like analysis (an occupational hazard for many of us trained as therapists!). She empowered us to become the Task Force for Cultural Responsiveness and Accountability. Momentum had shifted, and there was agreement from the start that departmental change had to happen.

THE TASK FORCE IN ACTION

One of the first decisions of the task force, supported by the CVC clinical director, was that we devote our existing monthly "brown-bag" clinical meetings to focusing on the effects of our own culture and privilege and its impact on our work with children and families. The meetings were open to all staff, including administrative staff. We noticed that there was rich conversation when we broke into smaller groups, but the silence and awkwardness reappeared when the group gathered as a whole. It seemed that there was mistrust between programs. We attempted to have programs introduce themselves and make explicit their thoughts about working with people from cultures with varying levels of culture, power, and privilege. The vocabularies and philosophies were so different that it was often hard to hear each other. There were undercurrents of grumblings about superficial political correctness, objections that conversations about culture threatened to eclipse clinical case conferences, and a repeated and well-justified refrain that "we want to talk about race, class, power, and privilege, but we don't know each other well enough to have these conversations."

From its inception, the task force has seen its purpose as guiding the CVC and its staff to reflect on how our own positions of power and privilege—as individuals and as an agency—affect the families with whom we work. Participation from all "levels" of staff was crucial: the fact that management, office staff, supervisors, therapists, and case managers were present with the intention of learning together was hugely significant. Since culture and racism were our initial focus, it also was significant that participants were Latina, Jewish, African American, and dominant culture white, and of course, within these categories, we had ranges of experience and identifications in terms of class, gender, sexual and affectional orientation, and generation. We agreed that though diversity was a shared value, it was no longer sufficient as even a minimum standard of care. If we were to work together toward providing ethical, high-quality care to the communities we hoped to serve, we would have to go deeper and wider in our anti-oppression work in order to build accountable relationships. We had to expose and understand the effects of historical and current injustices and power differentials among CVC staff, and between our agency and the families and communities we serve.

The road was not easy. Even within the task force, we differed in our experiences of thinking about these issues. We tried to operate by consensus and often disagreed and floundered. We met weekly at first and eventually settled into a bimonthly schedule, learning and adapting as we went. In an initial attempt to define our vision, we introduced Crossroads Ministry's "Continuum on Becoming an Anti-Racist, Multicultural Institution" (Crossroads Ministry, 2006). We thought it would provide us with an assessment tool and a map, a great way to name the limitations of white liberal racism, but there were snags. Not surprisingly, some of us with white-skin privilege thought we were further along than the people of color thought we were, and we stalled for weeks on this.

At about this time, many of us attended the first "ISMS" Conference sponsored by the University of California at Berkeley School of Public Health: "Privilege, Bias, and Oppression: Addressing Barriers to Eliminating Health Disparities Within Health Organizations." At the conference, we were heartened by presentations by other agencies on this journey, and we met two consultants, Laurin Mayeno and Jacqueline Elena Featherstone, who had helped them along the way (Mayeno & Featherstone, 2010). We had come to realize that we couldn't do therapy on our own family, and so we asked for their help (Bradley et al., 2008). They understood right away that we needed help not only with interpersonal communication but with institutional change. They held a long-term vision for us and said, "You can't let the hesitation of the few hold up the whole group."

Our managers, who were now actively prioritizing this work, secured funding and committed institutional time to mandatory staff training by the consultants. We were all ready to start afresh—and then it happened: we hit another patch of ice. In an exercise on "checking out assumptions," a clinician chose to practice in front of the entire staff by checking out with a program director the assumption that her program didn't talk about culture. There was a moment of breathlessness. Some staff became defensive. Most felt helpless, as chasms of old distrust reopened. The facilitators, in an effort to accommodate multiple voices, changed their format and original presentation to a conversation about hierarchy and honoring different personalities. Once again, we veered from the topic of racism. This was painful for some, hopeful for others, and confusing for many.

But once again, what could have been a breakdown became a breakthrough. At our next task force meeting we did not know how to proceed. Some blamed the facilitators, and we asked them to join us. One of the facilitators arrived at our department within 15 minutes. She heard the task force's fears, complaints, and confusion. She took responsibility for some of the day going off course and committed to helping us out of the tangle.

Instead of ignoring what had happened, in the next staff training the trainers and the managers modeled accountability, stating clearly what they had done and not done that had contributed to minimizing the effects of racism and power differentials, and the actions they would take to rectify this. These statements had a profound effect on all of us. The managers enacted humility and accountable leadership and demonstrated a commitment from those in power to keep the agency growing toward culturally responsive and ethical treatment of families and of each other. This made institutional change an agency priority, and conveyed the intention to take a piece of the burden off the women of color who had been working so hard to raise the standards of cultural accountability and responsiveness in our practice.

The facilitators led discussions that helped us to identify our priorities, and helped lead us to find common ground. This was the success we had needed, and along with the commitment of management, it sent the clear message that discussions of culture and power were now part of the expected standard of practice. Cultural responsiveness and accountability were now part of "the CVC way."

The consultants then met with the task force and proposed that we move forward in an intentional way toward developing a cultural strategic plan. If we continued just to talk, it would lead to our demise, they said. We needed to take action and create small successes (Mayeno, 2007). On the basis of the priorities identified by the staff at one of the trainings, they proposed that the cultural strategic plan be based on five work groups, focusing on the positive work environment of the department, community outreach, bigger systems (i.e., outside the department), department policies and procedures, and clinical practice (Mayeno, 2007). Every staff member would become a member of one of the work groups, which would be facilitated by task force members. A strategic planning group with staff members from different positions within the department was enlisted to coordinate efforts. The consultants suggested that each work group create a vision, define an issue in need of attention, and devise a sequence of recommended actions to address the issue. These were compiled in a Handbook for Cultural Responsiveness and Accountability. Although the original intent was to meet one or two times, the groups themselves decided to continue, and have done so for the intervening three years.

The groups did profound work, partly because their membership cut across programs, so people knew each other in new ways. There was from the start a "no repercussions agreement," which addressed the fact that work groups included but were not run by managers and supervisors. Management set aside time each month for meetings, and participation was mandatory. The creative initiatives of the groups made inroads into real institutional change (Bradley et al., 2008). There are impressive examples of what was accomplished.

For example, the positive work environment group attended to our frayed morale and addressed the "we don't know each other well enough" problem by replacing some meetings with potluck gatherings, organizing a staff barbecue with games, initiating a newsletter, and incorporating icebreakers and appreciations in meetings. They also created a culture of acknowledgment, a "goodie basket" of nurturing teas and snacks in the front offices, and a "birthday fairy" who acknowledged birthdays by sending good wishes and online cake and balloons. They made a real departmental change by developing polices governing greetings and good-byes, and clarifying program supervisory responsibility in acknowledging staff accomplishments and milestones.

The clinical practice work group, consisting of office staff along with clinicians, worked diligently to hear and respect one another across theoretical and experiential differences. They developed a set of "essential questions" to be included at clinical meetings so that when clinicians described the children and families with whom they worked, they also had to describe their own power and privilege and the impact of it on the relationship with the family. A laminated copy of these questions is in every conference room at the CVC. The group also developed a statement of commitment that the strategic planning group adopted as the foundation statement of our work. It reads:

> Our Promise, Our Commitment: we commit to cultural accountability to each other and our clients in every interaction. We are guided by our awareness of the impact of oppression and marginalization, membership in target and non-target groups, and the central impact of historical and institutional racism. We will be sensitive to our role in institutional oppression and we will seek consultation from the communities with whom we work. We will strive to be transparent and explicit in our process.

The policy and personnel group reviewed forms, hiring policies, and competencies. They altered performance evaluations to include cultural responsiveness and instituted policies to address continuity of care when trainees leave. They created a new orientation procedure to welcome new employees and trainees. Throughout this process they used surveys to make sure staff voices were included in the changes.

BACK TO THE PRESENT

The Task Force for Cultural Responsiveness and Accountability has been an important part of CVC culture since 2006, operating in an advisory capacity with management. Using Tatum's analogy of institutional racism as a moving sidewalk, we try to keep walking in the other direction (Tatum, 2003). We operate as a process group, challenging and supporting each other, and as a leadership group, ensuring that issues of culture and power stay central to the CVC's work with families and with other institutions. We are often stuck between action and reflection. And we have to keep asking ourselves: What might we be missing as we become mainstream? In what ways are we participating in oppression?

We at the CVC are still not all in agreement about the meaning of cultural responsiveness and accountability, and we do not all equally prioritize these issues or see their relevance. "Dead zones" of silence still happen in meetings sometimes, and inadvertent injuries, frustrations, assumptions, and personality conflicts occur. We try to reflect on where we've come from, and acknowledge the changes made in "the CVC way." We need to be reminded that hurts and awkwardnesses are inevitable as we try to expose things that have thrived for centuries in silence and obfuscation. And it is our hope that as people raise these issues—and the issues of which we are not yet aware—they will not have to do it alone anymore.

REFERENCES

Batts, V. (2002). Is reconciliation possible? Lessons from combating modern racism. In J. I. Douglas (Ed.), *Waging reconciliation: God's mission in a time of globalization and crisis* (pp. 35–76). New York: Church Publishing.

Batts, V. A., & Brown, J. L. (2009). *VISIONS, Inc. A personal approach to multiculturalism: Changing racism and other ISMS. Assumptions and definitions.* Paper presented in Cambridge, MA, July 14–17.

Bradley, K., Miller, J., Svingos, D., & Driscoll, J. (2008, April 25). *The CVC's journey towards cultural responsiveness and accountability: Where we come from and where we are going.* Paper presented at the 2008 ISMS Conference, Building Inclusive and Multi-Culturally Competent Health Organizations: A Healing Approach to Addressing the Isms, University of California, Berkeley, School of Public Health.

Chisom, R., & Washington, M. (1997, February). *Undoing racism.* Paper presented at the National Training for Organizers meeting, Waveland, MS.

Constantine, M. G., & Sue, D. W. (2007). Perceptions of racial microaggressions among black supervisees in cross-racial dyads. *Journal of Counseling Psychology, 54* (2), 142–153.

Crossroads Ministry. 2006. Continuum on becoming an anti-racist, multicultural institution. Adapted from original concept by Baily Jackson and Rita Hardiman, and further developed by Andrea Avazian and Ronice Branding. Reprinted in S. Spellers, *Radical welcome.* New York: Church Publishing.

Greene, M. P., & Suskind, A. (2006). Foreword. From a multicultural institution to an antiracist institution: A traditional Jewish organization meets the challenge. *Journal of Emotional Abuse, 6*(2/3), xxi–xxviii.

Hardy, K., & Laszloffy, K. (1995). The cultural genogram: Key to training cultur- ally competent family therapists. *Journal of Marital and Family Therapy, 21,* 227–237.

Hays, P. (2001). *Addressing cultural complexities in practice: A framework for clini- cians and counselors.* Washington, DC: American Psychological Association.

Jackson, V. (2002). In our own voice: African-American stories of oppression, sur- vival, and recovery in mental health systems. *International Journal of Narrative Therapy and Community Work, 2,* 11–31.

Leary, J. D. (2005). *Post traumatic slave syndrome: America's legacy of enduring in- jury and healing.* Milwaukie, OR: Uptone Press.

Lewis, L., Torres, E., Orfirer, K., & DeVoss, L. (2010, August). *Good intentions are not enough.* Presentation at Clinical Supervisors' Meeting, Children's Hospital and Research Center, Oakland.

Madsen, W. C. (2003). *Collaborative therapy with multi-stressed families.* New York: Guilford Press.

Mayeno, L. Y. (2007, July). Multicultural organizational development: A resource for health equity. In *Multicultural organizational development in nonprofit or- ganizations.* Organizational Development and Capacity in Cultural Compe- tence series. Los Angeles: California Endowment. Retrieved March 21, 2013, from http://www.mayenoconsulting.com/pdfs/CP%20Cultural%20Compe- tence%20Lessons%20FINAL%20RPT.pdf.

——. (2010, July 21). Transforming communication: When breakdowns become breakthroughs. Message posted to Mayeno Consulting—Lessons from the Field Web Log. Retrieved September 16, 2011, from http://mayenoconsulting. blogspot.com.

Mayeno, L. Y., & Featherstone, J. E. (2010, June 21). Balancing flexibility and ac- countability in working relationships. Message posted to Mayeno Consulting— Lessons from the Field Web Log. Retrieved September 16, 2011, from http:// mayenoconsulting.blogspot.com.

Pinderhughes, E. (1989). *Understanding race, ethnicity, and power: The key to ef- ficacy in clinical practice.* New York: Free Press.

Sue, D. W., Capodilupo, C. M., Torino, G. C., Bucceri, J. M., Holder, A M. B., Nadal, K. L., & Esquilin, M. (2007). Racial microaggressions in everyday life. *American Psychologist, 62*(4), 271–286.

Tamasese, K., & Waldegrave, C. (1993). Cultural and gender accountability in the "Just Therapy" approach. *Journal of Feminist Family Therapy, 5*(2), 29–45.

Tatum, B. D. (2003). *"Why are all the black kids sitting together in the cafeteria?" and other conversations about race.* New York: Basic Books.

Tervalon, M., & Murray-Garcia, J. (1998). Cultural humility versus cultural competence: A critical distinction in defining physician outcomes in multicultural education. *Journal of Health Care for the Poor and Underserved, 9*(2), 117–125.

Turner, H. A., Finkelhor, D., & Ormrod, R. (2006). The effect of lifetime victimization on the mental health of children and adolescents. *Social Science and Medicine, 62,* 13–17.

Vasquez, H., & Macgraw, S. (2005). Building relationships across privilege: Becoming an ally in the therapeutic relationship. In M. P. Morlas, K. L. Sunyemoto, & B. F. Olsen (Eds.), *Psychotherapy with women: Exploring diverse contexts and identities* (pp. 64–83). New York: Guilford Press.

Waldegrave, C., Tamasese, K., Tuhaka, F., & Campbell, W. (2003). *Just therapy—a journey: A collection of papers from the Just Therapy team, New Zealand.* Adelaide: Dulwich Centre.

CHAPTER 5

Rediscovering Positive Work Relationships Within a Diverse Relationship-Based Organization

SERVING CHILDREN IN TRANSITION

▸ *KAREN THOMAS*

THE CVC IS AN ORGANIZATION THAT strives to lessen the life challenges of children and families in transition, including homeless families and children in foster care. The CVC is also a relationship-based organization. This means that the CVC's clinical services are founded on the belief that therapeutic change can best take place within the context of a positive, empathic relationship with the clinician. Further, clinical supervision is built around a belief in, and commitment to, the parallel process between the patient-clinician and clinician-supervisor relationships. Clinicians can best support client families when they are afforded a similar level of support in the supervisory relationship. Jeree Pawl's "platinum rule," held in high regard, reads as follows: "Do unto others as you would have others do unto others" (Pawl, 2001, p. 4). This belief that clinicians can be most effective in supporting the families they serve when they are themselves treated with warmth, nurturance, and respect is especially important when clinicians are tasked with forging therapeutic relationships with the highly traumatized children and families served by the CVC. Despite this belief in the centrality of relationships, positive collegial relationships were nonetheless left primarily to chance at the CVC, until recently. Little was done, on an organizational or individual level, to conscientiously acknowledge or address differences in power, privilege, personality, or opinion in order to maintain an optimal working environment. In this way, the CVC neglected to consider the impact that less-than-optimal collegial relationships would ultimately have on the quality of services provided. Staff who are feeling disgruntled and disempowered within an organization are unlikely to be as effective in supporting highly traumatized and disempowered families. The CVC's history demonstrates how even relationship-based organizations need, at times, to focus inward on developing more-positive relationships among staff members. This chapter discusses the CVC's approach to building positive work relationships on organizational, program, and individual levels, including recent efforts initiated by the positive work environment (PWE) work group and approaches utilized by the CVC's SEED program to strengthen clinically focused teams and address conflict between team members. The chapter illustrates strategies through which organizations desiring to improve the work climate and culture can ensure that change initiated at the organizational level will indeed permeate all levels of the organization. Further, the chapter discusses ways in which individuals can be supported to improve the quality of collegial relationships, one relationship at a time.

REDISCOVERING POSITIVE WORK RELATIONSHIPS
AT THE ORGANIZATIONAL LEVEL

In 2007 the CVC was an organization gravely in need of a morale boost. The staff had been grappling with a steep learning curve to master the style of charting required to bill under the EPSDT program (Early and Periodic Screening, Diagnosis, and Treatment, a Medicaid program), and the organization had grown from about 10 clinicians in 1993 to more than 25 in 2007. The increased number of positions had given the CVC the opportunity to increase services and staff diversity, in terms of ethnicity and culture as well as languages spoken. Such changes had been needed for some time to improve the cultural responsiveness of the CVC's clinical services and to increase the organization's capacity to serve non-English-speaking families. However, the expansion was a blow to the CVC's equilibrium. This small, family-like organization, comprising a core group of employees who had been on board for many years, suddenly became much larger and much more diverse. On an organizational level, little was done to purposefully integrate the new staff and the old. Some new staff complained that they did not feel welcomed, especially by staff with whom they had few ongoing interactions. The CVC staff had no specific space. Instead they were placed in offices that were scattered throughout a large building along with staff from several different programs. Opportunities for staff to become better acquainted were not available, since interactions were mostly limited to awkward chance encounters in the hallways or stress-filled monthly staff meetings in which the organization's shortcomings in complying with billing requirements were regularly discussed. Newcomers, who were more likely to represent minority and disadvantaged communities, felt that the primarily Caucasian senior staff did not adequately consider or address the impact of institutional racism on the CVC's clients, especially in their interactions with child protective services.

Efforts were made, early on, to support staff in examining these issues as a group. The ADDRESSING framework (Hays, 2001) was presented as a tool that could heighten awareness of the ways in which cultural and power differences between clinician and client might influence the work with client families. Designed to deepen one's understanding of identity as complex and multidimensional, each letter of the title "ADDRESSING" stands for a different dimension of identity and affiliation with disenfranchised versus privileged groups: age and generational influences, developmental disability, disabilities acquired later in life, religion and spiritual orientation, ethnic and racial identity, socioeconomic status, sexual orientation and affection, indigenous heritage, national origin, and gender. Guidelines for effective communication across differences, proposed by consultants from whom the CVC sought advice (Mayeno & Featherstone, 2008), helped to direct staff and increase feelings of safety during these early discussions. However, as a staff member pointed out at one such meeting, as a group we did not know each other well enough to have built a foundation of trust upon which such difficult discussions could be supported. In short, the CVC was ripe for misunderstanding and resentment to develop among the staff. It was in this context that the Task Force for Cultural Responsiveness and Accountability was created, and it, in turn, launched the positive work environment work group (PWE), one among several smaller work groups that involved the participation of every CVC staff member, including all managers, clinical staff, and administrative staff.

POSITIVE WORK ENVIRONMENT WORK GROUP (PWE)
AT THE ORGANIZATIONAL LEVEL

Fast-forward several months after the PWE's inception. The setting is a hallway at the CVC. Twenty-five or so staff members are milling about, and it appears as if they are writing on the walls. Jill says, "Oooh, I've got to get my camera!" More than one staff member, including the CVC's clinical director, has tears in her eyes. What is happening here? It seems that staff members are actually writing on rectangular pieces of yellow paper taped to the walls: appreciation certificates made out in the names of all CVC personnel. Colleagues of the person named on each certificate are adding their own appreciative comments. Weeks and months later, a virtual tour of the CVC shows many of these certificates affixed to workstation walls, apparently valued as much as the framed diplomas that grace office walls elsewhere.

This was one of the many projects initiated by the positive work environment work group (PWE), a committee of CVC staffers dedicated to improving the work environment within the context of a multicultural workplace. The PWE was one of several staff committees launched by the cultural task force. All CVC staff were required to participate in one of these committees, and each committee, by design, comprised a mix of staff from the CVC's various clinical programs and administrative roles. At the same time, staff assignments to specific committees were based on individual preference. Thus, I and other staff participating in the PWE were all committed from the outset to identifying ways to improve the work culture at the CVC. In addition, we represented a range of programs and clinical and administrative roles. Some PWE members were managers. Some, like myself, were clinicians, and some were support staff. The cultural task force assigned one of its members as a facilitator for the committee, and by chance or design, the PWE facilitator did not happen to be a manager. This later emerged as a significant component of the work group's success. Power dynamics between staff roles, while still present, were neutralized to some extent by the fact that the facilitator was not the person in the group who held the most power within the organization. The resulting message was that one person's voice counted as much as any other person's.

The non-hierarchical structure of the PWE had a far-reaching impact on the way in which we PWE participants viewed our mission. Rather than adopting a top-down focus for improving workplace culture or climate in order to improve productivity or staff retention, which might have been the underlying agenda had management been in charge, we were motivated to improve the work environment because of a strong commitment to the mission of the CVC and the everyday work of improving the life circumstances of clients. From this passion came a desire to create a more positive, supportive experience for every staff person involved in furthering the organization's mission and day-to-day work. Instead of a top-down effort with the demands coming from the management, change began with various groups that included every member of the organization's staff. While the PWE was charged with focusing specifically on strategies to improve the workplace culture and climate, other work groups were charged with increasing the cultural sensitivity of the organization through its policies and procedures, approaches to training, clinical practice, and other areas of organizational business. Additionally, since every staff member was involved as a member of one of the groups, the effects of power within the organization were minimized. In this way, macro-level strategies became micro-level experiences and there was no part of the organization that was not touched by the cultural task force's efforts to shift the agency climate and culture.

All of the work groups met monthly for about an hour, during a time that had previously been reserved for staff meetings. One hour per month was not much time, but it was significant to all of us in the PWE that this hour already had been allocated. In order to meet, we did not have to carve extra time out of our busy and disparate schedules.

The first task of the PWE, as with all of the work groups, was to identify our group's mission. After some discussion, we agreed that relationships were central to improving the work culture at the CVC. The CVC had started out as an organization employing a very small number of individuals and had quickly grown to almost three times its original size, yet it still functioned in many ways as if it was a small family. There were positive aspects to this, yet PWE participants recognized that the problems between staff that had sparked the formation of the cultural task force in the first place were in part problems of relationships. As the organization grew, staff did not have much opportunity to interact across programs. Lack of familiarity with one another created ample room for misunderstanding. Keeping in mind this central concept of relationships, and the mission to improve them, the PWE got to work. The one directive we received from the CVC management team was that few funds could be spent to accomplish PWE's work to improve the workplace culture and environment. I expect that this is a challenge familiar to other human service organizations as well. While limited funding did restrict our options, we saw that this barrier could be overcome with a little creativity.

The fruits of the PWE's labor included the previously described appreciation certificates annotated by CVC staffers. Borrowing a few minutes from the CVC's monthly staff meeting and requiring only a little advance computer graphics know-how and paper and ink, creating the certificates required not much in the way of agency resources, yet the impact was extraordinary. We also used the monthly staff meetings to further strengthen connections among staff members by occasionally opening meetings with a sometimes silly get-to-know-you-better icebreaker, gaining permission to supplant the meeting agenda with an all-staff potluck brunch on a rare occasion, or, on an ongoing basis, adding a few minutes for positive acknowledgments at the end of every monthly staff meeting. Intuitively, the last change felt like the right thing to do to ensure that we didn't lose sight of what the CVC was doing well. In fact, mental health theorists suggest that taking time to focus specifically on the positive is one small step in beginning to train our brains to shift from innate patterns of remembering and reacting primarily to negative experiences to taking in and incorporating positive life experiences as part of who we are (Hanson, 2009).

These small but significant changes have contributed substantially to bringing balance to the CVC's monthly meetings. As is likely the case in most organizations of this size, the CVC's periodic staff meetings serve as a forum to communicate information that the organization needs its staff members to incorporate into the daily workflow: changes in billing procedures, funding cuts, etc. Often, the information shared is not welcome news, but information that staffers need to know in order to do their jobs or to be kept abreast of factors affecting the organization as a whole. When the emphasis is solely on adaptations that the organization needs its workers to make, even when delivered with empathy and apology, organizational morale can seriously suffer. When conscious efforts are made to balance the hard news with time out to laugh together and appreciate and acknowledge what is working well, organizational morale improves.

Fairness and perceptions of fairness are further essential components of an emotionally healthy workplace, one where diversity can thrive. The importance of fairness in employment contexts has been well documented. Individuals want to be treated fairly in recruitment, compensation, mentoring, promotion, and even dismissal. The belief that events in one's own life are just has a positive association with confidence in self-efficacy, satisfaction, and involvement with work, as well as higher levels of commitment to the employing organization (Otto, Glaser, & Dalbert, 2009). Although studies have shown that a personal belief in a just world is a fairly stable construct that is dependent on neither specific personality traits nor position in the organizational hierarchy, researchers suggest that it can be degraded by difficult life experiences, perhaps repeated experiences of injustice (Otto, Glaser, & Dalbert, 2009). Thus, organizations can likely do much to increase the commitment and contentment of their employees by striving for fair treatment of employees in policy and procedures throughout the organization.

Attending to inequities and developing an organization-wide policy for celebrations and formal acknowledgments was another PWE priority. The intentions to treat people fairly is a good place to start, but that must be followed by thoughtful action. In a diverse workplace, efforts to treat everyone the same are not the same as fair treatment, since that practice does not take into account individual differences and preferences. Some staff are quite comfortable with making known their interest in acknowledgment of life events (birthdays, family births, deaths, career milestones, etc.), while others, for personal or cultural reasons, cannot imagine asserting themselves in this way. Yet, who gets acknowledged and how they are acknowledged have a lot to do with perceptions of workplace fairness within the organization as a whole. For example, though the CVC management did not intend to create an unfair environment, in the absence of an organization-wide policy, some workers were sent on maternity leave with lavish baby showers that took the place and space of organization-wide staff meetings while other mothers-to-be who might also have appreciated such high-profile treatment received no more than a card from their closest coworkers.

We faced several significant challenges in developing a fair and realistic policy to acknowledge the life events of CVC staff. First, staff members had different expectations regarding celebrations and acknowledgments. Second, some program directors were more interested than others were in organizing and implementing celebrations or formal acknowledgements for the workers whom they supervised. Another challenge was that CVC had no money to spend for this purpose, so any form of celebration or acknowledgment had to be funded by staff donations. In our discussions about how to increase fairness in CVC's approach to honoring or acknowledging life events, we considered whether PWE members should directly assume the role of celebrating and acknowledging all noteworthy events. We ultimately decided that PWE members did not have the time to take this on for the entire CVC. Also, we felt that staff morale would benefit more directly if management participated. Ultimately, we presented the management team with our proposal for an organization-wide policy that was adopted by the department. The policy sets a minimum standard for recognizing major staff achievements, newcomers, and voluntary good-byes via a department-wide e-mail and a timely announcement at an all-staff meeting. Finally, the policy sets the expectation that program directors will strive for fairness in their treatment of the staff they supervise, should they wish to do more.

Fairness further inspired the advent of the "Birthday Fairy." Now an honorary member of the PWE, the Birthday Fairy does not exist other than in my head, but still manages to send e-mailed birthday announcements, complete with virtual "cake" and "ice cream" on a monthly basis. Not only are these treats delicious, but they are also free from calories! The Birthday Fairy's announcements are scheduled in advance, through the greater hospital e-mail system. By downgrading from the commercial e-cards that are now widely available, we avoided the problem of the system's spam filter, which intercepts commercial e-cards. Announcements are sent according to each staff member's preference: publicly, privately, or not at all.

Another important effort initiated by the PWE that is worthy of mention includes a "self-care" basket, filled with healthy snacks, teas, and other self-care items, such as a guided-meditation CD. The basket is funded by small-change donations to a jar and goodwill (during lean times). In order to reinforce the importance of opportunities for staff to connect in a social context, away from the day-to-day pressures of work, the PWE also was able to organize several social events during, and outside of, work hours, and on-site as well as away from the facility. These were primarily potluck events, with some small contributions from the agency budget.

None of the PWE's initiatives required major changes in the way business was done. None were innovative breakthroughs. Nevertheless, none were prioritized or implemented by the CVC prior to the PWE's creation. Through the task force's creation of the PWE and the other work groups, the CVC ensured that its positive intentions in fact were followed up by thoughtful action. Each of the strategies discussed here helped steer the CVC toward a process that more mindfully supported staff. Each helped to shift the focus toward the positive and stressed the importance of equity. The efforts of the PWE work group were complemented and enhanced by projects undertaken by many of the other work groups launched by the Task Force for Cultural Responsiveness and Accountability. Some had a very direct impact on improving workplace culture, such as the efforts of the policy and procedures work group to revamp the performance evaluation process and create opportunities for all staff to give feedback on the performance of supervisors, program directors, and managers. Collectively, these changes had a significant, transformative impact. Organizations that conscientiously cultivate a climate of humanity indeed find that they reap a multitude of benefits, such as a decrease in work-related errors, and employees with improved health and a higher level of contentment and commitment to their work (Sutton, 2010). In my opinion, the intervention that had the most far-reaching impact was the creation of the work groups themselves. By involving every CVC staff member in efforts to improve the CVC's awareness of, and responsiveness to, cultural and power differences within and outside of the organization, the CVC gave each staff member a voice and the power to shape the organization's future. Further, relationships among staff members, across programs and roles within the CVC, were strengthened through the process of determining work group goals and seeing projects through from concept to action. Such multi-level planning and problem-solving groups, involving staff from varying levels of the organization's hierarchy, have indeed shown promise in positively affecting workforce turnover in a related field (Strolin-Goltzman et al., 2009). Research further indicates that when positive contact between individuals of different races is facilitated, as was the case in the CVC's work groups, prejudicial attitudes decrease significantly and interracial friendships increase (Mendoza-Denton, 2008). This was the very salve that the CVC needed.

BUILDING POSITIVE RELATIONSHIPS BETWEEN INDIVIDUALS WITHIN ONE CVC PROGRAM

Top-down, organization-wide efforts to improve the work culture can go only so far. Without parallel efforts to improve the quality of individual

relationships and address conflict between staff members within the organization, strategies such as those undertaken by the PWE have the effect of
pristine frosting on a putrid cake. Collegial relationships need to be genuine and authentic, in good times and bad, in order to create a context of
goodwill in the workplace. This section describes efforts that took place,
in parallel to those of the PWE, to strengthen staff relationships within
one CVC program and to improve collegial collaboration to further the
program and agency mission.

The SEED program is unique among the CVC's many programs aimed
at supporting the mental health and development of children who are
homeless, at risk for homelessness, or in foster care. SEED is a collaborative
effort of a team of mental health clinicians and a developmental specialist
employed by the CVC, child welfare workers within two designated SEED
units at the county child protective services agency, and a team of public
health nurses employed by the county and a neighboring city. The goal
of SEED is to integrate developmental, mental health, child welfare, and
public health services in order to more appropriately and effectively serve
children ages three and under who enter the county's foster care system.
The SEED program therefore focuses on a subset of the population of children and families in transition that the CVC serves: children and families
involved in the child welfare system. Each child is served collaboratively
by a child welfare worker, a mental health clinician, and a public health
nurse on the SEED team. SEED children may also receive the services of
the team developmental specialist, as needed. Each week, this multidisciplinary team meets to discuss the specific needs of individual children and
their families, both foster and biological. Thus, although SEED team members are employed by different agencies, we sit at the same table and serve
the same families. SEED mental health clinicians further act as consultants
to the child welfare staff in considering the mental health needs of the children enrolled in the program (Orfirer & Rian, 2008).

At a SEED team meeting a while back, Monica, our psychology intern,
was discussing her progress and concerns in attempting to assess the mental health and service needs of a particular child and family. She sought
the team's input about how best to proceed. During the discussion that
followed, multiple opinions were voiced by many members of the team,
some more forcefully stated than others, with some differences of opinion expressed between clinical and child welfare roles and levels of power

within the program hierarchy. As members of the SEED collaboration sought to consider the full picture of the child and family's situation and what service strategies might best address the family's multiple needs, the discussion drifted from Monica's particular question to other areas. Later, when Monica again raised the question about how she should proceed with her assessment, Julia, another member of the team, spoke up to state that she thought the issue had already been discussed and settled earlier in the meeting. Feeling that perhaps power differences in the room created the perception that the topic was closed, I suggested that power dynamics might be having an influence on the discussion. This was new territory for us, as a program and a team. At this point in our program development, we were just beginning to bring observations regarding the team process to the table as an area for discussion. We weren't yet able, with any ease, to talk about process observations openly, in order to consider the impact they might be having on the ways in which the team functioned and their ultimate impact on the families we served. In this context, my words were met with silence. When the discussion continued, no reference was made to what I or Julia had said. Later, I unknowingly offended Monica by sharing my disappointment with an experience I'd had with a clinician from another agency, who I had made clear in my criticism was also an intern. The meeting ended a short while later, with nothing said by anyone about the feelings that had been aroused by the discussion. Monica left feeling disrespected and undervalued, while I, as a senior clinician, worried that I might have overstepped my role and upset the clinical and child welfare supervisors on the team.

Awkward moments and missteps such as those that occurred in this meeting probably take place in other meetings many times a day, every day of the week, in human service organizations across the country. Such uncomfortable moments, however, were what propelled us forward to more actively consider what was needed to form a more effective collaboration within the SEED program, for the benefit of all program partners and our clients and their families. Often, difficult feelings are triggered when we turn our attention to the challenging life circumstances of the children and families we serve at the CVC. Our roles as case managers and therapists for children and families in transition and crisis, who are facing insurmountable barriers to their well-being, regularly evoke strong feelings in all of us. This is particularly apparent in the SEED program, where the needs of infants and toddlers for stability and speedy routes to placement permanency contrast sharply with the more measured pace required to address substance abuse problems or other factors that impede a parent's ability to safely care for a young child. Awareness of the disproportionate representation of children of color in out-of-home care further increases the urgency of emotions raised. Feelings of inadequacy, outrage, frustration, confusion, hopelessness, anger, and anxiety are a regular part of the job. Not only do such feelings create challenges for individual clinicians, but they frequently interfere with forming effective professional collaborations within and between organizations. When such feelings are left unacknowledged and unaddressed, they impair the clinician's effectiveness and efforts to work well with other helping professionals. This, in turn, has a deleterious effect on the quality of services delivered to vulnerable children and families. The CVC and its SEED program are certainly no exceptions. It was, after all, strong feelings regarding the predicaments of CVC client families that created a climate of resentment and mistrust among CVC staffers and ultimately gave rise to the Task Force for Cultural Responsiveness and Accountability.

Organizations that support a diverse staff are blessed and challenged by a range of perspectives grown from a diversity of life experiences. Sue (2010) writes about the prevalence of racial and other forms of microaggression, which are defined as "brief and commonplace daily verbal, behavioral and environmental indignities, whether intentional or unintentional, that communicate hostile, derogatory or negative racial, gender, sexual-orientation and religious slights and insults to the target person or group" (p. 5). Such moments are probably unavoidable in an organization as diverse as the CVC. Not only do they have challenging impacts on their targets, but when brought to attention, they can raise difficult feelings among the perpetrators of microaggressions. The work further awakens our own "ghosts in the nursery" (Fraiberg, Adelson, & Shapiro, 1980), subconscious reminders of past trauma or relational difficulty and disappointment, and sets off strong feelings that are tied to past experiences. Within the SEED program, staff feelings about how families are brought to the child welfare system's attention and differing ideas about how to prioritize the child's and the parent's needs create the potential for heated conflict between collaborative partners on a daily basis. Further, the burden of responsibility for the child's safety, which our child welfare partners most acutely carry, increases the emotional weight of each decision regarding the child's care. Thus, effective collegial relationships, in the context of the SEED program, truly require work and cannot be left to chance.

The SEED program and the challenges inherent in partnering so closely with child welfare have in fact increased awareness within the CVC of the need to conscientiously support and maintain effective professional collaborations, more generally. How, then, does SEED promote effective working relationships in a context that so regularly and forcefully challenges them? Willing participants are a necessary base, but they are hardly sufficient. From my perspective as a senior SEED clinician, the key ingredients include reflective supervision, the willingness and resources to cultivate self-awareness, and an interest in applying that awareness and reflection to one's work relationships. Further, in recognition of the impact of moments of microaggression and other forms of interpersonal conflict on the work climate and effective collegial collaboration, the SEED program and the CVC as a whole have been making efforts to thoughtfully address such moments as they occur. Supported by leadership, SEED staff have made commitments to processing microaggressions and avoiding UWIBs (unnecessary words indicating bias) during weekly team meetings. At least once a year, the SEED supervisors and the program director convene a retreat day to improve team process and collaboration. Despite positive intentions on the part of leadership, opportunities to address injury and repair in the moment are sometimes missed, however, and efforts are then made to follow up later, to ensure that injuries are acknowledged and steps are taken toward collegial relationship repair. Both in vivo and in retrospect, a validate-confront-request process for addressing injury and repair (van der Zande, 2009; Visions, Inc., 2011) has been used. In the organization, there is a firm belief that when interpersonal injury takes place in a group setting, the entire group is affected and it is important not only to seek repair on an individual level but to include the group that was present when the difficulty arose.

Further, we are guided by the belief that efforts to address microaggressions and other forms of interpersonal injury not only improve the work environment and collegial relationships but have a significant impact on the effectiveness and cultural sensitivity of our work with client families. Our efforts to examine and address bias as it arises within the workplace may also bring us closer to addressing barriers that stand in the way of our effectively serving the children and families in our community who need our help (Snowden, 2003; Xanthos, 2008). Reflective supervision, self-awareness, and an organizational commitment to thoughtfully addressing moments of interpersonal injury can provide the courage and support necessary to acknowledge and work through microaggressions, countertransference, and conflict, with the goal of strengthening team relationships and increasing mutual understanding.

Reflective supervision is the core supervisory process for SEED mental health clinicians. It is the means through which clinicians are given the support and safety needed to thoughtfully examine their work and the feelings it evokes. A reflective process is also cultivated at SEED team meetings. While nonreflective processes tend to be more task- and action-oriented, a reflective process gives space to pause and consider the feelings aroused in oneself and others and provides the support needed to consider the meaning or impact of such feelings (see Weigand, 2007 for an eloquent description of the process and power of reflective supervision). Opportunities to reflect on team dynamics and strategies to improve team relationships are valued as much as any other intervention topic during supervision sessions. Asking questions such as the following can open avenues for conflict resolution and relationship repair where none were apparent before: "What were you feeling?" "What do you think the other person may have felt?" "Can you imagine talking with the other person about this directly?" "If so, what concerns do you have about doing so?" "How might you approach him/her?" Without the reflective space cultivated at SEED team meetings and regular reflective supervision, SEED clinicians could not be as effective in serving the children and families referred to SEED, nor could we collaborate effectively with our child welfare partners.

After the SEED meeting that I described earlier, I was feeling unsettled and anxious. I decided to contact Julia and talk with her about our exchange during the meeting. Meanwhile, the SEED program director pulled me aside and alerted me that Monica had spoken in her supervision session about feeling offended by my comments regarding the other intern. Hearing this, I agreed to follow up with Monica directly. During a private discussion, when Monica and I reflected on our experiences during the meeting, I acknowledged my dismay at the impact of my words. We both felt some relief upon repairing the unintentional damage to our relationship. This difference between one person's intent and the impact on others likely lies at the center of many interpersonal injuries. When there is recognition that both experiences are valid, relationships can move forward. When talking with Julia, I was surprised to learn that her comments had little to do with the power dynamics in the meeting, as I had assumed. She stated that she was irritated by the fact that the meeting did not start on time and that she was feeling distressed about meeting her work responsibilities within the limited time she had available once the meeting adjourned. It was then that I realized how the exchange between Julia and Monica had triggered familiar feelings in me about its not being safe for me to express my views when they differ from the views put forth by the supervisors in the room. Further, these feelings had led me to make an incorrect assumption about what was happening between Monica and Julia.

The next time the team met, I asked for some time to talk about the awkward moments the team had experienced during the prior meeting. I felt I was taking a risk, but decided that the prospect of a better outcome for all of us was worth it. I took a deep breath and informed the group about my efforts to follow up with Julia and Monica, summarizing the outcome of my behind-the-scenes discussions with each of them. I disclosed that the experience had caused me to reflect on the ways in which power differences on the team were inadvertently reinforced by the language I had used. In this case, it was irrelevant that the clinician who had disappointed me earlier also happened to be an intern. Perhaps, I suggested, it would have been better to leave that information out. Also, the experience illuminated my own sensitivities and helped me to appreciate how they could lead me to make incorrect assumptions. I felt vulnerable in making these disclosures, but several of the supervisors and line staff responded with appreciation for my transparency and shared their relief upon hearing that there had been behind-the-scenes relationship repair.

Proponents of the "narrative therapy" approach suggest that every individual has an alternative, "absent but implicit" (White, 2005), narrative or story about who they are and who they might become. These alternative or subjugated stories can be thickened or strengthened with the aid of a therapist trained in the narrative methods (Freedman & Combs, 1996). In a similar fashion, the opportunity to practice self-reflection in supervision gradually supports the clinician in owning this capacity and becoming a person who can be self-reflective at other times, in other contexts. What begins as a light pencil mark on paper becomes more visible each time it is traced over, until finally it is no longer hidden but is visible to all. Reflective supervision provides the supportive platform from which the clinician can take the risks required to acknowledge and address problems in collegial relationships and one's own role in maintaining them. It supports the pursuit and practice of what some call "emotional intelligence."

As defined by Salovey and Mayer (1990), emotional intelligence is the "subset of social intelligence that involves the ability to monitor one's own and others' feelings and emotions, to discriminate among them and to use this information to guide one's thinking and actions" (p. 189). Emotional intelligence is theoretically linked to personal success and well-being and has recently been shown to have a positive association with self-esteem, life satisfaction, and self-acceptance in an employment context (Carmeli, Yitzhak-Halevy, & Weisberg, 2009). This suggests that when we, as helping professionals, begin to develop greater self-awareness and apply this awareness in the workplace, not only may our effectiveness as clinicians improve, but so may our work relationships. As helping professionals, many of us endorse the concept of using countertransference to inform and guide our work with clients. We are less accustomed to thinking of these skills as being useful, and perhaps necessary, in our relationships with colleagues. Perhaps we feel that we need not work so hard in dealing with fellow professionals and can set self-awareness aside when we are not "on," as we know we should be when in the company of our clients. Much of the time, this works out fine. Then one day, a word is said, a reaction triggered, and it becomes clear, as the CVC has seen, that developing more effective collegial relationships requires our energy and attention, too. We need our emotional intelligence turned "on" in order to support our relationships with our colleagues.

If emotional intelligence, or self-awareness, is important for work, how can it be cultivated? There are likely many paths. Some mental health practitioners might find it through their own therapy or through mindfulness training such as that taught by Jon Kabat-Zinn (Kabat-Zinn, 1990). In my personal quest for greater self-awareness, I have felt lucky to be part of an infant mental health program, one that has a strong relationship and attachment focus. My mailbox is often filled with continuing education announcements that provide opportunities to develop a greater understanding of myself as a person and as a clinician while also honing the skills I need for my job. Attachment theory is at the heart of infant mental health work, and it is the foundation upon which all human relationships are built. When one studies how attachment works in infant-parent relationships, one also stands to increase an awareness of one's own functioning in relationship to others. Expressly intended to help the clinician intervene with families, training in infant mental health competencies may have the secondary benefit of helping the clinician to become more aware of the impact of his or her own history on the work (Heffron, Ivins, & Weston, 2005).

Implicit knowledge incorporates those things that we know without having to think about them, knowledge that we take for granted. The knowledge about how to ride a bike, once learned, is an example of implicit, or procedural, knowledge. The "knowledge" that each of us holds about our own emotional triggers can be thought of as another form of implicit knowledge (Seligman & Harrison, 2012). We know in a vague way what it is that might trigger a particular kind of response, what sorts of situations, in relationship to others, make us feel insecure, shamed, angry, and so forth. Mostly, we don't think about it and we go about life reacting rather than feeling and reflecting. When, through reflective supervision, therapy, or other supportive experiences, we begin to make the shift from implicit understanding to explicit knowledge, a more complete and active way of knowing, we begin to be able to use this knowledge to our advantage rather than helplessly reacting and being controlled by it. Business writer Srikumar Rao suggests that greater happiness at work is a matter of recognizing and shifting mental models and that change can be effected through exercises that alter one's perspective (Rao, 2010).

For me, an epiphany came, somewhat painfully, in the middle of a training that I attended hoping to learn something that would help me to better help my clients. I was sitting in a Circle of Security (Powell, Cooper, Hoffman, & Marvin, 2007) training, expectantly (and somewhat passively) waiting to be infused with knowledge about ways to help parents better understand and respond to their children, when suddenly I was jolted awake, terror-stricken, by the presenter's words and the creeping understanding that his words were likely true. What was he saying? Did he really mean that each and every one of us goes about life reacting to "Shark Music," a symphony composed of all of the unsatisfactory relationship experiences that have come before (Cooper, Hoffman, Powell, & Marvin, 2005)? Not only that, but each and every one of us has a "core sensitivity," a kind of sore spot that when poked, tends to lead to a particular type of defensive response. Clearly, I could be described as "esteem sensitive"—a characteristic that "in a rigid and pervasive form is narcissistic personality disorder" (Powell et al., 2007, p. 178). One had only to examine my reaction to determine that. According to the Circle of Security model, "Esteem sensitive parents have come to believe that who they are is not enough to be valued. Therefore, to protect themselves from abandonment, they must prove that they are special through performing, achieving and acquiring the acknowledgement of others" (Powell et al., 2007, p. 178). Yes, there I was, feeling upset with the presenter for suggesting that there was something "wrong" with me. However, what began as cognitive dissonance has since become part of my explicit knowledge and, consequently, a tool that I can apply to my work and work relationships rather than an impediment that I must carry around.

Positive collegial relationships, in fact, require the same attention to countertransference and the same kind of empathic, nonjudgmental stance as clinical, therapeutic relationships do. This, however, is a challenging proposition, especially when emotions are heightened and opinions differ. It is hard enough to maintain this stance when both partners in the conversation have an equal investment in mental health principles and processes. It is even more challenging when the partners in conversation have disparate levels of training or investment in a reflective process. Within the SEED program, our differing roles and training result in differing levels of ease with, or investment in, a solution-focused process vs. a reflective process. Generally speaking, child welfare work is, by necessity, more task-oriented and solution-focused, while mental health training directs the clinician to reflect on the moment-to-moment emotional and psychological experience.

In this way, the role of the SEED clinician regularly calls for the clinician to provide consultation to other team members, clinicians and child welfare workers alike, regarding the feelings that are evoked by the work. When such feelings are acknowledged and supported, there is greater potential to consider the impact they are having on our collaboration and on the work with our clients and families. As a SEED clinician, I can be more effective in performing my role when I am not only aware of the feelings that the work evokes in me, but able to support my colleagues with feelings that the work brings up for them. When I express empathy rather than irritation toward my colleague, a child welfare worker, who just returned from vacation and feels completely swamped, our conversation can go more smoothly and she is more likely to cooperate with the request I need to make of her. Similarly, I may purposefully name and offer support regarding the anxiety that a child welfare worker is feeling, putting my own frustration or impatience aside, anticipating that this support may remove invisible barriers that limit my colleague's responses, thereby allowing us both to collaborate more effectively to meet the needs of the client and family in question. When I can become conscious of my own countertransference during difficult interactions with colleagues, the potential exists to explore and support my colleagues regarding the countertransference responses evoked in them. Instead of being locked into a predetermined pattern of interacting with each other, together we can discover a new way forward. This new way forward further increases the effectiveness of our efforts to help children and families in transition.

•   •   •

Efforts to address problems in collegial relationships and improve work culture on macro (organizational) and micro (individual or program-based) levels can be thought of as two sides of the same coin: neither holds much value in the absence of the other. The growing pains experienced by the CVC during its expansion compelled the organization to reexamine its climate and culture and seek ways to increase acceptance and support for the diversity reflected in the community in which it is located, as well as in its own community of employees. Along with a focus outward, toward its client base, the CVC turned its focus inward and recognized that it had not been doing as good a job as it could to strengthen staff relationships, improve equity, and acknowledge the positive contributions that staff make each day toward furthering the organizational mission. The creation of the positive work environment work group and other work groups demonstrated efforts to ensure that the vision and values of the cultural task force did not just float at the top of the organizational hierarchy but, in fact, filtered down through all levels of the organization. The process of learning to collaborate more closely with the child welfare system further compelled the SEED program to thoughtfully examine how effective professional collaborations can be formed and maintained and what strategies are most useful when conflict arises between individuals. Through polishing both sides of the coin, the organizationally-based, program- and individually-focused strategies I have shared have moved the CVC toward rediscovering more positive work relationships and, in turn, more effective and culturally sensitive services for the vulnerable children and families it serves. I am sharing these stories and strategies in the hope that they may be useful to other organizations facing similar challenges.

REFERENCES

Carmeli, A., Yitzhak-Halevy, M., & Weisberg, J. (2009). The relationship between emotional intelligence and psychological well-being. *Journal of Managerial Psychology, 24*(1), 66–78.

Cooper, G., Hoffman, K., Powell, B., & Marvin, R. (2005). The Circle of Security intervention: Differential diagnosis and differential treatment. In L. J. Berlin, Y. Ziv, L. M. Amaya-Jackson, & M. T. Greenberg (Eds.), *Enhancing early attachments: Theory, research intervention, and policy* (pp. 127–151). New York: Guilford Press.

Fraiberg, S., Adelson, E., & Shapiro, V. (1980). Ghosts in the nursery: A psychoanalytic approach to the problems of impaired infant-mother relationships. In S. Fraiberg (Ed.), *Clinical studies in infant mental health: The first year of life* (pp. 164–169). New York: Basic Books.

Freedman, J., & Combs, G. (1996). Shifting paradigms: From systems to stories. In *Narrative therapy: The social construction of preferred realities* (pp. 1–18). New York: W. W. Norton.

Hanson, R. (2009, November). Taking in the good. *Greater Good Magazine.* Retrieved November 4, 2009, from http://greatergood.berkeley.edu/greatergood/2009november/Hanson.php.

Hays, P. (2001). Seeing the forest and the trees: The complexities of culture in practice. In *Addressing cultural complexities in practice: A framework for clinicians and counselors* (pp. 3–16). Washington, DC: American Psychological Association.

Heffron, M. C., Ivins, B., & Weston, D. (2005). Finding an authentic voice. Use of self—Essential learning processes for relationship-based work. *Infants and Young Children, 18*(4), 323–336.

Kabat-Zinn, J. (1990). You have only moments to live. In *Full catastrophe living: Using the wisdom of your body and mind to face stress, pain, and illness* (pp. 17–30). New York: Bantam Dell.

Mayeno, L., & Featherstone, E. (2008). *Guidelines for multicultural interactions* [Material adapted from VISIONS, Inc.] Paper presented at the Building Inclusive and Multiculturally Competent Health Organizations: A Healing Approach to Addressing the Isms. Retrieved September 13, 2011, from http://chl. berkeley.edu/images/stories/isms/conference08/guidelinesformulticulturalinteractions.pdf.

Mendoza-Denton, R. (2008). Framed: Rodolfo Mendoza-Denton argues that we must look to our prejudices, not our genes, to explain achievement gaps between ethnic groups. *Greater Good: The Science of a Meaningful Life, 5*(1), 22–24.

Orfirer, K., & Rian, J. C. (2008). Mental health treatment of infants and toddlers: Creating an integrated system of care for infants and toddlers in the child welfare system. *The Source, 18*(1), 1–6.

Otto, K., Glaser, D., & Dalbert, C. (2009). Mental health, occupational trust, and quality of working life: Does belief in a just world matter? *Journal of Applied Social Psychology, 39*(6), 1288–1315.

Pawl, J. H. (2001). Jeree Pawl on reflective supervision. In R. Parlakian, *Look, listen and learn: Reflective supervision and relationship-based work.* Washington, DC: Zero to Three.

Powell, B., Cooper, G., Hoffman, K., & Marvin, R. (2007). The Circle of Security project: A case study— "It hurts to give that which you did not receive." In D. Oppenheim & D. Goldsmith (Eds.), *Attachment theory in clinical work with children: Bridging the gap between research and practice* (pp. 172–202). New York: Guilford Press.

Rao, S. (2010) It's your model—not reality. In *Happiness at work: Be resilient, motivated, and successful—no matter what* (pp. 147–153). New York: McGraw-Hill.

Salovey, P., & Mayer, J. (1990). Emotional intelligence. *Imagination, Cognition, and Personality, 9*(3), 185–211.

Seligman, S., & Harrison, A. M. (2012). Infant research and adult psychotherapy. In G. O. Gabbard, B. E. Litowitz, & P. Williams (Eds.), *Textbook of psychoanalysis* (2nd ed., pp. 239–252). Washington, DC: American Psychiatric Publishing.

Snowden, L. R. (2003). Bias in mental health assessment and intervention: Theory and evidence. *American Journal of Public Health, 93*(2), 239–243.

Strolin-Goltzman, J., Lawrence, C., Auerbach, C., Caringi, J., Claiborne, N., Lawson, H., et al. (2009). Design teams: A promising organizational intervention for improving turnover rates in the child welfare workforce. *Child Welfare, 88*(5), 149–168.

Sue, D. W. (2010). *Microaggressions in everyday life: Race, gender, and sexual orientation*. Hoboken, NJ: John Wiley.

Sutton, R. I. (2010). Strive to be wise. In *Good boss, bad boss: How to be the best . . . and learn from the worst* (pp. 71–98). New York: Business Plus, Hachette Book Group.

van der Zande, I. (2009). Fullpower boundaries for adults with people we know. *Kidpower Teenpower Fullpower International*. Retrieved August 16, 2011, from http://www.kidpower.org/resources/articles/adult-boundaries.html.

Visions Inc. (2011). *VCR—Validate, Confront, Request*. Retrieved September 5, 2011, from http://www.visions-inc.org/index.htm.

Weigand, R. F. (2007). Reflective supervision in child care: The discoveries of an accidental tourist. *Zero to Three, 28*(2), 17–22.

White, M. (2005). Identifying the absent but implicit. *International Journal of Narrative Therapy and Community Work, 3–4*, 15.

Xanthos, C. (2008, July). The secret epidemic: Exploring the mental health crisis affecting adolescent African-American males. *Community Voices, Healthcare for the Underserved* Morehouse School of Medicine. Retrieved August 10, 2011, from http://www.communityvoices.org/Libraries/Community_Voices_Documents/resourceLibrary_mentalHealth_theSecretEpidemic.sflb.ashx.

PART 3

Promising Programs and Culturally Informed Interventions

The chapters in this section describe an array of different programs and interventions targeting children living in transition. Effective programs begin with effective practitioners. For that reason, the first chapter of the section, Chapter 6, is an autobiographical account of entering the foster care system, written by a psychologist who reflects on how the memories of those events inform her current clinical practice. This narrative clearly illustrates the importance of respectful, culturally informed clinical interactions to promote trust and reduce further trauma. The same themes are echoed throughout the section. Each chapter describes: (1) the program's interventions and the evidence on which they are based, (2) the referring agencies that provide the client population, and (3) at least one clinical example of the program's interventions.

Although there is a paucity of strong community-based services available to families living in transition, the best programs agree on three unifying concepts. First, all interventions begin with forming a respectful relationship. Second, most programs receive client children and families referrals based on their current living situation in a way that suggests that this condition is a permanent rather than a transient condition. For example, if the program received referrals from child welfare agencies, all children were identified as either "foster" children (if the child was entering or remaining in foster care) or "reunified" children (if the child had been in foster care but would be or had already been reunified with the birth parents)—even if the child was entering foster care because of family homelessness and parental charges of neglect. Third, each intervention must consider the context, including the unmistakable chasm between the position of power and privilege of the clinician and the position of the families living in transition.

Still, of the three elements, the most important element of any interventions is the program's and the staff's understanding that gaining trust is the first step. No intervention will be successful without attention to this aspect of the process.

CHAPTER 6

Transforming Shame

ALLOWING MEMORIES IN FOSTER CARE TO INFORM INTERVENTIONS WITH FOSTER YOUTH

▸ *LOU FELIPE*

DURING ONE OF MY TRAINING years as a predoctoral clinical psychology intern, I worked at a program serving foster youth and their families. As a person who was once part of the foster care system, I find that my past has given me a unique sense of empathy and compassion for working with youth who are currently involved in the foster care system. Albeit brief, my experiences as a youth under court supervision were undeniably impactful, and there have been many ways in which those experiences have informed my decisions as a child and family therapist. My decision to become a psychologist certainly stemmed from my life experiences with trauma, with the judicial system, with foster care, and with therapy. Some of these experiences were further traumatizing and painful; others opened my life to new possibilities.

REMEMBERING THE PAST

My internship years started with a flurry of trainings to inform me and my fellow interns of the various systemic issues that affect our client population. One of the first trainings offered to the psychology interns outlined the structure of the county's child welfare services agency. I learned how families and children are referred to child welfare services and was informed of the process by which they can move through the intricate system of foster care. Much of what I learned was unknown to me when I myself was an adolescent moving through the foster care system. I had court dates, but I was not quite sure of their purpose and what decisions resulted from them. I had a number of social workers, but I was unclear about the reasons behind the constant transitions from one social worker to the next. I found myself having intense emotional reactions to the training. As the trainer spoke, my mind frequently visited memories of the past, and I connected information from the training to the experiences I had as an adolescent. At the same time, I held that information as a clinician, as an intern, who was now expected to provide therapy for foster children and families. It seemed that the information being offered to me as a therapist was information that was more difficult to obtain as a child involved in the foster care system. A system that had been mysterious to me as an adolescent was being demystified in my first month of training as a psychology intern.

When I started my first week as a predoctoral intern, I held some fears that my past as a foster child would become known to my colleagues. I saw my past as potentially stigmatizing and believed that I should keep that part of my life concealed in my professional role as a therapist. I always understood my history as one that drove my interest in working with foster youth, but I never saw it as something that could inform how I related to my clients. I treated my history as something shameful that should be known to only a few people who knew my work as a clinician. I later learned that this feeling of shame is not an uncommon experience among those who were formally placed in foster care. The shame that I carried into adulthood stemmed from adolescence.

In 1997 Susan Kools conducted a study in which she interviewed adolescents involved in long-term foster care. She writes of how adolescents quickly internalized their devalued status of being a foster child immediately upon their placement into the system: "The status of 'foster child' is conferred on the child upon foster care entry, and the child soon learns that it is not a status of which to be proud. Foster child status was perceived by the study participants as neither familiar nor positive but rather, abnormal, bad, or damaged" (p. 266). Through their interviews, the youth revealed factors that contributed to feelings of depersonalization and stigmatization, including the institutional structure of the foster care system, the diminished status of being a "foster child," and the negative stereotypes placed on foster children (Kools, 1997).

I eventually came to a different realization about how to frame my foster care experience after a conversation I had in supervision. I disclosed to my supervisor that I was once a child in foster care, and I described some of the emotional reactions that I was having during the trainings. I wanted to inform her about this piece of myself so that we both could be aware of what countertransference issues may be stirred as I begin therapy cases with my clients. Carrying this piece of my history with shame, I was expecting a response of concern or pity for my situation. I certainly was not expecting my supervisor to respond with harsh judgment, but I was anticipating some level of sad empathy. Instead, her reaction completely surprised me: she was excited about the possibilities that such news would have for my profession. My supervisor said that my history could be used as a source of strength and that I had access to emotional experiences that few other clinicians have had. I was reminded that my history could be informative and useful to a field of professionals who are outsiders to the world of foster care. Her response completely relieved the internal sense of stigma that I had been carrying. Though I did not immediately share in her excitement, I had a wonderful reframe of how my past could inform the way I engaged in therapy with my clients.

ALLOWING PAST EXPERIENCE TO INFORM
CURRENT INTERVENTION

With a new perspective of my own history in the foster care system, I started accessing old memories of the period of time during which I was in foster care. Having let go of feelings of shame and devaluation for having been a foster child, I viewed my memories with less criticism and judgment. Rather, I started to allow my past experiences to inform the decisions I made in psychotherapy with my clients. While working with a child who had disclosed to me a trauma that he had endured, I was immediately reminded of my own experience of disclosing trauma to a county social worker when I was a teenager. In my own moment of disclosure, the social worker met me at my school. I was not given any notice of her arrival, and she asked me directly about the details of my trauma. I hesitated to speak to her, reluctant to give voice to an event that had not existed outside of me, that was not yet real—until the moment of saying it out loud. Impatient with my hesitation, the social worker prompted me to hurry up and tell my story, telling me that she had heard these stories a number of times and that whatever I had to say would not be new to her. I experienced this woman as callous and bullying, and whatever nervousness I had already been experiencing was further heightened by her impatience. Moreover, what I came to understand from her statement was that my story, which was painful and deeply influenced how I viewed myself and my world, was unimportant and small. From this woman, I understood that my story, once told, would become just one more story among the many that she had heard that were tragic but commonplace. As insignificant as I had already believed myself to be from the years of trauma that I had endured, this social worker walked into my life abruptly and reinforced that very belief within the first ten minutes of meeting me. It was within this context of insensitivity that I first spoke of the details of my life's tragedies.

In the moment that I sat with my child client, seeing the fear in his eyes, I was reminded of my horrible experience of having to disclose my trauma to an adult. Flooded with images of my experience with the social worker, I felt confident about how to respond to my client with sensitivity. Remembering the callous way with which I was prompted to tell my story, I first addressed my client by saying that I was grateful that he felt comfortable enough to tell me what had happened to him. I reminded him that I was not going to hurt him or touch him in any way and welcomed him to tell me if anything I said or did was making him uncomfortable or nervous. I told him that he was not bad in any way and emphasized that he did not do anything wrong. I also expressed how sorry I was that he had experienced such a horrible thing and empathized with how scary and confusing the experience must have been. I told him that I thought he was brave for being able to tell an adult that someone had hurt him and made him uncomfortable. Guided by the memories of my past, I felt driven to respond to my client with genuine concern, empathy, sensitivity, and patience. I truly felt honored by his bravery and recognized how powerful that moment was, the moment when he could directly acknowledge that something painful and traumatic had happened to him. It was only after establishing some level of safety and sincere respect with my client that I began asking him specific questions about his trauma.

I should mention that the primary reason for asking the child about the details of his trauma was to assess his level of safety. It was important to clarify whether his safety was currently being threatened. Initially, this client disclosed his trauma to me in writing, and though it was clear that a trauma occurred, it was not clear whether the event was in the past or was part of an ongoing situation. To determine whether the child was currently in danger, it was necessary to explore the details of the event, so that I could intervene for the sake of the child's safety. If circumstances surrounding the therapy had been different in that the child was referred to me with the knowledge that he had endured past abuse or trauma that had previously been reported to authorities, and was currently safe, my approach to uncovering the details of the trauma might have taken a different trajectory. For example, it has been suggested that disclosure among children who have been victims of sexual abuse takes place over a period of time (Bruck, London, Ceci, & Shuman, 2005). However, the scope of this article will not permit me to directly address specific interventions for working through trauma with children.

RECOGNIZING AND BUILDING UPON RESILIENCY

As a therapist for children who have experienced complex trauma, I am often struck by the resiliency that many of my clients exhibit. Despite layers of historical oppression and deep-seated histories of intergenerational trauma that affect their lives, many of them show amazing strength and fortitude. They remain hopeful, determined, and compassionate regardless of the challenges that are before them, and they stand in contrast to the hopelessness of the people surrounding them. Throughout my internship year, I often reflected on the ways in which I was afforded the opportunities to reach a high level of education, have meaningful and loving relationships, and come into a profession that I find valuable. I know that there were factors in my own life that helped me recognize my talents and strengths. There were relationships that were fulfilling, reciprocal, and loving; these relationships carried me through times of hardship, and there were people who loved me through the times in my life when I was sure that I was unlovable. I had clients who showed different levels of resiliency, and my hope as their therapist was to illuminate the ways in which they already possessed strength and build upon those strengths, so that they, too, could be sustained through the times when their own self-love was compromised by the influence of the oppressive forces around them. I remember gaining strength through athletics, through academic success, and through social events. I remained close to teachers, neighbors, and other adults who showed an interest in guiding and mentoring me. It was not the interventions of a single individual that helped me survive my childhood and adolescence; rather, it was a network of activities and concerned people who propped me up and pushed me through some of the most difficult times of my life. School, friends' homes, and after-school sports programs provided me with safe spaces where I could explore my interests and values. Research on resiliency supported what I had already learned from personal experience. Gilligan (1997), for example, suggests that for children in public care resilience is strengthened through participation in sports, cultural pursuits, or other activities, such as caring for animals. Furthermore, helping children identify their personal strengths and encouraging them to develop hobbies can build a positive self-image and strengthen self-esteem (Rink & Tricker, 2003). Children's environmental contexts are also key in developing protective factors and building resiliency. Just as I experienced school to be a safe haven where I could connect with caring adults and develop my abilities, research has shown that schools can strengthen children's resilience through developing social competence, forging teacher-student bonds, setting high academic and social expectations, and promoting meaningful student participation in school activities (Brooks, 2006).

Knowing the importance of these resiliency factors in my own life helped me as a therapist working with children who often had few opportunities to discover their own talents and strengths. It was common for the children in my caseload to have little connection with school and to have no awareness of their own interests and skills. As their therapist, I often focused on helping them discover the positive relationships in their lives, the people who recognized and nurtured their best qualities. I also worked with parents to educate them on the value of extracurricular activities as a way to give their children an outlet for their emotions, to stave off symptoms of anxiety and depression, and to give them a sense of importance and value in the world. If they were not able to participate in the family or in their communities, their sense of value and worth would never be acknowledged or sustained. As a student athlete, I understood my value to my team; it was imperative to attend practices and develop my skills in order to be a key team member. Being accountable to a group of individuals, my team, I remained involved in activities that built my self-esteem, kept me physically healthy, and offered me a space to release my emotions. I was once a sullen and withdrawn child, but through athletics I was able to build my social skills. I felt strongly that my clients also deserved such opportunities.

I once worked with a parent who had difficulty providing structure for her daughter, who was incredibly anxious and often displayed dangerously risky behaviors. Craving a sense of predictability and safety in her world, the child frequently behaved in explosive and sometimes aggressive ways in order to prompt her mother to provide her with safety and nurturing. Unsure of how to contain her daughter's behaviors, this mother wanted to treat her daughter's soccer practices as a privilege and threatened to take away her participation in athletics as a way to discipline her for not following directions at home. This child also had a tenuous connection with school (she was often suspended and often refused to attend), lived in an impoverished neighborhood that struggled with community violence, and had infrequent contact with caring and nurturing adults. Since I knew that she had few places where she could develop a positive sense of self, it seemed clear that her participation in sports played an important role in the improved stability in her behaviors. Also, she always looked forward to participating in this sport, and she continually expressed an unbridled sense of pride in her identity as an athlete. Witnessing her pride as an athlete and her appreciation of her involvement in soccer, I was reminded of how focused I myself was on participating in various sports activities as a child. I know that organized sports helped me survive a turbulent adolescence, and I remember how I had to plead and negotiate with adults in order to remain involved in sports. When I entered foster care, I moved from one home to the next fairly frequently. The distance of some of my homes from school often challenged my ability to sustain my involvement in athletics because transportation became a barrier. I do not have any memories of service providers or foster parents advocating for or protecting my involvement in athletics and extracurricular activities. However, my basketball coach did offer to give me a ride back to my foster home after practice for the rest of the season. This allowed me to finish out a basketball season that would have otherwise been cut short because of my placement in foster care. Reminiscing about my own experience, I felt confident about protecting my client's involvement in soccer. I explained to her mother that athletics benefit her daughter's emotional development in the same way that school develops her intellect. I encouraged her to treat sports as a necessary part of her daughter's week, explaining that exercise is important in the regulation of emotions, just as school is a necessary part of building a child's fund of knowledge and intellect. However, I wanted to empower the mother's authority as well as protecting the child's involvement in soccer, so I encouraged the mother to remain strengths-based with her daughter and helped her set up a behavioral incentive for her daughter that promoted positive social skills. I offered the mother other alternatives that could serve as consequences for poor behavior, such as setting an earlier curfew or taking away her cell phone. These options allowed the mother to set reasonable limits and allowed her daughter to remain connected to an activity that built her confidence.

REMAINING AWARE OF POWER DIFFERENTIALS

During the years of court involvement in my life and that of my family, I was very aware of how various service providers misunderstood my family's culture. Though I was often angry with my parents and appreciated the ways in which service providers challenged them and advocated for my needs, I also knew that my parents were often vilified. My parents were raised in the Philippines, then migrated to this country as young adults with two young children. I was their third child, the only one born in the United States. The differences between dominant U.S. culture and Filipino American cultures can be incredibly vast. Yet the history of U.S. domination over the Philippines has left Filipinos with a keener understanding of U.S. culture than the Americans have of Filipino culture. In addition, those years of colonization by the United States have left a number of Filipinos admiring U.S. culture to the point of wanting to emulate it unquestioningly, while simultaneously devaluing Filipino culture (David & Okazaki, 2006a, 2006b; Nadal, 2009).

Every social worker, lawyer, teacher, and therapist who worked with me during my adolescence was representative on some level of the larger U.S. culture or government. In essence, they were outsiders to my family, yet their connection to a powerful court system left my parents feeling powerless to combat any of the intrusion that had occurred. To have our family's secrets leaked and then to be chastised was horribly shameful to my parents. They were quickly disempowered, and while many providers seemed to have constant consultations with one another, it did not seem to me that my parents were often involved in those collaborations. I was fortunate enough to be reunified with my family, an outcome that is not often experienced by foster youth. I realize that the courts and the connected service providers must have viewed my parents with some positive regard for my court case to have been resolved in such a way. However, I often wonder what could have happened if my family's cultural and familial values had been viewed with less alienation; perhaps an outside home placement could have been avoided and family therapy could have been more effective and enduring.

The thought that an outside foster home placement could have potentially been avoided if my parents had been supported differently by social workers, lawyers, and therapists is a painful one. I recognize the missteps of my parents, and now that I am an adult reflecting back on my family's history, I can also appreciate the ways in which they were overwhelmed and misunderstood. As a therapist, I hold on tightly to these memories, and I am especially aware of the disproportionate number of children of color, especially African American children, who are involved in the foster care system (Morton, 1999). I have grown into a psychologist who is passionate about learning the ways in which community contexts and historical oppression affect certain cultural communities. I do not forget about the injustices surrounding families that exert enormous, often unsustainable pressure on them. The layers of systems created to disempower certain communities and to empower others are still very much in place, and though I do not excuse the atrocities that are perpetrated against helpless children, I can acknowledge how historical and contemporary racism, classism, sexism, homophobia, and religious persecution can make family stability an impossibility. Those of you who are reading this chapter likely have access to a quality of education that a number of children, especially those in foster care, will never have the opportunity to experience. Without education, community support, and role models of success and autonomy, the communities most affected by family court systems and foster care will continue to have a future of disproportionate involvement with such systems. Working within an impoverished and historically oppressed community, I am obligated to stay attuned to this fact, and I have experiential knowledge that such oppression does, indeed, occur.

When I come across a closed family unit, a family that maintains unwavering secrecy, I am frustrated at not being able to reach them. Yet, I remind myself that I am an outsider to the family values that have helped this family survive over generations. I have encountered situations in family therapy during which a parent describes to me a way of operating in the world that is incongruent with my worldview and my sense of logic. Remembering how quickly my parents' points of view were often dismissed by service providers, I try to retain a sense of humility in therapy situations, reminding myself that I am a complete outsider and have no understanding of a great deal of the family's culture. I do not compromise with regard to the safety and protection of the children with whom I work, but I can simultaneously hold compassion and empathy for the parents who are struggling to raise their children in an unjust and chaotic environment. I work hard to find the strengths in each family, remaining cognizant that there are positive elements to every family, and believing that possibly, with support, these positive elements can overpower the deficits. In many instances, the families are far too stressed for parents to have the capability to adequately monitor and uphold their children's safety. Yet I work determinedly to offer each parent an earnest chance to engage meaningfully with their children and to provide their kids with protection, security, nourishment, and love. I try sincerely to engage parents in a collaborative way and work hard to own and understand my judgments when I have them. In several instances, I encounter parents who love their children deeply, have regrets about many of their past decisions, and hold out hope that their children will have bright and successful futures.

My own experience in foster care prepared me as a therapist working with foster families in that I am more sensitive to the ways in which I am dealing directly with people's lives. I consider my actions carefully, remaining aware of the power of my words and recommendations. I also remain cognizant of how much I do not know, remembering the limits of my knowledge and wisdom. I continually work in connection with my colleagues, other professionals, but most importantly, I remain closely connected with parents and children. I do not make plans for children or families without first consulting them, requesting their feedback, and remaining transparent about my actions. My hope is that those of you reading this article who work with foster youth and families will remember the humanity of their families when providing services and advocacy.

REFERENCES

Brooks, J. E. (2006). Strengthening resilience in children and youths: Maximizing opportunities through schools. *Children and Schools, 28*(2), 69–76.

Bruck, M., London, K., Ceci, S. J., & Shuman, D. (2005). Disclosure of child sexual abuse. *Psychology, Public Policy, and Law, 11*(1), 194–226.

David, E. J. R., & Okazaki, S. (2006a). Colonial mentality: A review and recommendation   for Filipino American psychology. *Cultural Diversity and Ethnic Minority Psychology, 12*(1), 1–16.

——. (2006b). The colonial mentality scale (CMS) for Filipino Americans: Scale construction and psychological implications. *Journal of Counseling Psychology, 53*(2), 241–252.

Gilligan, R. (1997). Enhancing the resilience of children and young people in public care by mentoring their talents and interests. *Child and Family Social Work, 4*, 187–196.

Kools, S. (1997). Adolescent identity development in foster care. *Family Relations, 46*(3), 263–271.

Morton, T. D. (1999). The increasing colorization of America's child welfare system: The overrepresentation of African-American children. *Policy and Practices of Human Services, 57*(4), 23–30.

Nadal, K. L. (2009). *Filipino American psychology: A handbook of theory, research, and clinical practice.* Bloomington, IN: AuthorHouse.

Rink, E., & Tricker, R. (2003). Resiliency-based research and adolescent health behaviors. *Prevention Researcher, 10*, 1–3.

CHAPTER 7

Crossing the Border and Facing the System

CHALLENGES IMMIGRANT FAMILIES EXPERIENCE WHEN A CHILD IS REMOVED FROM THEIR CARE AND PLACED INTO THE CHILD WELFARE SYSTEM

▸ *ROSARIO MURGA-KUSNIR*

"LATINO" IS A CLASSIFICATION THAT INCLUDES people from Mexico, Central America, South America, and part of the Caribbean islands. They are from urban and rural areas, from different ethnic backgrounds (Indigenous, Caucasian, African, Asian, and mixed races), economic statuses, sociopolitical histories, and cultures. In 2010 more than 16% of the U.S. population was Latino or Hispanic; this represents a 43% increase from 10 years earlier (U.S. Bureau of the Census, 2010). Not all Latinos immigrate to the United States for the same reason. Some are forced to leave their countries because of war, violence, displacement, or natural disasters. Others voluntarily make the decision to immigrate for business, professional, or academic reasons. Some are fleeing abusive, violent relationships or family conflicts. Still other men and women decide, because of the lack of opportunities in their countries, to enter the United States without documentation. The peak of unauthorized immigration in the United States occurred in 2007; of the 12 million immigrants who entered, an estimated 7 million came from Mexico (Passel & Cohn, 2011). They crossed the border hoping to provide a better life for their children or to reunite with family members already in the country. Families in Mexico, as well as in Central and South America, have struggled to support themselves through years of instability as their home countries experienced a cycle of conquest, oppression, defeat, and struggle for liberation (Garcia-Prieto, 2005).

Each person who crosses the border has his or her own unique story, but there are some common issues that families share, among them the barriers that they face during their journey and the reception that they get in this country. Another similarity among families is the shock and despair that they feel if they become involved with the child welfare system. The story of a young undocumented couple, "Lety" and "Roberto," and their daughter, "Mayra," illustrates the psychosocial stressors in navigating the cultural differences in childrearing practices, the fear of being deported, the lack of knowledge about what constitutes child abuse and the consequences of it; gives a glimpse of life in a Mexican town; examines their decision to immigrate; and describes the obstacles they encountered along the way.

In this situation, the mental health clinician takes on the roles of "interpreter" for the family, advocate, case manager, cultural broker, provider of concrete assistance, parental support guide, and psychotherapist. These roles form the basis of a relationship with the family, while holding the impact of the abuse, empathizing with the pain of the separation, and helping the family through reunification. These roles are the products of a theory initially developed by Selma Fraiberg to address mental health problems in infants from birth to three years of age. In "Ghost in the Nursery" (Fraiberg, Adelson, & Shapiro, 1975), she emphasized the understanding of the subjective experience of the parents as part of the therapeutic process. Increased research on early brain development and the impact of trauma in young children led to different models of dyadic psychotherapy and the use of different interventions (Hoffman, Marvin, Cooper, & Powell, 2006; Lieberman & Van Horn, 2000; McDonough, 2000).

MEETING MAYRA AND HER FAMILY

Mayra was almost 19 months old at the time when the clinician met her and her parents. She had been in foster care more than three months. Every week she traveled in a van for more than an hour with a strange adult and several other children to meet her parents in a small room at the social services office for a one-hour visit.

Mayra was a sweet little girl with brown skin and black hair. Her mother was a well-groomed, slightly overweight young woman. Her father was tall and light-skinned, with black hair. They were seated around a small table where Mayra was eating *arroz con pollo* (rice with chicken). The clinician introduced herself. The family seemed to feel "at home," perhaps because the clinician was speaking to them in their native language. Mayra was quiet most of the time, making eye contact with neither the clinician nor her parents. She displayed very little emotion. The clinician listened to the parents' questions, many of which appeared to have been held inside during the past three months since the parents did not know whom to ask. They talked about their understanding of Mayra's removal, acknowledging neglect and denying intentional harm. The clinician empathized with their pain and their helplessness; she responded to their immediate questions and verified the imminent court date, being careful not to promise anything to the family. "I will work with you during this process," she told them, feeling that the parents were viewing her as a mother who would rescue them. The clinician explained the goals of the SEED program (Orfirer & Rian, 2008), and agreed to meet with them the following week.

GATHERING INFORMATION

SEED is a unique collaboration of three agencies: Alameda County Social Services Agency, Department of Family Services; the Center for the Vulnerable Child at the Children's Hospital & Research Center Oakland; and Alameda County Public Health Department Nurses. This program aims to integrate services, taking into account the "developmental/mental health needs of the child, and the child welfare mandates for reunification and permanency" (Orfirer & Rian, 2008). This collaboration between the SEED program and the child welfare system presents complex challenges. The child welfare workers (CPS) emphasize protection and the safety of the child, whereas the SEED clinician focuses on socioemotional development, with a deep understanding of the experiences and needs of young children (Lieberman, 1999).

When SEED clinicians receive a new case, they obtain information about the reason the child came into the system and when pertinent, the court hearing reports as well as the medical reports. Mayra was 16 months old when the doctors found a broken bone and bruises and notified the authorities.

Reading these reports and meeting the family brought up many questions about the additional challenges that undocumented immigrant families face when a child is removed. The court reports recommended "No Services," meaning that the parents would not be provided with the usual reunification services, such as parenting classes, referrals for individual therapy, anger management classes, etc.

The "No Services" recommendation usually is given when the family is not available (incarcerated or unknown whereabouts) or when the family has a long history with the child welfare system, drug use, mental illness, or homelessness. Such decisions often are based on the Adoption and Safe Families Act, which is intended to facilitate permanent or adoptive placements for very young children who are unlikely to reunify with their birth parents (Adoption and Safe Families Act, 1997). Yet this was the recommendation given in Mayra's case, and with this decision Mayra was placed in a foster home with a Latino family, whose primary language was English, in a city one hour away.

BUILDING A RELATIONSHIP

Many parents are resistant to therapy when it is mandated by the child welfare system. This is particularly true with our clients, given the SEED program's close collaborative relationship with CPS and the obvious power wielded by that agency. This was not the case with Mayra's parents. Instead, they saw the clinician as a rescuer, someone who would show them the pathway leading to reunification with their daughter.

The first clinical session was spent talking with the parents about Mayra and conducting a developmental screening using the Ages and Stages Questionnaire, Infant/Toddler Symptom Checklist (Squires & Bricker, 2009). This process is usually welcomed by the parents because they are eager to learn about the child's developmental performance in different areas. On the screening, Mayra's communication skills scored below the norm. The mother felt that Mayra "forgot" many of the words that she knew before their separation, and she expressed sadness that Mayra was forgetting Spanish. Language development is important, as it requires social involvement, and parents are the first ones to help their children understand their environment and culture (Fort & Stechuk, 2008). It was evident that the parents had difficulty focusing on their child; their minds were preoccupied with confusion and anxiety about the unknown.

The clinician communicated with the CPS caseworker, with the dependency investigator, and with the mother's attorney in order to advocate for services to work toward reunification. Many times, when needed, the clinician also served as a translator for the parents as they negotiated with the officials from the child welfare system. Fortunately, the initial recommendation of "No Services" was changed in the court hearing, and therefore the family became eligible for reunification services.

With this understanding, the agreement was to meet one hour a week for child-parent psychotherapy, with the next hour reserved for their one-hour visit. The treatment modality of child-parent psychotherapy involves a flexible integration of concrete assistance, emotional support, and developmental guidance, depending on the family's needs.

The assessment process began by providing a safe space that could encourage the family to tell their story. Through empathic listening the relationship began to develop. The clinician listened to the narrative and, using clinical judgment, decided which point of entry was most likely to be conductive to therapeutic change, given the receptiveness of the parties involved (Lieberman & Van Horn, 2005; Stern, 1995). Initially the parents wanted answers to their questions about the child welfare system. The clinician made sure they understood their case plan and the timelines to cover the court requirements. She also tried connecting the parents' anxieties with the child's reactions, making this interaction the focus of the intervention.

In terms of the treatment goals, the explicit agenda of this couple, as has been true for many families, was simply "to get my child back." It is important to acknowledge this overall goal and also to develop specific goals to deal with the impact of the removal on the parent-child relationship. Providing this treatment in the social services office had clear disadvantages because it was not the natural environment for the family. "I wish I can have my daughter back and they can put video cameras in my house to check how I take care of my daughter," the mother said, crying. The constricted space allocated for the sessions at CPS further heightened the negative experience, since for some families the CPS office is a constant reminder of the removal "nightmare."

Most of the families in the SEED program receive therapy in the home where the child lives. In this familiar environment the clinician can see the daily routines of the child's sleeping, eating, relating, bathing, and the various ways that the caregivers relate to their children, through pictures, objects, toys, and family members.

Gathering information about the child and the family is intertwined with the interventions. At the beginning of the treatment the therapist not only observes the parent-child interaction but also works on developing a relationship with the parents. It is common during the first sessions that the parents monopolize the attention, wanting to be heard, and as a result, the child might feel resented or excluded. To avoid this, the therapist can provide separate opportunities for the parents to talk about their needs. Mayra's mother expressed the need to talk about her depressive feelings, which triggered the removal of her child. As the history of the parents came out in the course of the sessions, "a picture of great hardship emerged that started long before the immigration" (Lieberman, 1990). The parents moved to this country to leave their pain behind, and now they found the separation from their child unbearable.

THROUGH MAYRA'S EYES

Mayra was a full-term, healthy baby. As is customary in her culture, an elder in the family took care of the new mother during the *cuarentena*, or the forty days after the birth, keeping her away from "the air and away from the heat." The mother lived in a small town with her great-grandparents, her maternal grandfather and six other relatives. Mayra was breast-fed, and she slept in the same bed as her mother in a room with other family members. Mayra's family used folk remedies when she was sick and rarely visited the clinic.

At 10 months old, Mayra was reaching developmental milestones as expected. It was at this time that her mother decided to join Mayra's father and migrate to the United States. Leaving her family, her town, and her social network to immigrate was a hard task. It was particularly difficult to say good-bye to her maternal grandfather, who so loved Mayra that he had asked Lety to please leave her in Mexico with him. From an attachment point of view, this was Mayra's first separation from the world that she had seen and known. At this age she was clearly bonded to her mother. The development of preferred attachment figures, stranger wariness, and separation protest is normal for a child from 7 to 12 months of age (Zeanah & Boris, 2005).

Mayra crossed the border before her mother did, with a family friend that she did not know. She was given medicine so that she would sleep during the crossing, and she arrived safely at Lety's family friend's home. Many children experience more traumas during emigration than Mayra did by being left behind, being mistreated, or having a prolonged or permanent separation from their parents. Mayra cried inconsolably when she woke up in a new home with new faces around her. After a long week, the mother reunited with Mayra. "I promise I'll never leave you again," she said.

Mayra and her mother entered this new world of freeways and billboards, arriving temporarily at the house of Roberto's father, who lived here with his new family. For the most part Lety and Mayra remained in one small room while Roberto went to work. Mayra's relationship with her father was just starting to develop.

At the time of the alleged abuse, Mayra was 15 months old. The family had rented a room with other adult acquaintances. Both parents worked and took turns taking care of Mayra. Mayra was injured while the father was taking care of her. The exact details seem blurry, but the parents are clear that it was unintentional. Still, we know that children remember traumatic events (Levine & Kline, 2007). Mayra was brought to the hospital by her parents. However, she left the hospital with an adult that she had never seen before. This strange person picked her up and took her away. This person knew nothing about her life, her likes and dislikes, her favorite tune, her favorite toy. Her parents, Lety and Roberto, did not say good-bye. There was no opportunity for that, because of a misunderstanding, probably the result of the language barrier, but Mayra did not know this. All she knew was that she was with a strange adult, and she had no idea where her parents were.

During the first years of life children have anxieties: fear of being abandoned, fear of losing the parent's love, fear of bodily harm, and fear of doing wrong (Lieberman, 1993). The most fundamental need for the child's developmental core is the capacity to trust that the parents are consistently available, able and willing to intervene effectively to fend off danger. The internal fears exist independently of circumstances, but they are exacerbated by external events. Consequently, the child's responses to stress and trauma need to be understood in terms of the convergence of both internal and external dangers. For Mayra this was the second separation from her mother, in addition to the injuries that she suffered while in the care of her father.

Mayra was placed in a foster home where the mother worked all day and the foster father was her primary caregiver. This was a Latino family who spoke English at home. Mayra's foster father reported that during the first week "she just stayed in this couch. She cried all day and she didn't want to eat or to be held." Mayra's constricted awareness or shutting down served to reduce anxious feelings (Levine & Kline, 2007) because she now perceived the world as a dangerous place. Young children cannot understand why they are not with their parents and cannot articulate their pain. They often misattribute frightening events, blaming themselves when parents are angry or when fights erupt between adults (Lieberman & Van Horn, 2005). The emotional cost of separation for toddlers is higher if the separation is prolonged, if it occurs abruptly, or if the child is left with unfamiliar caretakers.

Mayra was in a foster home where English was the main language. Language is a critical source of a child's sense of identity and cultural heritage (Chang & Pulido, 1994). She had visits with her parents only once a week, always after a long car trip. The parents were happy to see her. They took pictures, ate together, and made phone calls to their family in Mexico. And then, abruptly, her parents would say good-bye and go away until the next week.

THE TRAUMA OF CROSSING THE BORDER

Crossing the border is a traumatic experience for adults and children. Nowadays single mothers migrate in large numbers, leaving their children behind with grandparents, relatives, or neighbors (Falicov, 2005), but Lety decided to take Mayra with her. Lety knew that she was risking her life by crossing the border, and she had heard horror stories back in her town of women who had crossed. Many experienced theft, illness due to heat or cold, hunger, or rape.

All too often symptoms that lead to psychiatric hospitalization develop later from these experiences (Kusnir, 2005). This experience is not limited to families entering the United States from Mexico. An even worse journey is from Central America, where men, women, and children cross several borders and ride the dangerous freight trains called *el tren de la muerte*, hopping between seven and thirty trains to get through Mexico (Cammisa, 2010; Perez Torres, 2005). The journey can take months or even years and many attempts (Nazario, 2006). Some people never make it to their destination. Others give up because they cannot endure the hardships. Some families disintegrate, while others succumb to alcohol or drugs and never join their families.

After Mayra crossed the border, Lety started her journey by foot with a "coyote" (Guzman, Haslag, & Orrenius, 2002). She was taken to an old house and had to endure a man sexually harassing her. The next day she and a group of five walked 11 hours straight, only to be caught very close to their final destination. She went back to the Mexican side of the border and was confined to a small room with many men, some women, and children. She was filled with fear and uncertainty, spending several days with almost no food or water. When the "coyote" got the money that Roberto had sent, Lety had luck crossing the border in the trunk of a car.

THE MOTHER'S HISTORY/UNRESOLVED CONFLICTS

The weekly sessions linked past memories with the present. The parents saw their lives with a different perspective. They began connecting their emotions with their history. The therapist learned about Mayra's parents before they entered the United States. Traditionally, in a town like the one where Lety and Roberto were born, the man of the house would move "north" to do seasonal work. Those left behind would adjust to the new family structure, while the father provided financial support.

Lety was the second child in a family of five. Lety remembers her mother showing a clear preference for her brother—"Yo nunca quise una niña" ("I never wanted a girl")—and physically abusing her. Her mother found a job in a nearby town and moved there with Lety's older brother and younger siblings, leaving Lety with her father and her paternal grandparents. When she was 10 years old her father moved to the United States, promising a temporary stay, but it lasted six years. She went to live with her mother again, but life at home was miserable with her abusive mother and her abusive older brother. At age 13 Lety dropped out of school and ran away. At age 15 she got pregnant and had a baby boy. Unfortunately the baby had respiratory problems and died in her arms during his first month.

When Lety brought up the trauma of having her baby die in her arms, she looked at me and said, "When I saw Mayra with her eyes rolled, I thought she was dying and I shook her in desperation." The medical reports showed that according to the father, Mayra fell off the couch and had a seizure. There were many unresolved conflicts at many different levels that needed to be dealt with. First, there was the emotional and physically abusive relationship of Lety with her own mother. Next, there was the trauma of having her baby die in her arms, and the lack of support for adolescents to mourn for children who die. And finally, there was the lack of emotional support to help a new couple with a baby adjust to a new country.

Lety thought that she did not want to raise Mayra as a single mother, and when Roberto offered to pay a "coyote" to smuggle her and Mayra across the border, she thought that it was better to take the risk rather than staying in her town, where she could offer nothing to her daughter except poverty. It is possible that the conflictive relationship with her mother played a role in her decision to migrate. Adolescents tend to have a baby to fill an emptiness/longing that their mothers did not fill, or as a hope that they will be able to live another life (Fraiberg, 1987).

WHEN THE "DREAM" BECAME A "NIGHTMARE"

The parents reported being in shock when the social worker at the hospital told them that Mayra was not returning home with them. The parents explained some of Mayra's injuries, and even accepted responsibility for not immediately taking her to the hospital when she had the seizure. For example, according to the mother, Mayra got the broken bone while using "princess high heel sandals." Mayra had never had seizures before and they didn't know what to do. The parents' perception of the injury and her illness may have been influenced by their fear that taking Mayra to the hospital could lead to being deported. As a result, the parents had decided to use cultural remedies to treat the injuries.

Many immigrant couples remain with relatives or friends due to poverty and the lack of employment. In such desperate situations, several adults and children live in one room. The stress from such crowded and impoverished living arrangements may sometimes lead to neglect or abuse. It is also common that women can more easily find jobs, as babysitters or cleaning houses, thus creating tension in the couple because of the change in the traditional gender roles (Falicov, 2005).

New couples have to negotiate and adjust to the demands and stresses of living with a child. Compounding those difficulties is the additional fear associated with being undocumented and under constant threat of deportation. In 2009, according to the Department of Homeland Security, more than 70% of the deportees were Mexican (Hoefer, Rytina, & Baker, 2010). Lety got a job in the same restaurant where Roberto worked, but on a different shift. In this way they were able to take turns caring for their daughter. As is common, undocumented workers get paid less than the minimum wage, have no benefits, and rarely feel that they can refuse to work extra hours or to switch shifts (Garcia-Prieto, 2005).

Lety and Roberto stayed in the hospital day and night for two weeks, worried about their daughter's well-being. They were questioned about Mayra's bruises. Even when they had interpreters, they did not understand the meaning of the questions that were asked. The doctors were suspicious about the answers that the parents gave, and because of the severity of the injuries they performed a closer medical exam and found more injuries, including the broken bone. The doctors, as mandated reporters (required to report injuries that might be the result of abuse or neglect), called child protective services, and Mayra was placed in custody.

THE THERAPEUTIC PROCESS

Various different modalities were used. Besides family therapy, the clinician also provided treatment to the parents as a couple and sometimes to each parent individually. Sitting in one of the small chairs in the room around the table, the parents, the child, and the clinician played together, helping the child build a sense of self as a social being who was competent, cooperative, and emotionally connected (Lieberman, 1993). Week after week the therapist helped Maya's parents explore with curiosity the meaning of Mayra's behavior in the room. The role of the clinician is not to investigate the abuse, but to help the families in pain. The treatment process moves back and forth, between past and present, between feelings and behavior, following the flow of parental associations and interactions between parents and child (Lieberman, Silverman, & Pawl, 2000). The child-parent therapist brings the voice of the vulnerable child so that the parents can understand the child's internal world. The therapist holds both the allegations made by the court and the parents' views while working to help the parents empathize with the child.

Mayra's affect in play began to change from being withdrawn to being engaged. She also began seeking comfort from her mother. These breakthroughs were a fundamental first step for the parents' preparation for reunification. Child-parent psychotherapy included developing a relationship, exploring their cultural views, gaining a better understanding of their history, reflecting about the family's experiences, and bringing the voice of the child into the room by inviting parents to observe a specific reaction of the child or simply "wonder" about the internal world of the child. The parents were able to articulate a coherent narrative that included maintaining Mayra's safety. The quality of the relationship with the therapist became stronger, and the parents themselves increased their sense of being worthy persons and caregivers (Larrieu, 2002).

The sessions with the couple were centered on improving their communication skills and helping them understanding their daughter's emotional needs. Discussing their view of discipline and parenting in general was an important piece of the treatment. It also was important to ask about their longings, their traditions, what they wanted to keep and what they wanted to discard. The clinician gave them time to think about the connections among all these elements, and to discuss them without passing judgment. Individually each parent had the opportunity to talk about his or her perceptions and the meaning of Mayra in their lives. It was evident that Mayra's primary attachment continued to be with the mother and that often the father would feel jealous or left out. The aim of the therapy sessions was to repair the rupture that led to the separation by making the parents more aware of the interactions between themselves as well as those with their child. The mother questioned the reason for crossing the border, for living with her husband, and she even questioned her reason to live. By being provided the space to tell their story, the parents slowly regained their sense of self as well as their dreams and hopes

It was clear that this couple needed more psychological support. In collaboration with the child welfare worker, referrals were given so Lety and Roberto were able to receive both couples therapy and individual therapy.

Week after week the therapist's presence in the room became more familiar, and so Mayra would greet the therapist with great enthusiasm. The parents were following their case plan ("al pie de la letra"). Roberto was attending a year-long anger management group, in Spanish, and enjoying it. He also attended weekly individual therapy regularly. Lety joined a women's support group that became a real help in her life. Not all families take advantage of these services as this family did. Some families are eager to be out of the system, and involve themselves with services only as mandated by the child welfare system.

Mayra was developing appropriately. She was curious and ready to explore the room and the toys around her. The parents learned to read and respond to Mayra's cues and behaviors. They better understood the emotional needs of their toddler and were able to reflect about the child's inner world.

Therapy, concrete planning, and videotapes were used as a part of treatment. The videotapes are a therapeutic tool for parents to view their behaviors with their children (Larrieu, 2002). The use of videotaping was particularly useful for Roberto, as he was able to see his anxiety in his interactions with Mayra. He talked about his feelings during the process. At the same time, the mother became calmer and her depression decreased considerably as we began planning the reunification.

MAYRA REUNITED WITH HER PARENTS

The child welfare worker, the parents, and the clinician met to develop a transition plan for reunification. We discussed the changes that they would anticipate in the child's behavior, as well as in her sleeping and eating habits. We also talked about Mayra's memories that might bring fear, sadness, or other feelings. The SEED program pays special attention to "creating threads of continuity" when children in foster care are transitioning from one home to another (Frame, Orfirer, & Ivins, 2004). In Mayra's case, the transition was less than optimal because the foster parents and the birth parents had minimal face-to-face communication throughout the time Mayra was in foster case. This problem was partly the result of the logistical issues created by the distance and the lack of transportation, and partly a reflection of the difficulty that many foster parents have in facing the loss of a child who has been living with them.

Mayra returned to her parents' home close to Christmas Day. "Our best present," the parents said. The foster parents sent her clothes and some toys, along with a photo album.

The therapist continued to provide home-based child-parent psychotherapy, monitoring Mayra's adaptation. The parents became more empathic toward their daughter, checking her reactions and asking for help when needed. They also became more playful with Mayra.

Mayra now feels that she belongs to her family. The rupture has been repaired. Mayra can once again see her parents as a source of protection, safety, and reassurance. The little girl is rooted in her culture, and the family can once again make sense of risking their lives by crossing the border to have a better life. Roberto works hard. Lety has decided to stay home and take care of Mayra.

REFLECTIONS

From the moment this therapist received this case she became intensely involved and enraged about the injustices of seeing that a young family was about to be destroyed. As a Latina therapist, she wanted to help the family understand the system, an unknown and frightening entity for them. Reflective supervision provides an opportunity to find a balance among the internal experiences of the child, the relationships (therapist-parent-child), and the social/cultural context. Clinicians need a time to reflect and to confront their own "ghosts," as well as a space to be aware of their position of power, and the cultural differences and similarities. The job of the clinician is to help the parents understand the internal world of the child, and through the therapy help to repair the rupture that led to the removal.

The child-parent psychotherapist needs to respond to the families where they are, and this means understanding and addressing the specific challenges of undocumented families. This was a young and inexperienced couple, and the parenting models that they learned at home were not necessarily the ones that they wanted to follow. They themselves were in the adolescent stage, a stage of psychological separation from their own families, normally a stage in which teens can reflect about the childrearing practices that their own parents employed. Many adolescents, like Lety and Roberto, enter the adult stage before they are ready. Children and families who are newcomers to the United States, particularly those whose first language is not English, face considerable barriers to accessing programs and services. This lack of access contradicts the American value of equal opportunity. Children are not the only ones who lose; the entire society suffers from the loss of their human capital, creativity, and productivity as family members, workers, and community members.

Children of undocumented immigrant parents are often considered at increased risk of abuse because of the stress and the pressure that the family experiences. Latinos experience income disparities, poverty, and lack of education (Committee for Hispanic Children and Families, 2010). Many undocumented families live in constant fear of being deported (Cervantes & Lincroft, 2010). They tend to use culturally appropriate "medical" remedies rather than western medicine, and they frequently are uninformed about U.S. laws, particularly the child protective laws.

When a child enters the welfare system, immigrant parents face huge obstacles in reuniting with the child. For example, if a parent is detained or deported, he or she cannot participate in child welfare proceedings like family court or case plan requirements, and that creates the risk of permanent, unnecessary separation from their child.

One can say that this was a success story because this therapeutic approach promoted a good outcome. This family had the opportunity to stay together and to learn new ways to relate to each other and their child. One wonders what would had happened if they had not received support during this journey. What happens to all the families that "fall through the cracks"?

This journey described here suggests several reflective questions. What training is needed for clinicians so they can effectively assist undocumented immigrant families? How do clinicians work with the couple that lives under stress? What interventions are needed to assist young parents who have very little support in this country? How can child welfare agencies work with mental health agencies to help each other and to ultimately provide better interventions that support families? How might child welfare agencies better identify and help address immigration issues affecting the abused, neglected, and abandoned children they encounter? How can immigration attorneys and child welfare attorneys collaborate effectively in connection with juvenile court and immigration proceedings that affect children?

REFERENCES

Adoption and Safe Families Act of 1997. P.L. 105.89 (H.R. 867). 105th Congress, 1st Session. Retrieved May 18, 2011, from http://library.childwelfare.gov/cwig//ws/library/docs/gateway/Blob/56367.pdf.

Cammisa, R. (Writer & Producer) (2010). *Which way home* (Film). HBO Documentary Films presents in association with Good and White Buffalo Entertainment; a Mr. Mudd Production in association with Documentress Films.

Cervantes, W., & Lincroft, Y. (2010). *Caught between systems: The intersection of immigration and child welfare policies: The impact of immigration enforcement on child welfare.* From Migration and Child Welfare National Network and

First Focus. Retrieved February 13, 2011, from http://www.f2f.ca.gov/res/pdf/Caught_Between_Systems.pdf.

Chang, H. N., & Pulido, D. (1994). The critical importance of cultural and linguistic continuity for infants and toddlers. *Zero to Three, 15*(2), 14–16.

Committee for Hispanic Children and Families. (2010). *Creating a Latino child welfare agenda: A strategic framework for change.* A report by the Committee for Hispanic Children and Families. Retrieved October, 10, 2010, from http://www.chfinc.org/policy/Packard_report_for_chcf%20web7_15_03.pdf.

Falicov, C. (2005). Mexican families. In M. McGoldrick, J. Giordano, & N. Garcia-Prieto (Eds.), *Ethnicity and family therapy* (3rd ed., pp. 229–231). New York: Guilford Press.

Fort, P., & Stechuk, R. (2008). The cultural responsiveness and dual language education project. *Zero to Three, 29*(1), 24–28.

Fraiberg, S. (1987). The adolescent mother and her infant. In L. Fraiberg (Ed.), *Selected writings of Selma Fraiberg* (pp. 168–173). Columbus: Ohio State University Press.

Fraiberg, S., Adelson, E., & Shapiro, V. (1975). Ghost in the nursery: A psychoanalytic approach to the problems of impaired infant-mother relationships. *Journal of the American Academy of Child Psychiatry, 14*, 387–421.

Frame, L., Orfirer, K., & Ivins, B. (2004). Creating threads of continuity: Helping infants and toddlers through transitions in foster care. *The Source, 13*(2). Berkeley, CA.

Garcia-Prieto, N. (2005). Latino families. In M. McGoldrick, J. Giordano, & N. Garcia-Prieto (Eds.), *Ethnicity and family therapy* (3rd ed., pp. 153–162). New York: Guilford Press.

Guzman, M., Haslag, J., & Orrenius, P. (2002). *Coyote crossings: The role of smugglers in illegal immigration and border enforcement* (Research Department Working Paper 0201, Federal Reserve Bank, Dallas). Retrieved October 2, 2011, from http://www.dallasfed.org/research/papers/2002/wp0201.pdf.

Hernandez, D., Macartney, S., Blanchard, V., & Denton, N. (2010). Mexican-origin children in the United States: Language, family circumstances, and public policy. In N. Landale, S. McHale, & A. Booth (Eds.), *Growing up Hispanic: Health and development of children of immigrants* (pp. 169–178). Washington, DC: Urban Institute Press.

Hoefer, M., Rytina, N., & Baker, B. (2010). *Estimates of the unauthorized immigrant population residing in the United States: January 2009.* Washington, DC: Office of Immigration Statistics, Policy Directorate, U.S. Department of

Homeland Security. Retrieved March 15, 2011, from http://www.dhs.gov/xlibrary/assets/statistics/publications/ois_ill_ pe_2008.pdf.

Hoffman, K., Marvin, S., Cooper, G., & Powell, B. (2006). Changing toddlers' and preschoolers' attachment classifications: The Circle of Security interventions. *Journal of Consulting and Clinical Psychology, 74*(6), 1017–1026.

Kusnir, D. (2005). Salvadorean families. In M. McGoldrick, J. Giordano, & N. Garcia-Prieto (Eds.), *Ethnicity and family therapy* (3rd ed., pp. 262–264). New York: Guilford Press.

Larrieu. J. (2002). Treating infant-parent relationships in the context of maltreatment: Repairing ruptures of trust. *Zero to Three, 22*(5), 16–22.

Levine, P., & Kline, M. (2007). *Trauma through a child's eyes: Awakening the ordinary miracle of healing.* Berkeley, CA: North Atlantic Books.

Lieberman, A. (1990). Infant-parent intervention with recent immigrants: Reflections on a study with Latino families. *Zero to Three: Bulletin of the National Center for Clinical Infant Programs, 4,* 8–11.

——. (1993). *The emotional life of the toddler.* New York: Free Press.

——. (1998). Culturally sensitive intervention with children and families. *Newsletter of the Infant Mental Health Promotion Project 22.* Reprinted and adapted from *Child and Adolescent Social Work, 7*(2) (1990), 1–5.

——. (1999). The trials and rewards of being a clinical consultant to child protective services. *Zero to Three, 19*(3), 14–18.

Lieberman, A., Silverman, R., & Pawl, J. (2000). Infant-parent psychotherapy: Core concepts and current approaches. In C. Zeanah (Ed.), *Handbook of infant mental health* (2nd ed., pp. 472–483). New York: Guilford Press.

Lieberman, A., & Van Horn, P. (2005). *Don't hit my mommy! A manual for child-parent psychotherapy with young witnesses of family violence.* Washington, DC: Zero to Three Press.

——. (2008). *Psychotherapy with infant and young children: Repairing the effects of stress and trauma on early attachment.* New York: Guilford Press.

McDonough, S. (2000). Interaction guidance: An approach for difficult-to-engage families. In C. Zeanah, (Ed.), *Handbook of infant mental health* (2nd ed., pp. 485–493). New York: Guilford Press.

Nazario, S. (2006). *Enrique's journey: The story of a boy's dangerous odyssey to reunite with his mother.* New York: Random House.

Orfirer, K., & Rian, J. (2008). Mental health treatment of infants and toddlers: Creating an integrated system of care for infants and toddlers in the child welfare system. *The Source, 18*(1), 1–6.

Passel, J. S., & Cohn, D'V. (2011). *Unauthorized immigrant population: National and state trends, 2010*. Washington, DC: Pew Hispanic Center.

Perez Torres, A. (Writer). (2005). *Wetback: The undocumented documentary* (Movie). Washington, DC: National Geographic.

Rios, E., and Duque, S. (2007). *Bridging the cultural divide: Building a continuum of support services for Latino families*. The Committee for Hispanic Children and Families, Inc. Retrieved on October 23, 2010, from http://www.chcfinc. org/policy/BridgingtheCulturalDivide.pdf.

Squires, J., and Bricker, D. (2009). *Ages and Stages Questionnaire (ASQ-3)* (3rd ed.). Baltimore, MD: Brookes Publishing.

Stern, D. (1995). *The motherhood constellation: A unified view of parent-infant psychotherapy*. New York: Basic Books.

U.S. Bureau of the Census. (2010). *2010 Census results*. Retrieved May 29, 2011, from http://2010.census.gov/2010census/data/.

Zeanah, C., and Boris, N. (2005). Disturbances and disorders of attachment in early childhood. In C. Zeanah (Ed.), *Handbook of infant mental health* (2nd ed.). New York: Guilford Press.

Zeanah, C., and Fox, N. (2004). Temperament and attachment disorders. *Journal of Clinical Child and Adolescent Psychology, 33*(1), 32–41.

CHAPTER 8

"I Am Bad!"

▸ *ROBERTO MACIAS SANCHEZ*

IT WOULD NOT BE SURPRISING to hear adults label themselves as bad, but it is unusual—even painful—to hear 4- or 5-year-old children refer to themselves with this negative label. How could children with a still-developing identity already settle on the idea that they are bad? What experiences contributed to this negative self-image? These questions are not easy to answer. What is clear is that there are many layers to this complicated issue, and the more layers that we deal with, and the earlier that we do it, the easier it will be to reverse the self-perception of "I am bad" to "I am good."

This chapter describes the experiences of the children, caregivers, teachers, and clinicians who collaborate to support the interventions and goals of the SPARK program. SPARK specifically targets children in preschool who are homeless and experiencing behavioral issues. The term "homeless" is used to refer to children who are living in homeless shelters as well as to children who are living in extremely impoverished homes under very tenuous circumstances.

A TYPICAL REFERRAL

Generally, children are referred to SPARK because of their aggressive and disruptive behaviors. The children typically have difficulties interacting socially. Their emotions are intense, and they challenge their teachers' capacity to manage them. They are constantly on the move. They do not comply with behavioral expectations or follow established routines. Their frustration threshold is lower than that of the majority of their peers.

Unfortunately, "acting out" behaviors are motivators for referring children, while internalized ways of dealing with stresses are not. Children who are timid, quiet, and compliant receive little notice since they do not disrupt the class. For example, it is not uncommon for children with serious speech delays to go unnoticed unless the child is "acting out."

THE PROGRAM

SPARK was created in response to a social worker's observations that preschool children who had been living in homelessness were being expelled from preschools because of their challenging behaviors as well as the teachers' inability to meet their needs. SPARK's primary aim is to provide children of homeless families with the necessary skills to adjust to preschool life with the hope that these skills will carry over into their academic and personal futures. SPARK also provides screening and referrals recommending further examination or specialized services for children who demonstrate behaviors that suggest more than a "normal" variation in behavior. In addition, usually children referred for services in the classroom also need help with difficulties at home. Unfortunately, we do not always have the opportunity to work in the home with the caregivers, and this may hinder progress in the classroom. Still, ongoing efforts are made to establish relationships with caregivers, and to support them and their children.

SPARK believes that the first school experience has a lasting impact on the lives of children. It is at this stage in their lives that children first apply and expand their knowledge of basic human social coexistence outside the home environment. They learn to familiarize themselves with "strangers," to work collaboratively, and to communicate respectfully, assertively but not aggressively. These basic skills provide the foundation for essential tools throughout their lives, which are cherished in the school, work, and social environments. The SPARK approach employs a model that promotes socioemotional development and supports children's appropriate behavior while preventing and reducing challenging behavior (Fox, Hemmeter, Joseph, & Strain, 2003).

Since there is evidence that homeless children have more prevalent behavioral and emotional problems than the general population (Masten, 1992), early intervention is valuable. This is especially important since unaddressed behavioral challenges in young childhood are likely to fester and contribute not only to poor academic outcomes and social difficulties in later childhood but also to mental health concerns and psychosocial difficulties throughout adulthood (Dunlap et al., 2006).

THE TEAM

It is clear that the efforts of clinicians are likely to be most effective when they enlist the help of teachers, school administrators, and caregivers. This team is the foundation of successful interventions. The greater the involvement of all team members in the interventions and decision-making process, the more effective the interventions are. There needs to be consensus and consent from all team members. The input and expertise that each brings contributes to a successful intervention plan. The goals need to be clear and explicit. Whenever possible a home component that parallels the school's expectations is an excellent complement to the school-based action plan, as it creates consistency across both environments, with the caregiver serving as an indispensable extension of the treatment team. "Family involvement in the planning and implementation of interventions facilitates durable reductions in challenging behaviors of young children" (Dunlap et al., 2006).

THE SETTING

SPARK has focused on partnerships with two types of academic settings: Head Start programs and child development centers (CDCs). Different school systems have different expectations; therefore, children will need to use different strategies to adapt and become successful at their individual preschools. In addition, each Head Start or CDC may have additional expectations besides those mandated by federal or state standards. The clinicians must adapt to both the philosophy of the program and the specific site to address the child's adaptive behaviors.

With the referral, the clinician's very first step toward creating positive outcomes is forming relationships with all members of the treatment team; this includes the client, the caregiver, the school personnel, and when necessary other professionals who are involved in the child's care. Caregivers' and teachers' perceptions of the clinicians are likely to influence their support for treatment goals, and ultimately they have a greater influence than the clinician, since they have more daily contact with the client. Moreover, teachers and parents are more likely to support treatment goals when the goals respond to *their* concerns. Care meetings are an opportunity to discuss client concerns. Occasionally teachers and caregivers might be at odds with each other at these meetings. Clinicians can use such a situation as an opportunity to address the concerns of both. At these joint meetings, the clinician can emphasize what is usually the case—that both points of view are actually beneficial and complementary. This affords a unique opportunity to strengthen the therapeutic/working alliance with both caregivers and teachers, and it also supports collaboration.

THE WORK

Because preschool curricula concentrate on the development of basic academics, most SPARK interventions focus on social skills and psycho-emotional development that promote the child's preschool adjustment. Contributing factors to the child's healthy socialization and healthy preschool adjustment are the development of empathy and emotional regulation. Children must be able to regulate emotional distress, tolerate frustrations, and remain emotionally and cognitively flexible in the face of inconsistency. Building these skills is essential for their success in preschool.

Treatment usually incorporates dealing directly with the behaviors that are most disruptive. The goal is to replace maladaptive behaviors with adaptive ones, such as using words to express frustration instead of using aggression. Behavioral techniques are effective for this particular age group. However, once again it is important to stress that behavioral interventions require complementary relationships with clients, teachers, and caregivers, since support for the treatment plan and ongoing feedback inform the clinician on the direction of the interventions. The collaboration, cooperation, and mutual respect among the members of the treatment team help children adapt to the expectations and internalize these values.

SPARK assumes that children are more responsive to people whom they respect, trust, and who provide them with a sense of safety. This likely applies to caregivers and teachers as well. According to Cooper (2008), "At the heart of most successful therapies, is a client who is willing and able to become involved in making changes to her or his life [and] if that client then encounters a therapist whom she or he trusts, likes and feels able to collaborate with, the client can make use of a wide range of techniques and practices to move closer toward her or his goals" (p. 157).

In addition to direct classroom services, clinicians can address issues relating to family dynamics when they are relevant to the behaviors observed in the classroom. For example, if a client is aggressive and through the family history it is revealed that the child is currently or was exposed to domestic violence, then the clinician can make a connection between the expression of emotions, the context of an abusive relationship, and how clients express themselves in the classroom. Such delicate conversations can take place only when there is a solid therapeutic alliance in place. Cooper (2008) writes: "Clients' [and observers'] ratings of the therapeutic alliance . . . tend to be more predictive of outcomes" (p. 101) and "there is some evidence . . . that measures of the alliance in the early stages of therapy . . . are especially strong predictors of positive therapy outcomes" (p. 104); also, "negative feedback is likely to be accepted as accurate and useful" in the context of a solid alliance (p. 119). The last point is of particular importance, as many of the caregivers already have heard complaints about their children's behaviors before coming into contact with clinicians.

If the clinician suspects or knows that the caregiver disciplines the child harshly, and also learns that the caregiver has other stresses, the clinician can provide psycho-education while also providing concrete support that alleviates those stressors. High levels of stress may contribute to lower frustration thresholds; consequently, talking about alternative parenting practices before addressing the high levels of stress may risk losing the trust of the caregiver. Psycho-education can be an important and effective tool, but it must be used with respect and sensitive timing. At the same time, the clinician must always keep in mind the child's safety, as well as legal mandates such as the reporting of neglect or abuse.

Additional services include providing referrals for housing, legal, and other supports to help reduce the stressors affecting the family unit. Clinicians also advocate for services such as speech therapy. Advocating for client needs becomes an important role of clinicians. The rights of homeless children are oftentimes overrun by systems that are insensitive to their needs. Sometimes school districts struggling with financial woes appear to try to provide the least possible amount of support and may even find ways to justify a no-need-for-services conclusion. Clinicians advocate and provide support by sitting in on individualized education planning (IEP) meetings and stressing the need to implement plans that will address the concerning behaviors. Clinicians are consistent advocates, from the everyday conversations with teachers about their frustrations or hope for clients, to representing their clients' interests in IEPs. To be a good client advocate, clinicians must be aware of laws affecting homeless populations. For example, there are laws such as the McKinney-Vento Assistance Act, which mandates, among other things, that school districts facilitate the enrollment of children in homeless situations. This issue needs to be approached sensitively, as many families who need and want the advantages that such laws provide may nevertheless not want to be identified as homeless. Some may not even realize that they qualify as homeless—such as immigrant families who are doubled up and living "under a roof" rather than homeless and "on the street." Finally, clinicians benefit by creating a network of relationships with agencies that support the needs of homeless children.

CHALLENGES OF WORK

In working with teachers, the principal concern is to balance the expectations that teachers have for their class with the skills that the children possess. Children who need to be in control constantly can cause disruption by their ongoing desire to always be first, the only one, or the one in control of rules and goods. Conversely, teachers expect children to be able to wait their turn and follow directions. Clinicians can bridge the needs of both. For example, the clinician can make it a goal for the children to help set the table, if they sit down during circle time and listen to instructions. Here the expectations of both the child and the teacher meet. The children are in control of setting the table, and the teacher gains a helper who did not disrupt the class. The clinicians' highlighting the importance of teacher participation validates them as professionals and caring adults, and is a great way of ensuring the implementation of treatment goals. After all, as mentioned before, children spend more time with teachers than with clinicians.

Teachers also possess biases and specific expectations about how children should behave. With tact and sensitivity on the part of the clinician, these can be addressed in a parallel process. When working with the client on aggressive behaviors, for example, teachers can be made aware of the influences of their own behaviors on the clients' behaviors, particularly those that they desire to reinforce. This helps teachers develop greater awareness of their own efficacy or lack of it. Their efforts are validated. Equally important, teachers are empowered with the specific tools that they can use to work toward desired outcomes.

Another common challenge involves a mismatch between the teaching style or class expectations and the children's ability to comply. Culture can be at the heart of some of these discrepancies. Teachers may hold specific cultural values that can influence their perception of the behaviors for which children were referred. A teacher who emphasizes cleanliness may be upset by children who do not clean up after themselves. A second teacher may perceive "a little rough play" as appropriate while another one may not. Some will see children's jumping from the top of a play structure as "risky" and even "dangerous," while others may view it as a perfect way to practice gross motor skills. Helping a teacher reflect on these variations within a context of trust and collaboration is very useful. Clinicians have to balance their own values, those of teachers, the goals of the program, and the rules of the preschool setting, all while being aware of the needs of their clients and any safety concerns.

Many times children who are new to the school setting experience a period of adaptation. For some this initial adjustment period may be problematic. Sometimes children who exhibit initial difficulties are labeled, and once that happens, adults have difficulty seeing or accepting positive progress. Unfortunately, it is not unusual for clients, after making a reputation for themselves, to be blamed by teachers and peers alike for events that were not their fault. Moreover, children who exhibit difficulties in one area may find that improvements in other areas go completely unnoticed. If the improvements had been noticed, they would have been reinforced. Clinicians can highlight the progress by consulting with teachers frequently and underlining both the positive changes and the interventions that made the changes possible. In this way the clinicians ensure the continuity of progress and provide teachers with tools to deal with the behaviors of concern. A secondary benefit is that clients are seen in a different light. They begin to be evaluated as being capable of meeting social and academic demands, providing a balanced view of who they are.

According to Whitman, Accardo, Boyert, & Kendagor (1990), "Programmatic responses to . . . [homeless children's] . . . special needs . . . do not appear to take account sufficiently of the complexities of the impact of homelessness. This lack of awareness often leads to inadvertent insensitivities by service providers towards . . . [homeless children]" (p. 518). By making teachers aware of the challenges that children face and incorporating the teachers' experiences and expertise, we are likely to create a working alliance that not only helps the clinician but also is beneficial to the child. This is important, because when children experience genuine caring, compassion, and safe classroom spaces, they can become active participants in their education (Walker-Dalhouse & Risko, 2008).

Sometimes teachers inadvertently reinforce the behaviors they are trying to decrease. An example is when teachers respond to children who engage in disruptive behaviors by allowing the children to sit on their laps, thus ending the objectionable behavior. The children, of course, are likely to welcome this resolution, since they feel rewarded by the attention. Affection and praise are a great way of sending the message of "I value you," and children are likely to respond by repeating the behaviors in order to get more of the same kind of attention. Such situations generate a cycle of disruptive behavior. At the same time some children may genuinely need this attention, and it should not be denied to them. After all, teachers, generally female at this academic level, become a sort of surrogate maternal figure. Balancing the emotional needs of children with support for the development of emotional maturity becomes a tricky business, particularly for homeless children whose parents struggle to obtain basic needs and may themselves not have had nurturing models. Consequently, part of the work of the clinician can be helping teachers to figure out a balance between a healthy response to emotional needs and appropriate limit setting.

Like teachers, clinicians have to be aware of their boundaries and be clear on when to respond to emotional distress with affection. It is not a simple issue. One consideration is that children may already have experienced difficulties with attachment to a primary caregiver. Thus the child can become confused about the roles that the teacher and the clinician play in their lives. Children may see the teacher or clinician as a source of psychological comfort like their primary caregiver, and as a result, they may become distracted when they receive support from the teacher or clinician in class. In this case it may be useful to revisit the idea of boundaries with the child, but always in a warm and caring manner. Conversely, some children may not trust the adults and will be reluctant to approach them for support when warranted. Some children may even exhibit aggressive behaviors when they have a sense that adults are unable to meet their needs or keep them safe.

Aggression may become automatic as children lose trust that their needs for safety or support will be met by the adults around them. In such cases, bolstering children's confidence that adults will keep them safe can become a goal. Safety does not mean just physical safety. It is not unusual to see children at this age verbally hurting each other. Children are driven to fear, despair, feeling rejected, and other negative experiences when they are taunted, humiliated, and bullied. Sadly, this happens even in preschool and often goes unnoticed as adults tend to minimize children's experience and have difficulty understanding their perspective. Teachers need to be made aware that these emotions are important and that the distress and suffering experienced by children of this age are real. Adults looking at these interactions have a tendency to minimize their importance. This is a mistake. Children's feelings are just as valid as adults', and we must attend to them with the same seriousness and respect. In addition, setting consistent, clear limits in an empathic and caring way that adults can model pro-social, age-appropriate, empathic interactions and show children that they can be counted upon to help the children feel safe, decreasing the need for children to decide to undertake "personal justice," such as verbal and physical insults to peers .

Gaining the caregiver's trust is perhaps the most important task for the clinician in a complex web of relationships that are needed to support homeless children. Parents are often overwhelmed with life demands, and may feel further challenged by clinicians who ask them to become active participants in treatment. Promoting a trusting and supportive relationship facilitates the providers' ability to reach the desired outcomes. Clinicians must be aware that the clients' perceptions, and those of their families, are the ones that matter most; it is their perceptions that are ultimately linked to positive outcomes, as "clients, not therapists, make therapy work" (Duncan, Miller, & Sparks, 2004, p. 12).

Occasionally, caregivers do not believe that there is a problem. They may therefore minimize teachers' concerns or externalize responsibility for what is happening. They may blame teachers and the client's peers. Some caregivers may be in complete denial and will not follow through with referrals that could benefit their children, while others are unable to follow through. It is important to keep in mind that some caregivers may not trust the clinicians because of a long history of experiencing other agencies' hurtful and intrusive interventions. Other caregivers may be participating because they feel compelled to accept help to keep their children at school. Whatever the reason, it is essential to continue making efforts to build an alliance with caregivers. One strategy is to focus on what goes well. Another is to seek caregivers' opinions on their children; this is a great way of honoring their importance, participation, and feedback. Agreement on therapy goals and consensus on tasks in the context of a positive bond are the components of the therapeutic alliance (Cooper, 2008).

One way to bypass or minimize the caregiver's distrust is to focus solely on what the caregiver desires for the child's future. Almost all caregivers express a desire for their children to do well, and to live successful and happy lives. Addressing the behaviors that the caregivers' view as interfering with their vision of their child's future offers an opportunity to align with them and gain their active support for their child's treatment. Ultimately, it is important for the clinician to be empathic and earn the caregiver's trust, particularly since caregivers have the burden of having to "meet and talk" with the clinician after a long day of work.

Clinicians must be careful with the language used. Attempts to keep a caregiver informed can be perceived as ongoing complaints and may distance the caregiver from the process. Just as it is important to let children know when they do well, it is important to inform caregivers when their children do well. This feedback allows caregivers to feel good about their children's progress and about themselves as caregivers. This approach is also helpful with teachers. Meaningful feedback is important, but it must be provided in the presence of a solid relationship.

In the best-case scenario, clinicians must be flexible with their time constraints. It is hard for a single mother who has to work long hours to make ends meet to make appointments during regular work hours. Many caregivers do not enjoy benefits such as paid vacations or even sick leave. Taking time from work means less money is available for an already strained budget. Some caregivers say that it is physically exhausting to go from their workplace to taking care of family tasks at home, and then make time to accommodate meetings with clinicians. For this reason it is important to understand the caregivers' living situation and make accommodations so they are not perceived as not "doing their part." When face-to-face communication is difficult to set up, alternatives modes of communication such as phone calls, letters, e-mail, and texting are useful.

A common challenge of working in a classroom environment is lack of consistency. If the treatment goal is to decrease impulsive behaviors, for example, an intervention may be as simple as reminding the child to wait for his or her turn. However, if at the same time, the teacher is allowing other children to participate without waiting for their turns, this request becomes problematic. It is unfair to enforce behavioral expectations for one child but not for another. This difficulty comes up in other variations as well, such as when behavioral expectations are inconsistent from teacher to teacher, or when the particular behavior itself is treated inconsistently. Clinicians can facilitate the implementation of the treatment goals by making consistency an important aspect of the success of the treatment plan, communicating the goals and interventions, and checking with teachers about their acceptability. It is also important to adapt to situations that may require a change, but still to encourage ongoing consistency.

One global challenge when working with children is that of helping adults to understand the child's perspective. Many times disruptive behaviors are reactions to "simple" challenges of daily routines. For example, when teachers read a story, they often inadvertently position themselves such that some children can see and some cannot. This simple problem can become the trigger for disruptive behaviors as children begin to move around for better viewing of the book the teacher is reading. When they start moving around, they may cross the personal boundaries of others, thus creating conflict. Friction can result from social interactions. When these situations occur, teachers may not react. Their reasoning may be to encourage children to work out the conflicts by themselves. However, for children who do not have the necessary social skills to do so, this logic is implicitly unfair and incites aggressive or disruptive behaviors.

SCARCITY

A clearly challenging aspect of homelessness is the scarcity of resources. Limitations of one type or another and instability permeate the lives of homeless children. Many times this scarcity is clearly evident. For example, some children repeatedly wear ripped or poorly fitting clothing. These material limitations can also affect behaviors in direct ways. Children may be teased by their peers. Sometimes even teachers tease children without realizing the shaming effect it can have on the children and the potential to encourage similar interactions with peers (if teachers do it, it must be okay).

Sometimes scarcity of resources is revealed during intake, and caregivers may actively ask for support. At times it is disclosed only after a good relationship has been developed. This may be particularly true for immigrants, who may have insufficient knowledge of available community resources or of their rights to access them, or, in some cases, might be afraid to do so because of their legal status. Clinicians can have a positive impact by providing concrete resources, when their agencies provide them, or by referring the client to agencies that can provide such assistance. They can also help by finding the location of the facilities and even support the family by facilitating transportation. Assistance with filling out an application can be very helpful for caregivers who cannot read or write. Alleviating stresses due to a lack of concrete resources or helping the family to overcome obstacles to accessing those resources strengthens the therapeutic alliance, which in turn supports the likelihood of achieving treatment goals. Moreover, alleviating stresses by providing essential resources allows the caregivers to have more time for their children. However, it also is important to be clear about why support is provided and what the ultimate goal is. The clinician also needs to be able to recognize personal biases that may either hold back needed help or offer help that is not in the best interest of the client or family. Finding the balance between helping and empowering can be a difficult task, but ongoing consultation with supervisors and other experienced colleagues can help to clarify such sensitive issues. I would recommend consulting a number of professionals, not just a supervisor or a single professional, since all clinicians have their own set of biases and prejudices—despite believing otherwise.

NOURISHMENT

If children are to excel in school, their bodies must have the nutritional and physical resources to facilitate that success. Inadequate housing and inadequate food are hallmarks of the homeless experience and represent chronic challenges for the homeless family (Committee on Community Health Services, 2005). With limited resources families buy what is most affordable. One study found that obesity was the most prevalent nutritional problem faced by homeless children, as they have easy access to cheap fast food that is low in nutritional value and high in caloric content (Committee on Community Health Services, 1996; Fierman et al., 1991). Another study found that homeless children experience growth delays in height and weight compared to housed children; this was particularly true of homeless children in large families headed by single mothers (Fierman et al., 1991).

Advocating for a family to secure basic nutritional resources can be a very important step in improving children's behavior in the classroom and an opportunity to build trust and rapport with caregivers. As noted with regard to other challenges, alleviating stress not only contributes directly to the well-being of the clients and their families, but it also frees the caregivers to potentially have more time and space to meet the psycho-emotional needs of their children.

In some cases nutritional needs may affect the clinical presentation of clients. For example, one client was referred for excessive aggression and non-compliance. His aggression was particularly extreme toward teachers. Information gathered from the caregiver and from teachers revealed a pattern in his behavior: he would become most aggressive right before lunchtime. It may be that his breakfast did not sustain his metabolic needs. One solution discussed was to make snacks available to him, and a referral to a specialist helped the caregiver understand the nutritional needs of the child. That was half the battle. It eventually became clear, however, that the teacher was not a good match for this child, and so the child changed schools and is now thriving both academically and socially.

Other situations involve children who create disruption by impulsively reaching for their peers' food, or other children who eat past comfortable fullness to the point of vomiting, or yet others who aggressively defend their space at the table. Although some such behaviors may not be uncommon, those observed in these situations have greater intensity or frequency than expected.

LOVE, AFFECTION, AND EARLY STIMULATION

Love and affection are a necessity, indispensable for children to thrive. Feeling wanted and receiving ongoing attention and nurturing from caregivers not only creates deep emotional bonds that promote self-esteem and contribute to a basic overall sense of trust in the world but it also stimulates and facilitates overall development. In fact, failure to thrive is a well-known condition that exemplifies the importance of relationships. When children's emotional needs are not met, regardless of having access to food, development is impaired and children fail to develop psychologically and physically. Relationships are crucial to brain development and neural functioning throughout the life cycle; the brain develops through each social and verbal interaction (Fishbane, 2007). It is known, for example, that depressed caregivers, having little energy to interact with their children, may not be stimulating enough for their children, who in turn may develop delays. Attachment is crucial for a child's development, and it is based on the quality of the relationship between the parent and child. By being responsive to the needs of their children, parents create a bond. Through this bond, children develop a sense that the world is secure. When these relationships are problematic and the attachment is insecure, it becomes "predictive of behavior not only at three, five, seven, or fourteen . . . but also at twenty, thirty, and seventy" (Karen, 1990, p. 7). Children's attachment to their primary caregiver at infancy becomes the template for future relationships. Even so, it is important for the clinician to know that attachments can be changed later in life, and clinicians can become the catalyst for this change.

In contrast, some caregivers do too much for children. Although this practice may be perceived as loving and protective, caregivers who anticipate their children's needs and do everything for them actually interfere with the children's development of communication skills and of the ability to meet their own needs. This pattern can potentially result in developmental delays.

According to Risley and Hart (2006), welfare recipients, working-class caregivers, and individuals with advanced degrees varied in the amount of time they spent talking to their children. Their research found that welfare recipients talked the least to their children, followed by working-class caregivers, and those with advanced professional degrees. They assert that once the talk of "business" is out of the way, the extra talk tends to be more enriching, and that, despite the class differences noted, the amount of talk predicted children's "intellectual accomplishments." Children who are well-spoken might have a greater advantage over children who have difficulties expressing themselves, and "children who express their anger verbally are better liked" (Bradley, 2003, p. 33). Clinicians can offer psycho-education to caregivers about the importance of stimulating their children through everyday interactions by doing simple activities such as talking. This may be an overly simplistic statement, as some caregivers may not have the capacity to give extra time to their children because they expend all their energy on addressing the many challenges of daily survival. Yet it is still important to inform them of this basic need.

Clinicians have to be careful to take into consideration their client's family material resources and psychological abilities. Recommendations to stimulate children must build on the resources already available to the family, such as visiting existing parks, naming everyday objects, or reading at local libraries. Expensive items are not needed. Stimulation can be a natural consequence of their interactions. Ultimately, the most basic recommendations are the easiest and often prove to be the ones that provide the greatest academic and social advantages along with personal satisfaction.

EFFECTS OF HOMELESSNESS

Homelessness can affect both physical and psycho-emotional development of children. Some studies estimate that families with children are the fastest-growing subgroup of the homeless population, representing one-third of the total homeless population nationwide (Committee on Community Health Services, 1998, 2005; Rosenberg & Bassuk, 1990). Many caregivers of homeless children are single females, and from ethnic and racial minorities. Some have histories of physical or sexual abuse, misuse of drugs, and physical and mental problems (Committee on Community Health Services, 1996). Children who are homeless are more likely to experience substance misuse, higher rates of mental illness and health problems, and to struggle with academic challenges, family conflict, domestic violence, and physical and developmental delays (Committee on Community Health Services, 1996, 2005; Fierman et al., 1991; Garcia Coll, Buckner, Brooks, Weinreb, & Bassuk, 1998; Hernandez Jozefowicz-Simbeni & Israel, 2006; Masten, 1992; Zlotnick & Marks, 2002).

MEDICAL ATTENTION

Homelessness has been found to be an independent predictor of poor health (Weinreb, Goldberg, Bassuk, & Perloff, 1998). For homeless families, health becomes a lower priority as parents struggle to meet the families' daily demands for basic needs (Committee on Community Health Services, 1996, 1998). Homeless children have been found to be twice as likely as others to be seen in medical settings and have high prevalence rates of upper respiratory tract infections, scabies, lice, tooth decay, ear infections, diaper rash, conjunctivitis, trauma-related injuries, developmental delays, and neurologic deficits (Committee on Community Health Services, 1996). Yet it is not unusual for clinicians to have clients who do not have a primary care physician or dentist that they visit regularly. Clinicians can screen for this need, refer the clients, and advocate for them by informing them of their options and their rights to access the services. This issue is particularly relevant for immigrant families, who often do not know their options for medical care or may have been misinformed by others. Clinicians need to be knowledgeable about available resources in their communities. When addressing the mental health of children it is important to ensure that they are cleared medically to rule out the possibility that the behaviors are linked to a medical condition.

SOCIAL SKILLS

Social skills are fundamental to healthy development and are indeed perhaps the most important part of everyone's education. Humans evolved to be social: "Neither the individual neuron nor the single human being exist in nature. Without mutually stimulating interactions, people and neurons wither and die" (Cozolino, 2010, p. 179). The ability to work collaboratively, the ability to communicate one's needs and ideas respectfully, and the capacity to be assertive without disregard for the rights of others are but a few examples of qualities that are important for healthy functioning in our society. These interactions also serve the function of further stimulating the development of language, motor, and cognitive skills needed to thrive in our complex environments. When children are aggressive, exhibit difficulties playing with others, or cannot express their personal needs, they face social repercussions, running the risk of becoming isolated, receiving less support from teachers, and being labeled as a problem child. In ongoing consultation, the clinician can create an atmosphere that encourages the teachers and parents to pay attention to desired behaviors rather than focusing on undesired ones, and can reinforce for them the importance of sustaining and building upon positive social interaction. This effort usually elicits positive behaviors from children, and in response results in more positive perceptions of the child by teachers and parents.

NEUROLOGY AND ATTACHMENT

The debate about the importance of nurture versus nature has been ongoing, and most current research suggests that the two are synergistic and not exclusive. The individual affects the environment as much as the environment affects the individual. "Because the first few years of life are a period of exuberant brain development, early experience has a disproportionate impact on the development of neural systems" (Cozolino, 2010, p. 216). Some homeless clients have been or are suspected of being victims of abuse and/or neglect. Many others have been exposed to milder but chronic forms of neglect and abuse that can appear "justifiable" in light of the great demands placed on their caregivers. Regardless, children are vulnerable and can be deeply affected by these conditions. In fact, it is estimated that child abuse is underreported and that the official statistics probably reflect the "lowest level of child maltreatment" (Sharples, 2008). In the past decade more children have been killed in their own homes than soldiers in the Iraq and Afghanistan wars combined; and this figure may reflect only half of the true number (*Star Ledger* staff, 2011). It is important to acknowledge that child maltreatment crosses all cultural boundaries and that most often the abuse is perpetrated by primary caregivers (U.S. Department of Health and Human Services—Administration for Child and Family, Administration of Child Youth and Family, Children's Bureau, 2010).

Homeless children, for multiple reasons, are less likely to experience nurturing environments than are other children. Researchers have documented higher levels of social isolation and violence in the lives of homeless parents and families and "clearly, children who experience frequent violence are likely to model the aggressive behaviors that they observe" (Anooshian, 2005). No matter the reason—whether the caregivers are working longer hours, are depressed, feel incapable of responding to their children, are inexperienced at parenting, or reside in a shelter or other transitional situation that inhibits greater intimacy and thus opportunities for bonding—the potential for a negative impact on the caregiver-child relationship is the same

"Babies and young children need to have the opportunity to develop a close, trusting relationship or secure attachment with at least one special person. The ability to attach to a significant adult allows young children to become trusting, confident, and capable of regulating stress and managing distress" (Cohen, Onanuku, Clothier, & Poppe, 2005, p. 3). It is known that very young children are more attuned to caregivers' nonverbal communication, as that is the way young infants communicate. Very early in life, infants begin to smile, which delights the attentive caregiver and encourages him or her to provide even more attention, just to obtain the precious reward of the baby's smile, thus promoting attachment.

Helping caregivers to strengthen the parent-child relationship is vital, but it can be done only after the clinicians have developed a mutually respectful and trusting relationship with the caregivers. It is important that our interventions are co-created or have respect for caregivers' input so that they will be more likely to follow through with recommendations.

TRAUMA AND VIOLENCE

Trauma and violence are common experiences of many homeless families. Homeless children are more vulnerable to traumatic experiences by virtue of their age and the state of being homeless, with fewer buffers and more stressors than housed children. Many children referred to SPARK have been traumatized in one way or another. Some are traumatized in mild but chronic forms; others have experienced the acute and severe traumatic experiences that are typical of a post-traumatic stress disorder (PTSD) diagnosis. But the single most important variable affecting children's overall development is the quality of their relationships with their caregivers. This will determine an individual's ability to become a well-adjusted adult (Karen, 1998). Healthy relationships serve as buffers that help counteract adversity, and the advantages of these buffers extend past childhood and can propel children into a future as well-adjusted individuals.

When a child's relationships are affected by trauma and violence, the child's emotional foundation—essential for all aspects of development—is negatively affected. The child sees relationships through a new lens that reflects these early experiences, and if no help is provided to correct the viewpoint, it will taint all others to come. These early relationships become the mold in which future relationships will be shaped. It is also important to know that trauma can induce a permanent state of hyper-arousal, making it difficult for children to exercise self-regulation. Studies have shown that trauma can result in physically altering the development of the brain. According to Fishbane (2007), children who have been traumatized, abused, or neglected experience impairment in the brain's emotion regulatory system that negatively affects judgment, self-control, and emotional fluency.

Homeless families are often forced to live in communities where violence is endemic. The child's caregivers and the children themselves often report the loss of family members or acquaintances due to violence. Violence can become so common in the life of a given community that its impact on children is minimized by caregivers who have seen it all, too many times before. "In fact, many people assume that very young children are not affected at all, erroneously believing that they are too young to know or remember what has happened" (Osofsky, 1995, p. 783). Caregivers' thinking of crime and or violence as a "normal" aspect of daily life minimizes the negative impact of its effect on children and affects their will to reach out for help. Children are expected to just "get over it." Clinicians can provide insight into the damaging effects of violence in clients' lives through psycho-education. Parents' awareness of how violence hampers the overall well-being of their child may be pivotal in creating motivation for concrete changes to reduce exposure to violence. For example, a 5-year-old client during a session insisted that he would be the policeman and the clinician would be the "bad guy." The topic was not new, but this time it had an intensity and quality of play that was different from previous sessions. The clinician also felt that the play was much more "sadistic," and so decided to check with the mother to see if anything might have caused this change. She told the clinician that the client had been with his grandmother when there had been a shooting. "Some guy was shot on the front porch of the house, but he [the child] did not see anything." The mother said the child was inside the house with his grandmother; and when the shots were fired, the child had to throw himself on the floor (he knew what to do). The mother was certain that the child did not witness the crime. Unfortunately this was not his first brush with violence. Even at his young age he had already had many experiences like this one. His mother had little insight into why he would be affected when he was not the direct target of the violence. Regrettably, three years later he is attending a therapeutic school, continues to function poorly, and has lost a brother to gunfire.

Caregivers may not realize how the presence of domestic violence affects their children, particularly during the first years of life. As a matter of fact, witnessing domestic violence can be even more damaging than the direct effects of trauma (California Attorney General's Office, 2008). In addition, according to Fishbane (2007), the interpersonal environment helps shape the children's emotional brain. Thus it is what the children assimilate, not what they understand from an adult's perspective, that is important. When children witness an action, they not only see the action but read beyond it and infer the goal of the action (Faull & MacLean, 2010), so even if a parent tries to hide an act of discord, children are aware of the intent to hide it and are likely to be aware of the event that led to the efforts to hide it in the first place. According to Anooshian (2005), violence and aggression contribute to relationship problems and social isolation among homeless children, and children of mothers who are victims of domestic violence also exhibit more aggression. Finally, numerous studies confirm that even witnessing anger (not necessarily violence) or being on the receiving end of anger—verbal or nonverbal—is a stressor for children (Faull & MacLean, 2010). Unfortunately, violence of one sort or another is often part of the life experience of homeless children. Clinicians must understand, to the best of their ability, the complexities of their clients' lives so they do not over- or underreact to events that take place.

Caregivers who resort to harsh parenting may socialize children to use angry, aggressive, acting-out behaviors during conflict (Scaramella, Neppl, Ontai, & Conger, 2008). The notion that we will act the same way our parents did with us is evident (Karen, 1990). According to Scaramella and colleagues, even though young children may exhibit more-externalized behaviors, there is a typical decline over time; however, this decline is attenuated by harsh parenting. In addition, studies have found correlations between harsh parenting—spanking—and increases in aggression and decreases in IQ (Alice, 2010). Moreover, Gershoff (2002) asserts that "corporal punishment is associated with . . . increased child aggression" and a dozen other negative outcomes. Whenever possible, it is important to encourage parents to implement positive parenting practices to the best of their abilities. This is a particularly sensitive issue. Cultural concerns complicate and enrich the controversy surrounding parenting practices. It is ultimately the legal and ethical duty of clinicians to keep children safe.

Sometimes aggression—easily turned to violence—is actively encouraged by caregivers and is perceived as a skill that will reduce the possibility that children will become its victims. Anooshian (2005) states that aggression may be an adaptation to living in unsafe environments. Ironically, if aggressive behavior is not taught as a last resort, and in conjunction with other ways of responding to interpersonal conflict, it can become the child's first choice as a way to deal with discord. When children are quick to resort to violence, they have difficulty developing appropriate social networks, and so they can become isolated and have reduced choices for friendships. Consequently, it is not unusual to see aggressive children playing all by themselves as they are rejected by peers and teachers. This isolation can have grave repercussions for their social development.

Violence is unempathic. According to Brennen (2007), a lack of empathy is what may lead people to violence. Given that the family unit is the place where one acquires basic values of how to be in life, having caregivers who exhibit a lack of empathy by using harsh parenting practices may facilitate violence. Adding a layer of complication, one prevalent aspect of the lives of some homeless children is the involvement of their caregivers with the legal system. Some of these children have caregivers who are or have been incarcerated. Ninety percent of incarcerated parents are fathers, although maternal incarceration is on the rise. Many prisoners are of child-rearing age. Ethnic minorities, particularly African Americans, are overrepresented in this population (Blenner, 2008). More than half of the inmates grew up in a single-caregiver household themselves. Thus the possibility of perpetuating the cycle of violence seems very real. According to Blenner, there are many ways in which the incarceration of a caregiver can affect children: loss, trauma, attachment disruption, and modeling.

It is not unheard of that the same systems that are in place to protect children can paradoxically also cause a great deal of harm to their vulnerable psyches. Separation in itself is very damaging to children, regardless of the reason for it. For example, a client's caregiver was mandated to a rehabilitation program, and although the program allowed some children to reside with their parents, this caregiver's child was not admitted because at five years of age, he was deemed too old. The separation caused a great deal of resentment and feelings of abandonment on his part. Now, six years later, the child still struggles with "anger issues" and feelings of abandonment.

Some children may exhibit aggressive behaviors at home but not at school. An important part of the work is examining differences in behaviors at home and at preschool or in other settings in which the child functions. Sometimes parents may feel that their children are wrongfully judged by teachers. If there is a discrepancy, the clinician can use these differences as a rich field of exploration to understand the client's adaptive skills in each setting, thus identifying both strengths and areas that need improvement. For example, one mother reported that her child did not exhibit the serious difficulties with impulsive aggression that had been observed at school. A visit to the household confirmed that this was true. And the reason became evident: this particular caregiver was harsh and punitive at home. Unfortunately for this child, the school was the only place where he could test his limits and express his emotions "safely."

Modeling our culture and values is a very important way in which we transmit that information to our children. The ability of the child to imitate a caregiver, and therefore for the caregiver to influence the child's behavior, is present at a very early age. Newborns can imitate facial gestures such as sticking their tongues out and smiling. Many caregivers, unaware of how their interactions may affect their children's psycho-emotional development, may engage in various degrees of maladaptive behavioral patterns with little awareness of their influence on their loved ones. And others may have little control over what their children become exposed to even when they want to change their child's experience, such as in situations where community violence is a contributing variable to maladaptive behaviors.

Domestic violence is probably one of the best examples. From subtle verbal exchanges to overt physical violence that causes grave injuries, domestic violence, as mentioned above, is thought to have greater negative effects on children than trauma itself. Psycho-education about the impact of domestic violence on children's development is beneficial. Few caregivers are willing to purposely engage in activities that are potentially harmful to their children. As a matter of fact, the love that parents have for their children is the most important tool that clinicians have to support clients. Tapping into the caregivers' aspirations and hopes for their children is the clinician's gateway to a collaborative relationship.

The decision to bring to a caregiver's attention the ways in which their own behaviors may be affecting their child's development must be considered very carefully, particularly if the caregivers themselves are violent.

Sometimes the issues become charged when caregivers have limited insight and do not see the connections between their own behavior and their child's. It is important to remember that conversations such as these can take place with the hope of a good outcome only when there is a good relationship. It is not necessary to address the full scope of the concern at a single session. As a matter of fact, it would be best to work through the concerns over a period of time so that the caregiver has a chance to see the dots connecting the particular pattern the clinician is working to elucidate. Ultimately, this is the art of the work we do, being able to assess the needs of those we serve, so that we can discern how much to ask, how much to give, how much to repeat, how much to ignore, how much to suppress, in order to reach the best possible outcome for children and their families.

* * *

Preschool-based programs such as SPARK can provide children with the tools that they need to be successful in the classroom. Early interventions have the potential to effect changes in a child's behavior that will extend beyond the preschool years into adolescence and adulthood. The tools provided support better relationships with adults and peers, and contribute to overall development. Ideally, these tools promote a healthy balance of dependence and independence with peers and adults. The program also works with caregivers and advocates finding services and resources required to complement treatment goals in the classroom. When invited, it also supports home environment dynamics that in turn support classroom expectations. Although the interventions rely on behavioral techniques, it is always within the context of relationships that the program works best. Most importantly, in the context of relationships, respect, trust, and cooperation can flourish to help change the child's perspective from "I am bad!" to "I am good!"

REFERENCES

Alice, P. (2010, April 12). *Yahoo News*. Retrieved April 12, 2010, from Yahoo, http://news.yahoo.com/s/stime/20100412/hl_time/08599198101900/print.

Anooshian, L. J. (2005). Violence and aggression in the lives of homeless children. *Journal of Family Violence, 20*(6), 373–387.

Bassuk, E. L., & Rosenberg, L. (1990). Psychosocial characteristics of homeless children and children with homes. *Pediatrics, 85*(3), 257–261.

Bradley, S. J. (2003). *Affect regulation and the development of psychopathology*. New York: Guilford Press.

Blenner, Stephanie L. (2008). *Developmental and behavioral implications for children of incarcerated parents*. Retrieved August 9, 2010, from www.uptodate.com/patients/content/topic.do?topic .

Brennen, B. H. (2007, September). *Family and crime reduction in the Bahamas*. Speech presented at a town meeting on crime. Retrieved October 18, 2011, from http://www.soencouragement.org/crimereductionspeech2007/.

California Attorney General's Office. (2008). *First impressions: Exposure to violence and a child's developing brain*. Oakland, CA: Iron Mountain Films, Inc. Retrieved March 22, 2013, from http://www.youtube.com/watch?v=8kH4pmc79OE.

Cohen, J., Onanuku, N., Clothier, S., & Poppe, J. (2005, September). *Helping young children succeed: Strategies to promote early childhood social and emotional development*. Retrieved November 12, 2011, from http://main.zerotothree.org/site/DocServer/help_yng_child_succeed.pdf?docID=621.

Committee on Community Health Services. (1998). Health needs of homeless children. *Pediatrics, 82*(6), 938–940.

——. (1996). Health needs of homeless children and families. *Pediatrics, 98*(4), 789–791.

——. (2005). Providing care for immigrant, homeless, and migrant children. *Pediatrics, 115*(4), 1095–1099.

Cooper, M. (2008). *Essential research findings in counseling and psychotherapy*. Thousand Oaks, CA: Sage.

Cozolino, L. (2010). *The neuroscience of psychotherapy*. New York: W. W. Norton.

Duncan, B. L., Miller, S. D., & Sparks, J. A. (2004). *The heroic client: A revolutionary way to improve effectiveness through client-directed, outcome-informed therapy*. San Francisco: Jossey-Bass.

Dunlap, G., Strain, P. S., Fox, L., Carta, J. J., Conroy, M., Smith, B. J., et al. (2006). Prevention and intervention with young children's challenging behavior: Perspectives regarding current knowledge. *Behavioral Disorders, 32*(1), 29–45.

Faull, J., & MacLean, J. O. (2010). *Amazing minds: The science of nurturing your child's developing mind with games, activities, and more*. New York: Penguin Group.

Fierman, A. H., Dreyer, B. P., Quinn, L., Shulman, S., Courtlandt, C. D., & Guzzo, R. (1991). Growth delay in homeless children. *Pediatrics, 88*(5), 918–925.

Fishbane, Mona D. (2007). Wired to connect: Neuroscience, relationships, and therapy. *Family Process, 46*(3), 395–406.

Fox, L., Dunlap, G., Hemmeter, M. L., Joseph, G. E., & Strain, P. S. (2003). The teaching pyramid: A model for supporting social competence and preventing challenging behavior in young children. *Young Children, 58*(4), 48–52.

Garcia Coll, C., Buckner, J. C., Brooks, M. G., Weinreb, L. F., & Bassuk, E. (1998). The developmental status and adaptive behavior of homeless and low-income housed infants and toddlers. *American Journal of Public Health, 88*(9), 1371–1374.

Grogan-Kaylor, A. (2004). The effect of corporal punishment on antisocial behavior in children. *Social Work Research, 28*(3), 153–162.

Hernandez Jozefowicz-Simbeni, D. M., & Israel, N. (2006). Services to homeless students and families: The McKinney-Vento Act and its implications for school social work practice. *National Association of Social Workers, 28*(1), 37–44.

Karen, R. (1990, February 11). *Becoming attached*. Retrieved March 19, 2013, from The Atlantic.com, http://www.theatlantic.com/magazine/archive/1990/02/becoming-attached/308966/4/.

——. (1998). *Becoming attached: First relationships and how they shape our capacity to love*. New York. Oxford University Press.

Masten, A. S. (1992). Homeless children in the United States: Mark of a nation at risk. *American Psychological Society, 1*(2), 41–44.

Osofsky, J. D. (1995). The effects of exposure to violence on young children. *American Psychologist, 50*(9), 782–788.

Risley, T. R., & Hart, B. (2006). Promoting early language development. In N. F. Watt, C. Ayoub, R. H. Bradley, J. E. Puma, & W. A. LeBoeuf (Eds.), *The crisis in youth mental health: Critical issues and effective programs: Vol. 4: Early intervention programs and policies* (pp. 83–88). Westport, CT: Praeger.

Scaramella, L. V., Neppl, T. K., Ontai, L. L., & Conger, R. D. (2008). Consequences of socioeconomic disadvantage across three generations: Parenting behavior and children externalizing problems. *Journal of Family Psychology, 22*(5), 725–733.

Sharples, T. (2008, December 2). *Most child abuse goes unreported*. Retrieved October 16, 2011, from http://www.time.com/time/health/article/0,8599,1863650,00.html.

Star Ledger staff. (2011, November 6). *The scourge of child abuse in America: Q & A*. Retrieved November 9, 2011, from http://blog.nj.com/njv_editorial_page/2011/11/the_scourge_of_child_abuse_in.html.

Thompson, Elizabeth G. (2002). Corporal punishment by parents and associated child behaviors and experiences: A meta-analytic and theoretical review. *Psychological Bulletin, 128*(4), 539-579.

U.S. Department of Health and Human Services—Administration for Child and Family, Administration of Child Youth and Family, Children's Bureau. (2010). *Child maltreatment 2009.* Retrieved September 19, 2011, from http://www.acf. hhs.gov/programs/cb/stats_research/index.htm#can.

Walker-Dalhouse, D., & Risko, V. J. (2008). Homelessness, poverty, and children's literacy development. *Reading Teacher, 62*(1), 84–86.

Weinreb, L., Goldberg, R., Bassuk, E., & Perloff, J. (1998). Determinants of health and service use patterns in homeless and low income children. *Pediatrics, 102*(3), 554–562.

Whitman, B. Y., Accardo, P., Boyert, M., & Kendagor, R. (1990). Homeless and cognitive performance in children: A possible link. *National Association of Social Workers, 35*(6), 516–519.

Zlotnick, C., & Marks, L. (2002). Case management services at ten federally funded sites targeting homeless children and their families. *Children's Services: Social Policy, Research, and Practice, 5*(2), 113–122.

CHAPTER 9

"When Do I Get to Go Home?"

▸ *PEGGY PEARSON*

THE FAMILY OUTREACH SUPPORT CLINIC (FOSC)

THIS CHAPTER PRESENTS TWO VIGNETTES about children followed in our clinic in order to demonstrate a unique model that combines research-informed practices of case management and pediatric care. The Center for the Vulnerable Child (CVC) is a department within Children's Hospital and Research Center Oakland (CHRCO) that serves families who are homeless, those who are at risk for homelessness, and foster children. It was created in the late 1980s when a pediatrician at CHRCO, Dr. Neal Halfon, noted the vast array of needs of foster children and realized that those needs went beyond what a doctor could address in the scope of clinic visits. From his frustration and desire to help, a clinic specifically designated for foster children was conceived. It featured a multidisciplinary approach, with the doctor and a case manager working together to provide comprehensive medical care, case management, assessments, and referrals for the foster families. When indicated, mental health and child development services are offered. In the early days we called it the Foster Care Clinic, but as the children were adopted or reunified with parents, the name no longer fit the children. Worse still, it was insensitive to the fact that the children had left foster care. For this reason, the clinic's name was changed to the Family Outreach Support Clinic. Even as the child grows and his life evolves, he can continue to attend the clinic throughout his youth and into young adulthood. And many of them do!

THE WAY BACK HOME FOR DERRICK

Two-year-old Derrick hadn't seen his mother since that night at the hospital. His arm was hurting badly. He remembered his mom yelling at him earlier at home about something and then abruptly pulling him away from where he was playing. Then Dad came home from work, yelled at Mom, and put everyone in the car. The car stopped at a big place called the hospital. A maze of faces was before him, looking at him, asking questions, doing things to him. The night ended with his arm in a cast and Mom crying and leaving without saying good-bye. Dad cried too but didn't take him home. A lady told him he would go to someone's house. Derrick was bewildered and exhausted.

This was the second time in a year that Derrick had come to us with a broken bone. The first event occurred when the unattended two-year-old child fell off a high ledge and broke his leg. As a result, Children and Family Services (CFS), the county agency generically known as child protective services, came into the family's life. This agency sent social workers out to Derrick's home many times after that event, supervising the home situation under "family maintenance." This term indicates that Derrick and his three older siblings were dependents of the county court due to a first-time allegation of neglect; however, it also suggests that the children are considered safe with their parents as long as the parents obey specific court orders: family counseling, both parents submitting to regular drug testing, weekly monitoring, and the mother's participation in a substance abuse program.

The scenario described above began while Dad was at work and Mom was under the influence of methamphetamines at home. She had been failing court-mandated drug tests and had been absent from her drug treatment program. Her three older children were of school age and gone most of the day. With Derrick's broken arm, a new allegation of physical abuse was made, and the mother was told she must enter residential treatment to keep custody of her children. She refused, moved out of the house, and left the state. The father was despondent. He now was the single working parent of four young children.

The three older children were interviewed and found to be reasonably safe in the home with the father. Their day included attending school and an after-school program. For this reason, they did not enter foster homes. Derrick's situation was different. Although the father was not at fault for Derrick's broken arm, he was now in the precarious circumstances of single parents. He was overwhelmed with the additional task of caring for a child barely out of the toddler stage, in a cast, who would need substantial medical follow-up. He had no relatives or anyone else in the area who could assist him. Because of this combination of circumstances, Derrick was placed in a foster home.

The birth father wasted no time in working to get Derrick back home. He met regularly with the child welfare worker and submitted to drug testing. Weekend overnight visits were arranged and Derrick's responses were carefully noted. As the months passed, his child welfare worker documented that the father was fulfilling the terms laid out by the court.

Derrick had been placed in a two-parent foster home with an adopted four-year-old son who had special needs. The foster parents were experienced and the mother was home full-time. Derrick took to their son and they immediately became playmates. His foster parents understood that Derrick would have fears, confusion, and grief while missing his family. Their earlier experience with their son's infant development specialist, infant mental health professionals, and the Family Outreach Support Clinic (FOSC) prepared them well. The foster mother nurtured Derrick and worked with him to help him progress emotionally and developmentally. Every day she coached him on the idea of using the toilet. She read to him, and beckoned him to reply and verbalize his needs. He had very limited speech when he arrived, but soon his vocabulary began to grow. He began speaking in longer sentences. She also noticed that he seemed "tongue-tied" and that this was restricting his pronunciation. She brought this to the attention of the pediatrician at FOSC, who confirmed a condition called poor tongue mobility. The foster mother talked with the social worker and with the father. Soon after the diagnosis, and with the father's permission, Derrick had minor surgery to correct the condition.

Derrick also had severely decayed teeth when he entered foster care. He underwent extensive dental treatment, capping the baby teeth. He learned how to brush his teeth. The father and the foster mother decided together to have these procedures done while Derrick was in foster care so the father would not need to take more time off from work. He had already missed several days because of court appearances and meetings with the social worker.

It became clear that the father would have great difficulty in taking care of Derrick without full-time child care. Anticipating this "reunification" with his family, the worker arranged for subsidized child care from seven in the morning to six in the evening at the family's home. After six months, Derrick was returned to the house of his father and three older siblings. They continue to deal with the loss of their mother and wife, family therapy will continue for an indeterminate time, and they will be visited by a child welfare worker for at least six more months. Still, Derrick is home.

JOEY FINDS A NEW HOME

Joey was three years old when he was discovered alone in a car. Hunger, cold, loneliness, and fear were all he remembered about that experience. A policeman found him, determined that his parents had been taken to jail, and drove him to a place with many doctors and nurses. Then a lady took him to someone's house. Everyone was speaking a language he didn't understand. Nice people gave him food and a bed and tried to play with him, but he knew only a few of the words they spoke. Finally a man and woman he had known before came to the house and they talked to him in his language. He went with them to their house, and they explained that he would live with them and their two teenage daughters for a while.

We at FOSC first met Joey with this second foster family, after he had left the temporary emergency home. The couple he had been placed with knew his biological family from their neighborhood. Not being licensed foster parents, they nevertheless came forward when they heard that Joey's parents had been incarcerated. They underwent a home evaluation and became certified to care specifically for Joey, who now had no home. Joey's behavior indicated internal stress. He did not talk; he pointed. He responded eagerly to the nurturing care of the foster family. Reacting to the past abandonment, he clung to the foster mother if she went out of the house, even if just to go to the store briefly. He eventually began to play and enjoy himself, but the clingy behavior with his foster mother persisted. She brought him to FOSC for regular medical care and found that he was in good health.

More challenges arose. The foster parents reported that Joey hoarded food and would sometimes eat compulsively. He was once alone in the kitchen for 20 minutes and ate five bananas, one after the other, until he was sick. More than once, Joey tried to fondle a visiting younger child. Guidance and admonishments did not stop this sexualized behavior; he only became more secretive. When the foster mother described these events, we immediately referred him to a therapeutic preschool where he would have daily individual play therapy and learn to trust and relax in social interactions. He would learn appropriate boundaries, including which parts of the body were private, and he would learn to express himself in a positive way.

All the while Joey did not have visits with his parents. After they were released from jail, the mother's whereabouts remained unknown and the father failed to meet with the child welfare worker or to comply with the court's requirements. As the foster mother learned that there was no hope that Joey would be reunified with either parent, she considered adopting him.

However, the foster family was undergoing its own stressors, independent of this extra responsibility with Joey. A year later, the foster father had filed for divorce. The foster mother's life turned upside down. She was forced to grapple with the decision of caring for Joey on her own. She moved to a different home and struggled with the finances of running her household, but was able to continue her involvement with Joey's therapeutic preschool and medical appointments. Her older daughters provided moral and physical support, and assisted with Joey's day-to-day care. The county child welfare worker was very supportive. She assured the foster mother that she would receive an increased stipend for the extra work she was doing to meet Joey's needs. The decision to adopt was put off until the family had more time to adjust, stabilize, and prepare.

After thirteen months in this foster home, Joey learned that it was going to be his "forever home." After formally terminating the birth parents' parental rights, the court approved the foster home for adoption. Joey always had been pensive and somewhat anxious. His foster mother told us he had troubling memories of his earlier life. He had been encouraged to remember, to grieve, and to ask questions even when there were no answers to his questions. Now, at this important juncture in his life, he was asked in therapy sessions how he felt about his foster mother becoming his adopted mother. He did not respond right away. Finally he told his therapist he wanted to stay. Public insurance (Medicaid) will continue to pay for his therapy. Joey now has a home.

WHO ARE OUR FOSTER CHILDREN?

In September 2010, of the 75 million children under 18 years old, about 408,425 were in foster care (Children's Bureau, 2009). The percentage of

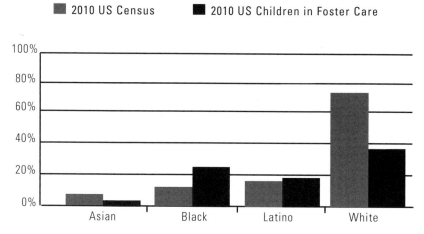

FIGURE 9.1 U.S. Population and U.S. Children in Foster Care by Race/Ethnicity (in 2010).U.S. Bureau of the Census (2008). U.S. Census Bureau—American Fact Finder. Retrieved March 24, 2008, from http://www.census.gov. U.S. Department of Health and Human Services—Administration for Child and Family, Administration of Child Youth and Family, Children's Bureau (2010).

children in foster care varies among states. Dense urban centers often have higher numbers of children in foster care, but it is too simplistic to assume that a county with a small population will be free from the serious social problems that lead to children entering foster care. By gender, the national percentages are 52% boys and 48% girls; by race, however, the percentages demonstrate a clear racial/ethnic disparity, with a higher representation of African American/black children and Latino children in foster care than would be expected based on the representation of those two groups in the general population (fig. 9.1) (Children's Bureau, 2009).

HOW LONG DOES A CHILD STAY IN FOSTER CARE?

Recent statistics do not track how long children stay in a particular foster care placement; however, the average length of foster care nationally is 25.3 months (Children's Bureau, 2009). This time has shortened substantially in recent years because of the change in laws during the Clinton administration (Williams-Mbengue, 2008). For children under the age of three, federal law under the Social Security Act, Title IV-E, now states that if there is no substantial progress on the part of the parent to reunify in the first six months of placement, the court can order that the child be made available for adoption. This fast-paced process is very different from that in the 1980s, when a baby could be in foster care for more than a year before the court approved an adoptive placement. A child could have had three or more foster care placements in that time. Of the children followed in FOSC, it is now common for a child to be in only one temporary foster home and then enter the adoptive home before the age of six months. It also is not unusual to see children adopted by the very first foster parent. Child psychologists have long known that the earlier an infant attaches to a consistent, loving primary caregiver, the better his chances for emotional stability throughout his life (Lieberman & Pawl, 1988).

WHY DO CHILDREN GO INTO FOSTER CARE?

Allegations that a child is being harmed, was harmed, or will be harmed if something is not done right away are reported to the county child protection agency (commonly referred to as CPS) or to the police, who later turn the matter over to CPS for further investigation. An allegation does not always lead to foster care placement. For example, the data from January to December of 2009 (the most recent tally for this particular count) show that only approximately one-quarter to one-third of the allegations entered were actually substantiated (U.S. Department of Health and Human Services, 2009). False allegations, lack of evidence, misunderstandings, and mistakes are not uncommon. Neglect is the most common charge, followed by physical abuse. Table 9.1 shows the types of allegations nationally (U.S. Department of Health and Human Services, 2010).

In cases of neglect, there is often a coexisting factor of parental substance abuse. For example, I typically receive a call from a foster mother asking for an appointment for a newborn baby she has just picked up from the hospital. She has been given the information that the baby was born with a positive toxicology screen for one of various illegal drugs and that "they" would not let the baby go home with the mother. "They" usually means the hospital staff, who alerted the child protection agency in Alameda County. It is not unusual for a mother under the influence of a stimulant drug like methamphetamine or cocaine to spontaneously go into pre-term labor, and

TABLE 9.1   U.S. Children in Foster Care by Type of Maltreatment (2010)

TYPES OF MALTREATMENT	PERCENTAGE
Neglect	78.3%
Physical Abuse	17.6%
Abandonment and other	10.3%
Sexual Abuse	9.2%
Psychological Maltreatment	8.1%
Medical Neglect	2.4%
Unknown/Unable to Determine	0.3%

Note: Some children were victims of more than one type of abuse or neglect; consequently, the total exceeds 100%.
Source: U.S. Department of Health and Human Services (2010), p. 24.

sometimes the mother is unprepared and ill-equipped to care for a very premature baby. The child may be challenging to care for, as he may have tremors, constricted muscle tone, feeding problems, and respiratory distress. Likewise, a child born exposed to opiates like heroin or methadone may suffer a very difficult withdrawal period. (Intensive care nurses and foster parents tell me that among newborns, babies withdrawing from methadone are the most challenging of all.) However, positive toxicology screens alone do not automatically result in removing babies from the mother. The issues of safety, shelter, and support also are evaluated. Racial discrimination plays a great part in this. The implications of data such as those in Figure 9.1 showing the disproportionally higher percentage of African American children being placed in foster care are compelling and alarming (Children's Bureau, 2010; U.S. Bureau of the Census, 2010). Are we sure of impartiality in determining whether a mother can provide safety and nurturing care to her child when our systems historically have been fraught with prejudice?

A determination of neglect is made when young children are not provided essential medical care, are unattended, unwashed, or fed inconsistently. Poverty makes parenting difficult, but as noted in federal reports, substance abuse is often behind the neglect (U.S. General Accounting Office, 1997). Some of these mothers have told me that addiction dictates their priorities and putting food on the table comes only after that need is met. My experience with their children's eating behaviors confirms the mothers' statements. Foster parents often describe how children hoard their food because they are not used to having food at regular intervals and do not know when they will get more.

As for sexual abuse, our clinic observations confirm the association that is frequently cited in professional literature, in newspapers, and on television: perpetrators of child sexual abuse are usually members of the extended family or are people invited into the family, such as a mother's boyfriend. In fact, this observation is validated by the finding that more than 80% of perpetrators of child maltreatment, including sexual abuse, are related to the child (U.S. Department of Health and Human Services, 2010).

THE CHILD IN FOSTER CARE

As professionals and caregivers, we are hopeful and relieved by the idea that the child will be safer in foster care. Of course, while some children may initially be very fearful of being taken away from all that is familiar to them, other children newly entering foster care respond as though they are on a field trip or a vacation, finding themselves in a nice home with lots of food, toys, and other children as playmates. In either case the child will soon register what is lost to him. We cannot talk about homeless children without discussing grief.

Besides losing their mother and/or father, children lose their homes and their neighborhoods. They lose the places they knew by heart, the world they could navigate. They often lose being with brothers and sisters. A "removal," as it is called when a child protection worker or a police officer takes a child away from the parent, is a very emotionally charged event, with unprepared families and no time to pack. The children lose their favorite toys and their clothes. They lose their school, classmates, teachers that understood them. Sometimes they lose their culture, and with it, familiar food and practices. The foster parents may even speak a different language. The children may suddenly be with people who do not tolerate the little habits they had. The new foster mother may not understand how essential that pacifier is to the three-year-old, and may decide to toss it out. She won't know how he calmed himself or how he needed to be handled when frightened. Children often lose their own sense of safety when taken to a new home, even when their family's home was actually unsafe. The strange faces, or even a dog, may terrify them. There may be other children in the home who are not accepting of the foster child, perhaps are even cruel.

Much has been written about the stages of grief that we experience when we suffer a loss. The model developed by Elisabeth Kübler-Ross is still considered very helpful in charting the course for countless people who are bereaved after losing a loved one, a job, an ability, etc. (Kübler-Ross, 1969). She describes denial, anger, bargaining, depression, and finally, acceptance. For children, the process of bereavement does not progress along a linear path. Rather, grief can be seen as cyclical and overlapping, revisiting the child at the dawning of each developmental stage, even though he may be well adjusted and have a loving permanent home. For example, an adoptive mother struggling to understand her troubled teenage daughter who was seeking her own identity once asked me, "Why can't she just get over it?" A foster child or adopted child may grieve the lost parent in a certain way at the age of 3, and again at age 7, and even more so at 13. The child or teen is experiencing the loss on a different intellectual level at each developmental stage: realizing more, remembering more, questioning more, hurting in different ways than he did when he was younger. It is reassuring to adoptive and foster parents to learn that this child is not regressing, but is actually moving through the stages of grief. Using the earlier Kübler-Ross stages as a starting point and incorporating the research on child development, one can observe characteristics in the stages that are unique for grieving children in foster care. For example, while some children do bargain, trying to be very, very good so they will get to go home, others try to assert control over the situation as a way of dealing with their grief. This control-seeking behavior often looks like retaliation or attempts to distance themselves from the foster parent.

Consider the following behaviors and feelings in this adapted model for a foster child:

Denial: Honeymoon period; waiting, believing, hoping the parent will come; wondering, "What happened to Mom?" "Where is she?" "When do I get to go home?"

Anger: Outwardly expressing rebelliousness; cursing; misbehaving, but inwardly feeling anxiety; sleeplessness; psychosomatic symptoms; anger

Getting control: Hoarding food; peeing on floor; regressing; stealing; manipulating other children; fighting; engaging in self-injurious behavior

Depression: Not feeling part of the family; despair at never being able to go back home; poor self-esteem; poor concentration; feeling unlovable or unworthy deep down inside.

Loss changes people. We give too much credit to the ideas that kids are so resilient, that they will recover in time from anything, that they won't remember. Attachment theory tells us differently. Some children struggle with poor self-esteem and unstable attachments for years and even into adulthood (Bowlby, 1988). This grief can lead to emotional unrest, interfering with children's ability to form attachments to the new family. We know that emotional distress impedes developmental and intellectual progress (Lubit, 2009). Children might unconsciously hold back, keep themselves from settling in at the new home, reject the new family's values, culture, and direction. Poor self-esteem can make them afraid to even try to succeed. It is easier to pretend complete apathy. Students may act out, repeatedly lose their homework, or refuse to do it as if they could not care less. Many foster children feel guilty for somehow being responsible for their family's breakup. If their parents do not come back for them, they feel unlovable, unworthy, untrustful of others or themselves. These kinds of feelings have an impact upon every relationship they have or will have in the future.

Some closure is needed before the wounds can heal and the children can move on. Closure will provide a touchstone from which to push off, to move forward in a new relationship and in a new definition of who they are. "Sometimes my mom says stuff but it doesn't happen." "They did the best they could." "They wanted better for me." "They cared but just couldn't do it" (Betzen, 2005). Even with a very committed new family, working through the grief process is an essential prerequisite before children can completely feel that they belong. Some adoptees report to me that they never quite achieve that sense of belonging to their new families.

THE BIRTH PARENTS, PRESENT OR NOT

We first meet foster children when their foster parents call to set up an appointment soon after their arrival in the home. In the scope of my job as a medical case manager in FOSC, I try to obtain a medical and birth history on the child. I find myself asking, "Is the mother in the area?" Often I learn her address is that of a shelter, a relative's home, a post office box, a drug treatment facility, or a jail. "Do we know where the father is?" The fathers are often less reachable, and some have not been involved with the mother and child before the removal to foster care. I meet some biological parents who attend the clinic appointments with their children, but more often I do not have that opportunity.

When we learn that the parent is actively trying to reunify with the child, we welcome that parent to join the foster parent at the clinic appointments. The meeting between the foster parent and the birth parent can be an emotional event, and some apprehension is understandable. Still, it is an opportunity to learn who the parent is, the nature of the parent-child relationship, what he or she can tell us about the child's history, characteristics, and culture. We learn from the parent and we can also inform the parent about the child's progress and development as we observe it in the clinic setting. In anticipation of the child's return to the parent, or even just for overnight visits, we can make sure the parent is up to date on the child's health, supplied with medications, and instructions. (For example, many of the babies that are born drug-exposed and/or premature require treatment for respiratory issues and gastroenterological reflux.) Involving the parents builds their confidence and capability, and, of course, this transfers to the child's sense of well-being.

Parental drug use is a factor for the majority of the children coming to the clinic. I believe that drug addiction usually is not the sole reason but rather a symptom of underlying causes. We have to look closer at the history of many parents in this tragic situation. When I have the chance to learn the stories from the parents themselves, the other family members, or even the children, I hear many accounts of the parents' own experiences of being neglected, abandoned, abused, and exposed to violence. (Sometimes it is clear that the trauma is multigenerational, passed down from parents to children.)

By the time they are reported to the authorities, the parents are often in very tenuous circumstances or homeless themselves. Consider the following typical scenarios, which I see over and over:

1. Mother is unable to support herself; lives with relatives
2. Father lives in a trailer or in his car
3. Mother and father split after removal, leaving mother homeless
4. Mother herself was in foster care when she parented this child

5. Father is in jail; mother depends on his relatives
6. Mother is in jail and will stay with relatives upon leaving jail

Homelessness does not in and of itself cause one's children to be taken away (there are various family shelters in our cities), but studies tell us it may be a determining factor for whether a child is placed in foster care (Zlotnick, Kronstadt, & Klee, 1998), and it most definitely can be a huge barrier to regaining one's children. For example, consider a parent who has a home and a job, whose offense was physical abuse to his child. He was required to complete a series of parenting classes, go to counseling, and demonstrate acquisition of nonviolent disciplinary skills before the return of his child. For the parent cited for a similar offense who had no job and no home of his own, the "reunification plan" would also include the requirement to have a stable place to live and an income to support the child. For homeless parents such as those described above, this challenge is daunting. What has been lacking for many people suffering from addiction, intergenerational poverty, discrimination, and broken families is social capital, or the norms and values that people hold that result in and are the result of collective and socially negotiated ties and relationships (Edwards, Franklin, & Holland, 2006). In other words, it takes a village. Considering the legacy of inferior education, closed doors, and lack of economic opportunities for African Americans and some other marginalized groups in the United States, it is easy to see that many lack the social capital that they could use as a starting point, support, and buffer in life's stressors, whereas many privileged people take such social capital for granted.

THE FOSTER PARENT

Foster parents choose what kind of home they will provide and what age range of child they will care for. When a child is first placed in foster care, he enters a "receiving home," meant to be a temporary situation while an investigation is being completed and a longer-term placement plan is created. Kinship foster homes with relatives are very common, as are homes of unrelated foster parents who also may be willing to adopt a child who cannot return home. Foster parents of older children who are not as likely to be adopted sometimes become their legal guardians. Group homes provide care to children, usually teenagers, for whom a family placement cannot be found. Although initially planned to be a temporary placement, many receiving homes become permanent adoptive placements. As one foster mother stated, "We just couldn't imagine him living anywhere else."

Placement decisions by the child protection agency should take into account a child's culture and ethnicity and try to minimize the trauma of foster care by placing children in similar homes. Fortunately, Alameda County has a very multicultural population and there are foster homes representing many different cultures, races, and nationalities. However, sometimes there is not an available "match" at the time it is needed, so we also see children going into homes where the child has to adjust to different foods, learn new ways, and do without cultural practices that were familiar. These differences add to the sense of loss. For example, some African American children find themselves in white homes and vice versa, which can lead to glaring and painful identity issues that must be dealt with as they get older. There are exceptions. Two African American brothers have grown up with a foster mother from South America and are now bicultural and fluent in Spanish. A white child placed with his African American foster family is now enjoying their Sunday church practices (with his mother's consent, since birth parents retain the right to determine the religious practices of their children while in foster care).

Just as we must consider the child's culture in placement, it is important to recognize the foster parents' culture. Their life experiences often led them to this work. Why do they do it? Foster parents are rarely thanked by the birth families and often feel unsupported by the overwhelmed foster care "system." I disagree with the idea that foster parents "do it for the money." It is a 24-hour-a-day job, but instead of being paid a salary foster parents receive a stipend that often does not cover all of the child's expenses. When reunification with the parent does not occur, the foster parents are often asked to adopt the child, and many do just that. At our foster parent continuing education classes, where foster parents meet and support each other, I have had the opportunity to hear their stories more times than I can count.

Often one's own childhood experiences laid the foundation for this vocation. Many foster parents revealed being adopted themselves and explained their desire to give back, repay, and repair or redirect their life in a positive and constructive way. One foster mother described how she was abandoned by her mother and left to be raised by relatives. She made a conscious decision to become a foster mother so that she could parent a child in the way she was never parented, drawing on the example of care that she received from other nurturing adults in her life.

Another foster mother described the happy childhood she had. She was loved and wanted, had family traditions to cherish, lasting relationships with extended family, and the wisdom not to take these things for granted. For this reason she chose to provide the same kind of family life for children who were missing such positive aspects of growing up.

The most frequent theme I hear when foster parents discuss their motivation to foster children is faith. Their spiritual beliefs, representing many religions, lead them to such altruism that they open their homes and hearts to the children of strangers.

I cringe when I hear a report of child abuse taking place in a foster home—for two reasons. The first, of course, is the abhorrence of the child's suffering at the hands of someone who was supposed to protect him; the second is the strong lasting impression that such a report makes on the general population. These accounts deserve our reactions of alarm and disgust, but I notice that far fewer stories are published about the *countless* selfless and terrific foster parents. Although not all foster parents have the same level of skill or commitment, it has been my privilege to know hundreds of foster parents over the years who are unsung heroes. Caring for someone else's child and doing it well takes a level of selflessness and compassion that is rare. Sometimes they arrive for a pediatric visit at FOSC after being up all night trying to console an infant who is experiencing withdrawal from methadone. They administer breathing treatments and give frequent feedings to premature babies who cannot keep food down. They perform range-of-motion exercises on tight little arms and legs stiffened by prenatal exposure to methamphetamines. They take children to specialists for skin grafts, physical therapy, play therapy, and special education. They embrace emotionally scarred children who exhibit challenging behaviors. They tell us that watching a child heal and thrive makes it all worthwhile.

RECOMMENDATIONS FOR WORK WITH FOSTER FAMILIES

The following suggestions, drawn from the clinical experience and the research discussed above, can be useful for social workers, therapists, clinicians, doctors, and others working with children in foster care.

1. *Embrace the foster parent's contribution.* Foster parents tell us they often feel disregarded by the child welfare staff in the assessment and placement planning for a child's future, and yet they are parenting the child daily. On the contrary, at FOSC, where the goal is not only pediatric care but also an opportunity to screen for mental health, behavioral, and development status, we respect the foster parent as our major consultant. The most important information we receive is the foster parent's narration of the child's symptoms, behaviors, responses, and progress. Our focus is not only on the child but also on the fit between the child and his foster parent. It is essential to bear in mind their relationship and what each brings to the other. Obviously, for example, a child who has severe asthma requires that his caregiver be very attuned to his symptoms and capable of providing the treatment protocol. In FOSC, the caregiver will be trained in administering these treatments and will need to make frequent follow-up visits to ensure competence in treatment administration. Likewise, for a child suffering from emotional trauma, we will discuss with the foster parents the behavioral symptoms they are seeing in terms of that past trauma. Suggestions and support will be discussed at each visit. This approach reduces the chance that the foster parent will give up in frustration, allowing for less placement disruption and more-satisfactory relationships and outcomes for the child. The foster parent's own strengths and limitations also must be considered. Even with the specialized help of therapists, teachers, and doctors, the foster parent is the agent of change who facilitates these other interventions while this child is in foster care.

2. *Support the foster placement.* While many doctors and clinics will not schedule a child without insurance, we will see the child before the insurance is in place. This allows the foster parent to start addressing the child's needs more quickly. As a pediatric hospital, we can offer a full range of specialty services as well—one-stop shopping, as it were. We offer bimonthly continuing education classes where foster parents can drop in, learn more about child development and behavior, and air their frustrations. They also earn continuing education hours for their foster parent license requirements. We have a specialized training series for those who are caring for medically fragile children. We assist them in applying for increased financial stipends for children with special needs, providing the court with written documentation of the child's needs based on our clinic reports. We instruct foster parents on the special education system and protocol, often

helping them start the process and attending school meetings to advocate for the child's services. We interface with the child welfare workers, other professionals serving the child, and the parents, with the goal of a holistic approach.

3. *Engage the birth parent.* Just as the foster parent teaches us about the child in foster care, the birth parent teaches us about the child's past, the family of origin, the culture, and the primary relationships of the child's life so far. By drawing the parent into the child's present health care and treatment issues, we are better informed as to how to help the child and build on their relationship. This is true even when reunification does not occur. The birth parent will always be part of who the child is. Even in cases where allegations of abuse and neglect were sustained, we can see the parent not as a perpetrator but as someone who is now trying to do the right thing for the child.

REFERENCES

Betzen, B. (2005). *Things I wish my adoptive parents knew.* Retrieved March 20, 2013, from http://www.openadoption.org/bbetzen/apknow.htm.

Bowlby, J. (1988). *A secure base: Clinical applications of attachment theory* (2nd ed.). London: Routledge.

Children's Bureau. (2009). *The AFCARS (Adoption and Foster Care Analysis and Reporting System) report.* Retrieved September 30, 2010, from http://www.acf. hhs.gov/programs/cb/resource/afcars-report-18.

Edwards, R., Franklin, J., & Holland, J. (Eds.). (2006). *Assessing social capital: Concept, policy, and practice.* Newcastle, UK: Scholars Press.

Kübler-Ross, E. (1969). *On death and dying.* New York: Simon & Schuster.

Lieberman, A., & Pawl, J. (1988). Clinical applications of attachment theory. In *Clinical implications of attachment* (pp. 328–335). Hillsdale: Lawrence Erlbaum Associates.

Lubit, R. (2009). *Child abuse and neglect: Reactive attachment disorder.* eMedicine World Medical Library. Retrieved October 1, 2011, from eMedicine.medscape. com/article.

Williams-Mbengue, N. (2008). *Permanency: A key concept for children in foster care. Moving children out of foster care. The legislative role in finding permanent homes for children*. National Conference of State Legislatures. Retrieved June 12, 2010, from http://www.ncsl.org/documents/cyf/movingchildrenoutofcare.pdf.

U.S. Bureau of the Census. (2010). *U.S. Census Bureau—American fact finder*. Retrieved March 24, 2008, from http://www.census.gov.

U.S. General Accounting Office. (1997). *Parental substance abuse: implications for children, the child welfare system, and foster care outcomes* (No. GAO/T-HEHS-98-40). Washington, DC: Subcommittee on Human Resources, Committee on Ways and Means, House of Representatives.

U.S. Department of Health and Human Services—Administration for Child and Family, Children's Bureau (2009). *Child maltreatment 2009*. Retrieved September 19, 2011, from http://www.acf.hhs.gov/programs/cb/stats_research/index.htm#can.

——. (2010). *Child maltreatment 2010*. Retrieved June 7, 2012, from http://www.acf.hhs.gov/programs/cb/pubs/cm10/cm10.pdf.

Zlotnick, C., Kronstadt, D., & Klee, L. (1998). Foster care children and family homelessness. *American Journal of Public Health, 88*(9), 1368–1370.

CHAPTER 10

The CATS Project

HELPING FAMILIES LAND ON THEIR FEET

▸ *VANCE HITCHNER*

SOME FAMILIES ENCOUNTER HARDSHIPS THAT overwhelm them. Often these hardships have roots that date back a generation or more, with repeated cycles of trauma and response.

For example, consider the family headed by Lena, a single African American mother whose life began a long downhill descent after she was raped when she was 10 years old. By the time she was 14 Lena had turned to alcohol and drugs to seek relief from the chronic nightmares, anger, irritability, and somatic complaints that began after the attack. She got pregnant when she was 17 years old and dropped out of high school soon after she gave birth to a son, Tyreke. When she was 21, she gave birth to a daughter, Alexis. Tyreke and Alexis had different fathers, neither of whom was involved with his child, so Lena was raising the children by herself in her mother's home. Lena's mother's ability to help with the children was limited by her own health problems. Her love for Lena was mixed with guilt, disappointment, and worry, and the two often bickered.

At age 23 Lena met Charles, a charming African American man who promised her the romance and support that she had always longed for, and she fell head over heels in love with him. Charles himself had a troubled childhood, and sometimes—when he had too much to drink, had problems at work, or was worried about the failing health of the grandmother who raised him—his outgoing playfulness would be elbowed aside by what he called his "demons," and he would withdraw into a sullen silence. Charles did not know how to accept help, let alone ask for it. After a couple of strongly rebuffed efforts to comfort him, Lena learned to give him room (she knew well the desire to hide from the world when despair came calling). By the next day the familiar cheerful Charles would be back, acting as if nothing had happened, and once again he would brighten the home.

At some point Lena and her children moved in with Charles, and Lena thought that at last she had created the family of her dreams. After a year and half of stability that Lena afterward always thought of as the happiest period of her life, with Tyreke settled in kindergarten and Alexis just beginning a Head Start day care program, Lena began making plans to get her GED, as a first step toward her lifelong dream of becoming a nurse. But just as she was about to set this plan in motion, Charles's grandmother had a stroke, and then another that led to her death. Charles was devastated, and withdrew deeper into himself than he ever had before. Lena felt helpless to comfort him, and she missed terribly the sunshine that he had brought into their lives. Charles, having no good way to find solace, turned to alcohol to numb the pain, and soon so did Lena.

The family began a downward spiral that kept picking up speed, and Lena felt powerless to reverse its course. She had a call from a counselor at Tyreke's school, asking her to come in and talk about his disruptive behavior. The counselor, not knowing that Tyreke was reacting to the stress at home, suggested that he had attention deficit disorder and encouraged Lena to have him evaluated for stimulant medication. Alexis, also reacting to the stress, became whiny and demanding, started wetting the bed and clinging to Lena when she dropped her off at her Head Start program. Charles had little patience for the children's distress, and started snapping at them, so Lena had to keep them out of his way. She resented this, and without realizing it, she too began to get short with her young children. Hurt and confused that their loving mother had become so irritable and distracted, Alexis and Tyreke started fighting with each other and having temper tantrums.

It is hard to get a straight story about what happened next. Official records mention crack cocaine and domestic violence. At some point Charles lost his job at a warehouse. On such and such a date Tyreke showed up at school with bruises, CPS was called, and he and Alexis were taken to the Assessment Center (the port of entry to the foster care system in Alameda County), and then to live with a Latino family in another town. Tyreke was seven years old, and Alexis was three. After a couple of weeks,

Lena got her children back; but Charles had to move out of the apartment, which Lena could not afford by herself, so she and the children had to move back with Lena's mother. At their grandmother's home Alexis and Tyreke seemed to be increasingly out of control. Tyreke, who was angry, aggressive, and defiant, stole some money from his grandmother's purse and insisted that he hadn't, while Alexis began hurting her grandmother's dachshund. Lena's mother became visibly more ill as the stress mounted.

Meanwhile, Lena came to view her child welfare worker as a heartless nag who was only interested in telling her what to do. And indeed, Lena was given a Department of Children and Family Services (DCFS) case plan that included a list of requirements: to get therapy for herself and for the children, to take parenting classes, to participate in an outpatient drug treatment program, and to submit to random drug testing.

Likewise, Charles had been ordered to take domestic violence classes, participate in a drug treatment program, and see a therapist. He requested and was granted weekly visits with Tyreke and Alexis, but these took place at one of the county's child welfare offices and had to be supervised. He was able to make it through a couple of visits during which Tyreke found various ways to let Charles know how angry he was at him. It was beyond Tyreke's capacity to communicate to his papa how much hurt and confusion fed his anger. Alexis clung to Charles and whimpered, breaking his heart bit by bit. This he had to endure with a white social worker supervising the visit and, Charles was sure, sitting in silent judgment of him all the while. He had been the target of enough racism over the years that he was not going to let down his guard and expose his vulnerable side to a white woman. When it came time for the third visit, Charles just couldn't bring himself to go. He wasn't able to put it into words, but he knew viscerally that the process was stirring up too many of his demons: his longing for his own father and mother and vestiges of his feelings of terror from the time that he was in foster care as a child, among others. Of course he couldn't talk about these things with the intern therapist that he was required to meet with. If he couldn't trust Lena, whom he loved, how could he trust a stranger?

The family was a shambles. Charles and Lena both were tormented and nearly incapacitated by a swirl of negative emotions and states of mind, including humiliation, guilt, loss, powerlessness, shame, confusion, and anger. Tyreke and Alexis also were angry, confused, and most of all more scared than they could bear, let alone understand. The four were drifting further from each other every day. Collectively and individually, their spirits were broken. If, instead of a family, this had been a failing small business, a careful look at the balance sheet might well have led to the conclusion that there was nothing left to do except to declare bankruptcy. Indeed, the child welfare system in effect had done just that; it placed the family in receivership when it removed Tyreke and Alexis, and ordered governmental restructuring of the family, as outlined in the family's case plan.

The help that is available for families like Lena's is limited. The courts assert nominal control, delegated to a caseworker. The caseworker provides material and emotional support, but within a framework that is essentially prescriptive: meet these conditions "or else." The conditions that are imposed—such as attending individual and family therapy, substance abuse and/or domestic violence treatment—are designed to improve family functioning, but suffer from a lack of specificity and coordination in their implementation, and often are viewed by parents as more punishment than opportunity. The logistical challenges of attending multiple meetings and sessions for services each week can be overwhelming. It is no wonder that many families become discouraged and do not follow through on their appointments.

THE CATS PROJECT

In Alameda County, a county in the San Francisco Bay Area, for families (like Lena's) in which the children have been made dependents of the courts but allowed to live with their parents, oversight is provided by child welfare workers in the Family Maintenance (FM) program of DCFS. In some FM cases the children have been reunified with their parents after living in out-of-home placements; in others the children were separated from their families for only a few days, or not at all. The CATS Project is one of the provider options when individual child therapy and/or family therapy is mandated for families under FM supervision. CATS is the only service in the county that works exclusively with referrals from FM, and it was designed and refined in consultation with DCFS personnel as a formal collaboration. The project was rolled out in January 2005.

The CATS Project attempts to take a holistic, integrated approach to bridging the gulf that often stretches between stressed families and therapeutic services. This approach is guided by an understanding of the impact of trauma not only on individuals but also on family systems, which shifts the work in the direction of making the whole family the focus of treatment (Ford & Saltzman, 2009, pp. 392–393). Formal understanding of the dynamics of families affected by multigenerational trauma is still in the early stages, but conceptualizing the family as an integrated unit affected by trauma on multiple levels provides a strong basis for creative and effective interventions. From this perspective, helping minors living under FM supervision naturally involves uncovering and addressing the ways that a parent's own trauma history can get in the way of effective parenting.

MULTIGENERATIONAL COMPLEX TRAUMA

The concept of "multigenerational complex trauma," which won't be found in the *DSM*, builds on recent advances in the treatment of trauma that recognize the distinction between discrete experiences of trauma and those situations—termed "complex trauma"—in which trauma is prolonged and occurs in an interpersonal context in childhood (Cook, Blaustein, Spinazzola, & van der Kolk, 2003). To some extent, adding the descriptor "multigenerational" to complex trauma is redundant, as children who experience complex trauma are very likely to have parents with similar experiences. Nevertheless, thinking in terms of "*multigenerational* complex trauma" can help the therapist situate the individual child or adolescent client within a family system that has been shaped in important ways by trauma in its various forms (Ford & Saltzman, 2009, pp. 392–393). Sadly, it is not unusual for the histories of such families to be marked by horrific trauma stretching back through several generations. The impact of trauma is registered at many levels in the family system, but most critically, from a therapeutic perspective, in the thoughts, feelings, and behaviors of the parents. The study and treatment of complex trauma in young people would benefit from formal research into the characteristic dynamics of such families (Ford & Saltzman, 2009, pp. 392–393).

The understanding of multigenerational complex trauma cannot and should not be separated from the social context in which it arises. A disproportionate number of families affected by it come from poor communities of color. This reflects the physical and psychological violence that our society historically has visited on these communities, which has not ceased. This context continuously impacts agencies and individual providers that strive to empower ill-treated families in order to mitigate some of the symptoms of this social problem. Progress toward the goal of empowerment is often undermined by new assaults on family well-being coming from multiple systems (education, mental health, and/or child welfare). As a result, a practitioner's work can be compared to that of an auto mechanic who labors to keep aging cars plugging along, when what is needed is a new transportation system. While the clinical work described below is focused on individual families, it is important not to lose sight of the broader need to address psychological, economic, and physical violence directed toward disadvantaged families.

FORMING THE THERAPEUTIC ALLIANCE

When families like Lena's are referred for mental health services, most have no basis upon which to welcome unfamiliar clinicians into their lives. Any parent considering child or family psychotherapeutic services takes a risk that the therapist will judge him or her as the source of the child's difficulties. When these services are mandated for parents involved in the child welfare system, that risk is multiplied. After all, the rationale for DCFS involvement is the presumption that these parents are not competent to raise their children without oversight. Like it or not, any therapist who takes a referral from DCFS enters the family sphere aligned with a formidable power that has violated the basic privacy taken for granted by most families. If the parents are able to see beyond this intrusion of state power, most are acutely aware of mistakes that they have made in raising their children, and the guilt and shame that they feel can be crushing. Often that shame is reinforced by humiliations thoughtlessly inflicted by a child welfare system that favors deference over autonomy and compliance over initiative. For example, these parents may need to get permission for their children to visit relatives, be told when they have to take their children to the dentist, or be criticized for their food and fashion choices for their children.

Such conditions as these hardly encourage parents to open up with a stranger about their family, yet if therapy is to be a collaborative process that is exactly what must happen. Consequently the therapist's first task is to establish sufficient trust with clients to allow collaboration, in order to transform the therapy from something that is imposed from above to something that truly belongs to the family. Success in building trust with our clients is far from guaranteed, as the loss of the ability to trust is one of the first and most long-lived consequences of interpersonal trauma (Kinsler, Courtois, & Frankel, 2009). The child who is not responded to adequately falls into a vicious cycle in which expressing the need for comfort is met by rejection, which increases the need for comfort, etc. Instead of learning to take comfort and nurturance for granted, such a child needs to build self-protective mechanisms to guard against feelings of isolation and abandonment. Often the chosen mechanism is to disconnect from one's internal awareness of need, a response that can become a lifelong obstacle to seeking and accepting help. In some cases, perhaps, help can be imposed on struggling families, but lasting change is more likely if they can truly accept the help, which means that first they must tolerate the vulnerability of accepting the need for help. To do so, they must develop trust in the therapist.

Creating this critical condition for therapy—sufficient trust to allow clients to accept and explore their own needs and desires—is the starting place for work with families mandated for treatment. This initial phase of therapy often lasts much longer for these families than for those who voluntarily initiate treatment (indicating at least some predisposition to trust the therapist). As Lieberman and Van Horn (2008) observe, "the very concept of mandatory treatment involves a contradiction in terms because inner change cannot usually be coerced but emerges from a person's awareness that things are not going well and one must develop new patterns of being and behaving."

The level of trust that the family has in the clinician serves as one measure of the progress of therapy. Many times in work with families in FM even the most skilled therapist is not able to build sufficient trust, and the therapy is stillborn. Often it is hard to even get in the door, and it can take months to get to the point where the client acknowledges that the clinician is a potential source of help. When this happens it is a moment to be celebrated.

The Johnson family came to the attention of CPS when a neighbor reported that the three young children were being left alone in their apartment by their single mother, sometimes for as long as two or three hours. They were referred to CATS for family therapy by their FM worker, who was worried that the oldest child, a 6-year-old boy, was being "parentified." Ms. Johnson was pleasant enough when contacted by a CATS therapist, but it was difficult to find a time when the therapist could come to the home, because of other appointments that Ms. Johnson said she had to attend to first. When the therapist was finally able to meet the family, Ms. Johnson seemed passive and somewhat vague, and was frequently distracted by the children or phone calls. Ms. Johnson did on a couple of occasions say enough about her life for the therapist to get a sense of the extensive trauma that she had experienced from a young age. The children, who were always friendly when the therapist stopped by, seemed to be disrespectful of their mother, who in turn would threaten them in frustration (but never follow through with her threats). Although Ms. Johnson could not identify any real problems in the family, she agreed to meet with the therapist in order to comply with her case plan. However, the meetings, which were scheduled to occur weekly, happened only sporadically. Sometimes the therapist would go to the home at the scheduled time and find no one there. Once she heard the children inside when she rang the bell, but no one came to answer the door, causing her to wonder if their mother had left them home alone again. Ms. Johnson never answered the therapist's phone calls, and the therapist found herself getting increasingly frustrated. When she communicated this to the FM worker, the worker encouraged her to keep working with the family. After a couple more months of frustration, the therapist decided to close the case, in spite of her lingering concern for the well-being of the children.

RELATIONSHIP-BASED TREATMENT

Developing trust with clients is essential if the ultimate goal is to help them recover other related social and emotional skills that develop in the context of interpersonal relationships, such as the ability to modulate and communicate emotions, the ability to maintain a balance between one's own needs and the needs of others, and the ability to adapt to the complexities of group dynamics. When there has been a history of relational trauma, most of the repair work will need to take place in the context of relationships. For children, this happens most effectively in the relationship with their parent(s) and other close contacts, and therapeutic efforts usually concentrate on repairing and revitalizing these relationships. On the other hand, when it is the parent who has not healed from the injuries of relational trauma, the parent's relationship with the therapist often assumes a central role in the therapy (Pearlman & Courtois, 2005). For this reason, at the CATS Project in most cases we assign one primary therapist to work with each family, although other models that we have drawn from, such as Trauma Systems Therapy, utilize designated treatment teams (Saxe, Ellis, & Kaplow, 2007, p. 11). Needless to say, placing the relationship between the therapist and the parent at the center of the therapeutic process adds greatly to the ambiguity and complexity of the work.

To earn the client's trust, a therapist needs to be trustworthy—reliable, emotionally stable, culturally adept, and honest—and able to maintain these qualities, well enough, during the crises and intense interpersonal dramas that often populate the world of multigenerational complex trauma. Most importantly, she or he needs to convey nonjudgmental acceptance of the parents, *and*, within reason, support their authority in the home. Since many families come under the supervision of FM precisely because of problems with parental exercise of authority (e.g., extremes of authoritarianism or permissiveness), meeting parents where they are may require conscious and active suspension of judgment and tacit support, at least temporarily, of less than perfect and even potentially counterproductive parenting practices. Examples of these include the use of shame or fear to manage child behavior, both of which can be especially destabilizing for the vulnerable sense of self of traumatized children. (It should come as no surprise that reliance on shame and fear to mold behavior would come automatically to many parents involved with child welfare, as these powerful emotions are readily evoked by their own experiences with the courts and the child welfare system.)

One of the consequences of involvement with CPS is that parents feel as if their actions are always "under the microscope" (as often they are), and consequently it is hard for them to have an accepting and curious attitude about the inevitable missteps that come with the job of parenting. Parents whose oversight of their children has been legally challenged are likely to be exquisitely sensitive to any criticism of their parenting, and just as likely, and with equal good reason, to view the therapist as the arbiter of what is acceptable parenting. If therapists are to help parents explore new ways of relating to their children, they must foster an atmosphere in which it acceptable to make mistakes. However, in the moment, granting the parent the space to find his or her own way of exerting healthy authority, and observing the persistence of habitual practices and attitudes, the therapist can have the uncomfortable feeling that she or he is supporting the parent at the child's expense, often experienced by the therapist as "colluding" with hurtful parenting. This is one of the many sources of strain that come with working with the family system in multigenerational complex trauma (Boyd-Franklin & Bry, 2000, p. 45).

Robert Nelson, a single father of two girls (4 and 6 years old), often found life confusing, especially with regard to parenting his daughters. His confusion was rooted in his own past—he had been raised in foster care himself—and he had serious mental health problems, which included delusional thinking. He was unpredictable as a parent, and might suddenly ask one of his daughters accusingly, "Why did you do that?" without making it clear what he was talking about. His daughters walked on eggshells, and they were used to responding deferentially to their father's intrusions, which would dissipate as quickly as they had formed. In the family therapy the therapist was always looking for ways to support Mr. Nelson's authority by clarifying the rules in the home and encouraging him to "catch his daughters being good" and to follow through on consequences for misbehavior. Sometimes the therapist found herself helping the father enforce rules that seemed capricious and/or developmentally inappropriate. For example, periodically Mr. Johnson would decide that the girls were not allowed in the kitchen, which he would convey to them by sharply asking, "What are you doing in there?" when they inadvertently ventured in. Since it was early in the therapy, the therapist chose not to advocate for less-restrictive rules, but instead worked with Mr. Nelson on signaling the rule more clearly by closing the kitchen door when the girls were not allowed access. While the therapist hoped that this would set the stage for her to engage Mr. Nelson in an examination of his parenting practices, she was not at all confident that he would ever be open to this, and she worried that she was letting the girls down by supporting their father. In the end she decided that this compromise was necessary if the work was going to continue.

LEVELING THE PLAYING FIELD

Another key feature of the CATS model designed to promote the growth of trust between clinician and families is the fact that most meetings take place in the client's home. While this alternative to seeing clients in the office also addresses a logistical imperative—many over-stressed families simply can't make it to an office on a regular basis—there are other important advantages to bringing the services to the home. Traditional therapeutic techniques were developed for the most part in a culture and under circumstances quite different from those of most families involved in the foster care system. As a result, therapists working with marginalized families are often in the position of introducing parenting and other interpersonal practices that may seem quite foreign to their clients. When the services are mandated by the courts, there is always the risk of imposing dominant norms and practices on disempowered families. Therapists trained to work with clients who voluntarily seek their services may lose sight of how culturally specific their own professional values are. In fact, the very idea of organizing the family around the emotional needs of its children contradicts the fundamental assumptions of many parents. Thus a critical part of building a trusting therapeutic alliance is creating a more equal and balanced field upon which the therapy can play out. Creating such a space is much more difficult, if not impossible, when these encounters occur on the therapist's home turf. Feeling "at home" makes it much easier for the therapist to miss asymmetric aspects of the therapeutic encounter, and as uncomfortable as it might be at times, meeting at the clients' homes goes a long way toward equalizing the power differential and building the therapeutic alliance (Saxe, Ellis, & Kaplow, 2007, pp. 170–171).

The establishment of a basic level of trust allows the family and the therapist to work as a team to transfer ownership of the therapy from the child welfare worker and the courts to the family. The case plan that mandates therapy and other services may be referred to as the "family's," but in reality it is the court's. If it were really the family's plan, it would be co-created. But since the child welfare system is organized under the rules and logic of the legal system, adversarial ways of thinking often impede cooperation. Thus when families first enter the system it is often the same child welfare worker who is building the county's case for making the children dependents of the court and is responsible for developing the case plan. Within this adversarial paradigm, the requirements of the case plan can seem like a "sentence" imposed by the courts for the "crimes" of which the parent has been found guilty. Unfortunately, the guilty-parent archetype permeates child welfare. There is a great need for reinvention of child welfare practices, including the creation of case plans, from a less legalistic, more strengths-based perspective.

AGREEING ON A FOCUS FOR TREATMENT

For the family and the therapist to form an effective work team, they need to agree on the essential problems that are to be the focus of treatment. Needless to say, framing the problems in terms of parental guilt can only lead to therapeutic dead ends. It is a crucial part of the opening phase of therapy to find out what the parents view as the problem(s). For some, the answer is easy: the problem is having CPS in their lives. This can be a starting point, as it is not hard to agree that it would be good for them to get their autonomy back, and if nothing else they can be helped to meet the terms of their case plan. From this point of agreement, to the extent that the family is open to therapy, the therapist and the family can work together to identify other problems. However, parents may have multiple reasons why they are not open to therapy, and it is worthwhile to question the assumption implicit in court-mandated services that therapy can be the solution for all family problems.

The co-identification of the problem(s) that will be the focus of the work should be part of a broader process of assessment that creates the initial structure of the therapy. This assessment touches on many levels of the child's environment. The more clearly therapists understand the needs and vulnerabilities of the children and their families, on the one hand, and their resources and strengths, on the other, the more strategic they can be in identifying realistic targets for change in families struggling with multiple problems on multiple ecological levels.

While establishing mutually agreed-upon targets for intervention helps to build the therapeutic alliance with families mandated for treatment, it can also set in motion a counterproductive process of "problem chasing," which distracts from the equally important task of developing an integrated clinical understanding of the underlying dynamics and processes that keep families stuck in maladaptive patterns of functioning. In fact, for some families the therapist needs to be careful not to inadvertently rein-force maladaptive relationship patterns by responding too ardently to cri-ses. It is always helpful to remember that the ultimate goal of the therapy is to empower the family so that they can find their own solutions (Boyd-Franklin & Bry, 2000).

Michelle Little was a single mother whose teenage daughter, Maxie, had a history of engaging in risky behaviors, such as binge drinking, cutting, and unprotected sex. Ms. Little bitterly resented the involvement of DCFS in her life—the agency had stepped in after her daughter made a serious suicide attempt—and tended to be dismissive of the therapist's efforts to help. Until, that is, Maxie would have one of her periodic blowouts. On these occasions Maxie would leave home for a couple of days to spend time with her boyfriend, whom Ms. Little disliked intensely. Suddenly the therapist was indispensable, called multiple times a day to serve as an intermediary between Maxie and her mother. At first the therapist—who had heretofore felt ineffective—was happy to get some traction with her work, but it did not take long for her to realize that she was being asked to play a role in a long-standing family drama, as a stand-in for Maxie's absent father, who had been in-volved in Maxie's life only on the occasions when Ms. Little could not handle Maxie's behaviors herself. Eventually the therapist and Ms. Little were able to agree that the therapist would focus on harm-reduction work with Maxie.

COMPLEX TRAUMA AND SELF-REGULATION

The concept of multigenerational complex trauma can help in ground-ing case formulations, with the impact of trauma on the regulation of emo-tion and behavior in a family and its individual members being of particular importance. Current treatments of psychological trauma share a focus on the way that trauma disrupts the normal functioning of the exquisitely cali-brated human stress-response system, a coordinated assembly of evolutionarily designed, automatic neurophysiologic processes and behaviors. Normally, after stressful experiences this system autonomously regains equilibrium when the stressor is removed (McEwen & Lasley, 2002). With extreme or prolonged trauma (e.g., complex trauma), however, equilibrium is not regained, and the stress-response system becomes chronically unbalanced and disconnected from feedback from the environment. This can be manifested in many ways, including chronic dysregulation of emotions and behavior. Thus many of the emotional and/or behavioral "problems" that parents and other observers witness in their children are symptoms of unresolved trauma. In families where the complex trauma is multigenerational, the emotions and behavior of children *and* parents may be dysregulated (and often recursively disruptive, with the dysregulation of one party triggering the dysregulation of the other). Thus the reduction of these chronic, destructive processes of traumatic dysregulation often becomes an underlying focus of therapeutic interventions.

Debbie Johnson was referred to the CATS Project shortly after she was released from a residential drug treatment program and reunited with her three sons, who had been living with her mother. Debbie had lost custody of the children 18 months earlier when police looking for her fugitive brother had raided her apartment and discovered drug paraphernalia. At the time of the raid Debbie had been addicted to methamphetamine for nine years. Frankie, her common-law husband, was also addicted to methamphetamine, and would regularly beat and humiliate her in front of the children. Although the boys' physical needs had been met, these scenes of violence, and the separation from their family for the six months when they were in out-of-home foster care placement, had left the children emotionally and behaviorally dysregulated. They were hyperactive and alternately defiant and clingy. Even after they were reunited with their mother (their father had refused treatment and dropped out of their lives), their dysregulated behaviors continued.

Debbie herself had experienced extensive childhood trauma, including neglect and sexual abuse, which had led to substance abuse as a form of self-medication. She was chronically depressed and tormented by nightmares, feelings of emptiness, and thoughts of suicide, and she would panic if she perceived there was any threat to her children. Her feelings of guilt prevented her from setting the limits that the boys desperately needed, and the whole household often spun out of control.

The work with Debbie and her family, which lasted for the better part of three years, started by addressing Debbie's own traumatic past, which she began to reveal freely once her therapist demonstrated that she could tolerate Debbie's pain. At first her children, who wandered in and out of the living room where the therapy was being conducted, perceived the therapist as harmful to their mother, because the therapist "made" her cry, but soon they came to recognize that with the tears came relief. As Debbie slowly became better regulated, her sons also stabilized. They became less clingy and were able to turn more and more toward the typical interests of other boys of their age.

In organizing our work to address the role that emotional dysregulation plays in multigenerational complex trauma, the CATS Project draws specifically on two contemporary treatment models, both of which were developed by clinical teams in the Boston area associated with the National Child Traumatic Stress Network (NCTSN). One of these models, Trauma Systems Therapy (TST), defines a trauma system as comprising "(1) a traumatized child who has difficulty regulating emotional states and (2) a social environment and/or system of care that is not able to help the child to regulate these emotional states" (Saxe, Ellis, & Kaplow, 2007). This succinct formulation is very useful for orienting a clinician working in the inevitably ambiguous and confusing world of multigenerational complex trauma. Using this definition as a starting point, TST offers concrete suggestions to help multidisciplinary clinical teams join with families, collaboratively assess their strengths and weaknesses, and construct treatment plans that strategically allocate clinical resources. The TST model lends itself to adaptation in a range of clinical settings, and its attention to the "system of care that is not able to help the child to regulate . . . emotional states" provides a useful framework for the elaboration of the family dynamics of multigenerational trauma.

The other model that we incorporate in our work, Attachment, Self-Regulation, and Competency (ARC) therapy, organizes assessment and treatment around nine clusters of psychological and behavioral functioning in family systems beset by [multigenerational] complex trauma (Blaustein & Kinniburgh, 2010). These areas of potential strengths and/or weaknesses are grouped into the three broad categories that give the model its name: attachment, self-regulation, and competency. These categories reflect interdependent lines of child development that are often disrupted by trauma. Each category provides goals for intervention. Thus the goal in working on attachment relationships within the family is to promote a "good enough" relationship between the child and the parent(s) by providing caregivers with skills and a context in which to understand their child's behaviors. Likewise, assessment and interventions in the area of self-regulation address the disruptive effects of the emotional and behavior dysregulation that accompanies complex trauma, while the focus on competency is intended to create the conditions for wide-ranging experiences of mastery, which are necessary for a child's healthy social and emotional development.

We integrate these two models with other clinical approaches, such as family systems (Ford & Saltzman, 2009, p. 397), cognitive behavioral (Cohen, Mannarino, & Deblinger, 2006), and psychodynamic (Heineman, 1998), as we attempt to identify the most pertinent clinical issues and formulate an initial plan of action. For example, when we began working with Debbie Johnson's family, we hypothesized that we were working with a "trauma system" in which there were three traumatized children who weren't able to regulate their emotions and behavior, and who could not be adequately supported by their mother, who was overwhelmed by her own trauma responses. Moving to the ARC framework to look at areas of family functioning that were in greatest need of attention, we concentrated on the categories of Attachment (especially the subcategory of "Caregiver Management of Affect") and Self-Regulation. This formulation provided a basic orientation from which to begin work with the family. Of course, before we could address any of this, the clinician assigned to the case had to convince Ms. Johnson that she might be a source of help, and not just one more attack by the system. It turned out in this case that after some initial wariness, Ms. Johnson was quite open to help, as long as it was delivered on her terms.

COLLABORATING WITH CHILD WELFARE

Too often, fragmented institutional responses to the needs of children in the foster care system compound their difficulties. When risk factors multiply and cases start to fall apart, it is easy for clinicians' and child welfare workers' approaches to become polarized, and even antagonistic. As Lieberman and Van Horn (2008) have observed, "The involvement of CPS and the legal system affects every aspect of treatment by mandating courses of action that are largely unrelated to the developmental stage and mental health needs of the child. Coordinating mental health treatment with the often contradictory demands of different systems of care should constitute standard 'best practice' for child mental health providers."

When therapists provide mandated services for families involved in child welfare, they become part of that system, and they must be clear with themselves, other professionals, and their client families about their role. From its inception the CATS Project was designed to be a working collaboration with DCFS. Regular joint meetings between therapists and child welfare workers were built into our model. Originally we worked with just one FM unit, and used our joint meetings to work out the details of the collaboration. Perhaps the greatest benefit of these meetings was the opportunity to form face-to-face relationships with each other. Unfortunately, as we began to offer our services to other FM units, the small size of our program worked against continuing the practice of meeting regularly with the FM units. The demand for our services simply outstripped our capacity, and the wait for openings grew from weeks to months. To limit the flow of referrals—and thus the frustration of the workers making the referrals—we gradually began meeting less frequently with the FM units. To reinstitute joint meetings we would have to expand our program and assign separate teams of therapists to each unit, and funds currently are not available for program expansion.

Child welfare workers and therapists come from similar professional backgrounds but operate under different but overlapping paradigms that fundamentally affect the roles they play and their relationship with families. Child welfare workers, representing the power of the government as administered by the courts, play a supervisory role in relation to the child's parents, and the balance of power is clearly on their side. Therapists often seek a fundamentally different balance of power, with the goal of empowering children and parents to assume as much responsibility for their own lives as possible. This involves helping people see their lives in new ways and providing them the tools to make changes that they desire. The therapist's role shares aspects of that of a supervisor, such as supporting and teaching, but is different in that the locus of control is clearly with the client. The therapist answers to the parent, while the parent answers to the child welfare worker. These competing lines of authority and responsibility usually remain in the background, as child welfare workers and therapists team up with parents to promote the best interests of the child. But occasionally—most often when safety concerns come to the forefront—the question of how much the therapist should answer to the child welfare worker becomes pertinent (e.g., establishing the correct balance between patient confidentiality and the therapist's responsibility as a mandated reporter of suspected child abuse).

In addition, in the most demanding cases, when the parent's ability to meet the basic needs of the child is in question, managing the differences in the roles and responsibilities of the therapist and the child welfare worker can require careful attention on both sides. Some families seem to be hope-lessly stuck in dysfunctional behavior. The parents in these families—due to unresolved trauma, serious cognitive deficits or psychiatric illness, severe personality disorder, active substance abuse, or a combination of these—are not able to meet their responsibilities to protect and educate their chil-dren (Barbell & Freundlich, 2005). Their offspring, usually adolescents, often attend school irregularly, engage in risky or illegal behaviors, and defy adult authority, especially that of their parents. These behaviors force con-sideration of whether the minor would be better off living in a foster place-ment, a group home, or a residential treatment program. This question is never easy to resolve, given the strength of the bonds between children and parents, on the one hand, and the limitations and uncertainties of alter-native placements, on the other. In recent years the pendulum has swung in the direction of maintaining youth with their families if at all possible. As a consequence of this trend and shrinking public resources, youth who previously would have been placed in residential treatment programs have become the responsibility of FM and programs like ours, which frankly are not designed to provide an equivalent level of structure and support. Thus some of the most vulnerable youth are left suffering from complex trauma without effective treatment for their debilitating disorders.

Clinicians can make recommendations for residential treatment and other alternative placements, but the responsibility for making the deci-sion is the domain of DCFS and the courts. When the decision is to keep the minors in their parent's home, therapists are usually urged by the child welfare worker to continue to provide services. This situation can create an ethical dilemma: should the therapist provide services considered to be inadequate in the hope that they will mitigate foreseeable harm, or is it bet-ter to move on to work with other families who might benefit more from the services?

AVOIDING BURNOUT

Working with families with multigenerational complex trauma puts a great strain on clinicians, who are daily witnesses to the impact on children and families of the destructive forces that thrive in our society. The desire to right the wrongs is persistent, and the feelings of guilt and ineffectiveness that arise when things can't be fixed are hard to bear. The difficulties that families experience are particularly vivid for the clinician who is working in the home. Managing all of these negative experiences is an important part of a clinician's job. To help offset the feelings of isolation and demoralization that come with this work, at CATS we attempt to share our cases conceptually as much as possible. This is accomplished through supervision, impromptu consultations, and most importantly through our weekly case conference, where we try to "hold" the families as a team. We are a small team (six clinicians, including trainees), carry small caseloads (8–12 families each for full-time clinicians), and collaborate with a familiar group of referring caseworkers at DCFS, so we are able to build the sense of collective containment of our cases to a significant degree, especially for those families who are frequently in crisis, and thus often the ones that clinicians bring to the case conference for consultation.

· · ·

At the CATS Project we have seen how flexible, comprehensive, and open-ended mental health services, working in conjunction with child welfare and other community agencies, can interrupt the cycle of trauma and response in families, and offer the chance of fresh beginnings. However, these interventions are labor-intensive, and will never be equal to the task as long as the families at the bottom rungs of society are the targets of widespread economic, political, and interpersonal hostility. Ultimately the best cure for multigenerational complex trauma is the transformation to a more humane society. For example, if the health care system expanded its definition of disease to include social maladies, it would open the door to addressing the impact of stress and violence on children and families more holistically. Similarly, activities that promote social and emotional learning should be integrated into the core curricula of our schools and day care centers. In the meantime, further study of the dynamics of multigenerational complex trauma could spur development of more-comprehensive and -effective services for children and families coming into the child welfare system.

REFERENCES

Barbell, K., & Freundlich, M. (2005). Foster care today. In G. P. Mallon & P. M. Hess, *Child welfare for the twenty-first century: A handbook of practices, policies, and programs* (pp. 504–517). New York: Columbia University Press.

Blaustein, M. E., and Kinniburgh, K. M. (2010). *Treating traumatic stress in children and adolescents: How to foster resilience through attachment, self-regulation, and competency.* New York: Guilford Press.

Boyd-Franklin, N., & Bry, B. (2000). A framework for home-based family treatment. In N. Boyd-Franklin & B. Bry, *Reaching out in family therapy: Home-based, school, and community interventions* (pp. 37–57). New York: Guilford Press.

Cohen, J., Mannarino, A., & Deblinger, E. (2006). *Treating trauma and traumatic grief in children and adolescents.* New York, Guilford Press.

Cook, A., Blaustein, M., Spinazzola, J., & van der Kolk, B. (Eds.). (2003). *Complex trauma in children and adolescents.* National Child Traumatic Stress Network. Retrieved August 30, 2011, from http://www.nctsnet.org/nctsn_assets/pdfs/edu_materials/ComplexTrauma_All.pdf.

Ford, J. D., & Saltzman, W. (2009). Family systems therapy. In J. D. Ford & C. A. Courtois (Eds.), *Treating complex traumatic stress disorders: An evidence-based guide* (pp. 391–414). New York: Guilford Press.

Heineman, T. V. (1998). *The abused child: Psychodynamic understanding and treatment.* New York: Guilford Press.

Kinsler, P. J., Courtois, C. A., & Frankel, A. S. (2009). Therapeutic alliance and risk management. In J. D. Ford & C. A. Courtois (Eds.), *Treating complex traumatic stress disorders: An evidence-based guide* (pp. 183–201). New York: Guilford Press.

Lieberman, A.F., & Van Horn, P. (2008). *Psychotherapy with infants and young children: Repairing the effects of stress and trauma on early attachment.* New York: Guilford Press.

McEwen, B., & Lasley, E. (2002). *The end of stress as we know it.* Washington, DC: National Academies Press.

Pearlman, L.A., & Courtois, C. A. (2005). Clinical applications of the attachment framework: Relational treatment of complex trauma. *Journal of Traumatic Stress, 18*(5), 449–459.

Saxe, G. N., Ellis, B. H., & Kaplow, J. B. (2007). *Collaborative treatment of traumatized children and teens: The Trauma Systems Therapy approach.* New York: Guilford Press.

PART 4

Needs for the Future

The saying "Pull yourself up by your bootstraps" has been directed with derision toward those who drop out of school, use drugs, or have trouble with the law. Rarely verbalized, but obviously present, is the hidden assumption behind this statement that everyone has access to the same amount of resources and privileges. Of course, if that were the case, the work of "pulling yourself up by your bootstraps" would be equally hard or easy for each of us. Sadly, evidence suggests that this assumption is highly erroneous. Adulthood health status, education level, and socioeconomic status can be predicted in a newborn simply by identifying race/ethnicity and family income level. Thus, the challenge of our society, particularly for those who have been born into privilege, is to identify strategies and to develop systems that will equalize the resources and privileges for everyone.

CHAPTER 11

A Systems Dilemma

INTERGENERATIONAL FOSTER CARE AND HOMELESSNESS

▸ *CHERYL ZLOTNICK*

LEONA'S STORY

LEONA'S EARLIEST MEMORY WAS HER mother's frenzied screams to not move or break anything. Now 25 years old, she vividly recalls absorbing her mother's anxiety as she rigidly sat on someone's sofa trying to "behave." They had just moved to a new place. Rarely did she and her mother stay any place longer than a month. Leona's other childhood memories were tinged with fear, frustration, and anger as she remembers living in a blur of different people's homes and homeless shelters. The short stays in people's homes were the most difficult. Not because of the locations— sometimes they lived in the garage and other times they stayed in the living room—but because Leona's mother would take off and leave Leona all by herself for days at a time. Leona felt scared and angry. She never knew where her mother was or when she would return. Her mother would just say she needed a break, some time to herself. Leona remembered that her secret fear was that one day her mother would leave and not return. Usually the conditions in the homeless shelters were less than ideal. Still, Leona preferred them to other people's homes. At least when they stayed in shelters, her mother had to stay with her and couldn't just take off and leave Leona with strange adults. Some of the shelters even had fun events, although those were rare. Most shelters were dreary and chaotic, with screaming parents and crying children. Sometimes there were fights. Leona knew it was bad when her mother had a fight with a shelter worker or another mother. The result was always the same. She and her mother would have to leave. From kindergarten to fourth grade, Leona lived in so many places and went to so many schools that she never ended the year in the same place where she started it.

Leona would never forget the last home where she stayed. It was at a great-aunt's apartment. Her mother, as usual, had taken off. It had been weeks this time. Somehow, even then, Leona felt it was different. Then it happened. Leona's great-aunt showed up at her school. Leona knew something was up. Her aunt had been asking her over and over again where her mother was and when she'd be back. As Leona got into her aunt's station wagon, she saw the suitcase in the backseat. Leona asked where they were going, but her aunt kept silent. Fifteen minutes later, Leona was standing beside the suitcase at the police station. Her aunt explained to the police that Leona's mother had left almost a month ago and that she no longer could care for Leona. The police officer started asking her aunt questions, but she ran out crying. Leona tried to run after her, but the police officer held her back. That day, Leona entered foster care. She was 8 years old. She never saw her mother again.

Leona felt petrified and alone. She couldn't sleep. She wouldn't talk. For a while, she bounced from one foster home to another. After living in four foster homes in two years, Leona, now 10 years old, was placed in a group home. It was chaotic and Leona's behavior reflected the chaos, becoming erratic, vacillating from being withdrawn one day to cursing out the teacher the next. The group home provided Leona with therapy. Every year for the next four years, she was transferred to a new therapist. She had liked therapy at first, but after she learned that the therapists were students and she had to change therapists every year, she became more and more resistant to it. As she was about to be assigned to her fifth therapist, Leona refused.

School was hard. Leona had missed so much school during her early years in homeless shelters and then with the various foster care and group home placements that she rarely understood the class work. She began skipping class often and barely attended a month of school in tenth grade.

Leona felt like a speck of dust floating through air. She was insignificant and practically invisible. No one cared or thought of her. She had no connections, few friends. Well, there was one friend, Ray. He was 25, almost 10 years older than Leona. He hung out near the group home entrance. At 15, Leona became infatuated with Ray. For the first time in her life, someone was interested in her. He always was eager to see her and waited for her every day. He told her she was desirable, beautiful, and the only one for him. Never had Leona garnered such attention. One day, Ray was short on cash and desperately needed to pay someone back. At least that was the story that Leona remembered. She wasn't exactly sure how it happened, but to pay Ray's debts, she began prostituting for him. Prostitution was not unusual among the girls at the group home; the place was well known among pimps. After a while, the relationship with Ray became physically abusive. Leona finally left him and returned to the group home, but not before she became pregnant.

Pregnancy also was not unusual for the girls at the group home. At 16, Leona found pregnancy a bit scary but also exciting. Finally she would have someone who would love her unconditionally. When her baby daughter, Betina, was born, Leona was amazed at how much she loved her. She was adorable. As Leona got less and less sleep, her dreams of being loved unconditionally became clouded. Feedings, diaper changes, doctors' appointments—keeping up with all of Betina's needs was simply too much. She simply could not handle it. Leona just needed a break, some time to herself; and so she did the same thing that her mother had done with her. She left Betina in the group home. When she returned eight hours later, three-month-old Betina was gone. Someone at the group home had reported that the baby had been left alone, and so Betina was removed and placed in foster care. A caseworker from the child welfare system (CPS) came to speak with Leona and discussed parenting expectations and behaviors. She gave Leona tips on how to find a babysitter when she needed a break, described her responsibilities as a parent, and explained that leaving an infant unattended was abandonment. The caseworker also gave Leona a sheet of paper called a case plan that listed the activities that had to be completed before Leona could regain custody of baby Betina.

The list of places where Leona could seek help with the case plan requirements was daunting. Worse yet, many referrals were useless. For example, the parenting class that the caseworker recommended only admitted participants who were 18 or older. Leona was 16. Supervised visitations with Betina took place at the caseworker's office, but Leona had to take three buses to get there. The last bus ran so infrequently that she couldn't get back to the group home before curfew. Eventually Leona gave up trying to complete the case plan's activities, parental rights were terminated, and Betina was put up for adoption. Leona never saw her again. She felt that the system had tricked her. She was angry, ashamed, and frustrated.

For the next two years, Leona alternated between living in the group home and on the street. She never went to school. Her drug and alcohol use increased, and she supported her habit by prostituting for a pimp who hung out in front of the group home. At the age of 18, Leona aged out of the foster care system and was on her own. Her life became a whirlwind of prostitution, drugs, beatings, and jail. At 24, she became pregnant again. She ignored her pregnancy and never attempted to obtain prenatal care. But in the delivery room, when the nurse handed the beautiful baby boy to Leona, her life suddenly came to a jarring halt. She saw her son's brown eyes peering up at her, and a strong wave of love overtook her. She named him Max and promised him that he would not have to grow up in the foster care system like she and her daughter, Betina, did. She wanted to be a good mother to little Max.

The doctors and nurses at the hospital had another perspective. Max exhibited some abnormalities at birth, including tremors and hypertonic motor function. Blood tests indicated that Leona had used cocaine while she was pregnant with Max. The hospital notified CPS, and a caseworker came to place Max in emergency foster care. To further complicate the situation, Leona's teenage history of having lost a child (Betina) to CPS appeared. Since Max was Leona's second child entering foster care, Leona was told that the court might put Max up for adoption. However, the court was sympathetic. Leona was told that she could regain custody of little Max if she completed her case plan, which required residential substance abuse treatment, parenting classes, therapy, and meetings with the caseworker. Leona agreed to the terms and immediately entered the residential treatment program—only three short blocks away from the group home where she had lived before. As required by the case plan, Leona began therapy. By the second session, Leona was diagnosed with clinical depression and prescribed an antidepressant. At first Leona was hesitant to take the medication, but she was persuaded when her therapist explained that depression may have contributed to her self-medication with alcohol and street drugs. Unfortunately, neither Leona nor her therapist had realized that the residential substance abuse program was not licensed to administer prescriptions, and consequently did not admit patients who needed medications for mental health problems. Since the substance abuse program was required by her case plan, Leona refused to fill the prescription for the antidepressant. Meanwhile, her depression made it hard for her to get out of bed, do her assigned chores, engage in therapy, participate in the Alcoholics Anonymous meetings, and demonstrate to the program's staff that she could care for her baby.

THE CURRENT SYSTEMS

Like many others living in the transitional situations of homelessness and foster care, Leona encountered myriad public and private systems, among them housing, child welfare, mental health, criminal justice, and substance abuse. The systems and services provided to Leona differed depending on whether she was viewed as a homeless child or as a foster care child. This chapter identifies the systems with which transitional families come in contact and explores ways that the systems could combine forces to become more effective and focused.

Housing

Like Leona, many families caught in the cycle of homelessness survive without a stable home for months, even years, as they live in a series of temporary places with relatives or friends. Since they do not live on the streets or in shelters, their living status is not apparent. This kind of situation is neither new nor unique. It was documented as long ago as 1988, when researchers noted that many families who would ordinarily seek shelter instead moved through a series of temporary accommodations with family members and friends, called "doubled-up" situations (Institute of Medicine, 1988, pp. 23–24). The instability of the "doubled-up" dwellings used by families living in transition is evident as these families seek refuge in the homes of impoverished rather than middle- or higher-income families (Bolland & McCallum, 2002). Thus, homeless families are borrowing resources from families who are already struggling with poverty.

Despite the problems, it is not surprising that many families prefer living in doubled-up situations rather than in shelters. First, compared to shelters for single adults, family shelters usually have fewer beds and allow longer stays (U.S. Department of Housing and Urban Development, 2007). Next, many family shelters prohibit admission of male adults and male children over the age of 12 or 13. As a result, two-parent families are forced to separate, and families with older male children are put in the untenable position of placing their sons elsewhere. Third, these initial barriers make shelters the refuge of last resort.

Most families entering shelters already have experienced long periods of instability and often have exhausted the goodwill of their family and friends. Family shelters provide communal living situations. Families must submit to a list of shelter rules, must participate in required activities with strangers who are in similarly stressful circumstances, and must parent their children and function while under the scrutiny of other parents and shelter caseworkers (Friedman, 2000). Also, disproportionately more parents who require homeless shelter placement, compared to other low-income parents, have substance abuse and mental health problems (Shinn et al., 1998). Parents suffering from such problems may feel compelled to hide their difficulties because of the very real fear of being watched, judged, and even reported to CPS.

On the other hand, living in homeless shelters has some advantages when compared to doubled-up situations. Families staying in doubled-up situations are virtually invisible, since providers of health and social services would need to ask the family members in order to determine a family's living situation. Entering a shelter signals the family's need and request for assistance, and many homeless shelters have case managers who can respond to those needs. Other parents also become resources for permanent housing, child care, and schools. Since many families entering homeless shelters arrive after long periods of transiency, the children and families have multiple physical and mental health concerns that require services (Bassuk, Rubin, & Lauriat, 1986; Burg, 1994; Hausman & Hammen, 1993; Rafferty & Shinn, 1991; Wood, Valdez, Hayashi, & Shen, 1990; Zima, Wells, & Freeman, 1994; Zlotnick, Kronstadt, & Klee, 1998). Additionally, children living in these transitional situations often have many unaddressed social and academic concerns that require assessment and follow-through (Bassuk & Rosenberg, 1990; Burg, 1994; Zima, Wells, & Freeman, 1994). Some shelters can address these needs, since they have connections to physical and mental health providers.

Not all shelters are the same. Leona remembered a shelter that provided social events, was immaculately clean, and had a warm family environment. Unfortunately, most others contained bunk beds in cold and dreary rooms, and were a chaotic maze of children and parents.

Shelters have different goals. Some enlist case managers to help families with their children's physical, psychological, social, and academic needs, and have assembled strong networks to a variety of systems and services with the goal of helping families gain independence and stability. Other shelters merely strive to provide temporary respite for homeless families and have very few resources to help families with other needs.

The variation in shelters reflects the absence of a governing body to oversee the vast number of private, public, and faith-based shelters, and the lack of service requirements for shelters. Of course, many of the shelters are funded solely through philanthropic donations and volunteers. Limited funding is reflected in the hours of shelter operation as well as the amount and quality of its services. Remarkably little research has focused on shelter quality and capabilities, with the exception of those designed for single individuals with substance abuse issues or mental illness (Tsemberis & Asmussen, 1999; Tsemberis, Gulcur, & Nakae, 2004). Moreover, although shelter admission is the single best indicator of homelessness and service need, few researchers have seized the opportunity to identify the optimal environments or types of services that family shelters need to facilitate family stability, function, parenting, or child development.

Homeless and Child Protection or Welfare Systems (CPS)

Transiency introduces other problems. For example, although homelessness is *not* a reason for a child's removal and placement in foster care, sequelae from extended periods of homelessness may have the appearance of child neglect. This problem is apparent when parents prioritize basic needs, such as food and shelter, above other needs, such as pediatrician appointments or teachers' meetings. Moreover, parents have difficulties obtaining transportation and this too creates obstacles to attending appointments or arriving at school on time. For older children, school tardiness or absenteeism may be a problem. These lapses clash with the definition of medical and educational neglect in the 1996 Child Abuse and Prevention Treatment Act (P.L. 104, 42 U.S.C. 5106h). Others, more conscious of the impact of poverty on family life, have added caveats to further refine the definition of child neglect as "the failure of the child's parent or caretaker, who has the material resources to do so, to provide minimally adequate care in the areas of health, nutrition, shelter, education, supervision, affection or attention and protection" (Wolock & Horowitz, 1984, p. 531). Still, it is not always clear to CPS or others which activities are the results of poverty and which are indicative of neglect.

Many studies have noted the high prevalence of out-of-home and foster care placements among children who once lived with their homeless families. More than three-quarters of homeless single women were mothers of children under 18 years old, but only 15% of minor-age children were living with their homeless parents (Burt et al., 1999). The other children were living elsewhere. In one county, almost half of the young children entering foster care had been removed from homeless parents (Zlotnick, Kronstadt, & Klee, 1998). Current evidence suggests that approximately 25% of homeless parents' children were in the foster care system (Park, Metraux, Brodbar, & Culhane, 2004; Zlotnick, Tam, & Bradley, 2007), while the other 75% were staying in out-of-home placements, including those that had been arranged by the homeless parents or their families.

Moving among shelters, doubled-up situations, and other transient living circumstances are extremely difficult for parents, but for children it can be frightening. Leona's story illustrated the trauma of entering a series of places, each of which had new rules, new people, and new routines. When formerly homeless children enter foster care, the one constant that they had in their lives, their parents, is removed. Sometimes children are placed with relatives or friends, but just as frequently they are placed with foster parents who are strangers to them. Children in foster care may move from one place to another. At each placement, the child must adjust to the new surroundings and the new caregivers. CPS has units that help with reunification and family maintenance, but no study has tabulated the prevalence of homeless parents who were offered these services or the outcomes that result.

The Mental Health System

Shortly after Leona's entry into foster care, she was referred to therapy because of multiple behavior problems. Children in transient, compared to stable, living situations are more apt to have behavioral and mental health concerns (McMillen et al., 2005; Zima, Wells, & Freeman, 1994). However, for children entering foster care, it is difficult to tease out whether the trauma and behavioral concerns exist as a result of the conditions before entry into foster care or as a result of entering foster care, which usually includes moving to a new location with new caregivers (Breslau, 2009; McCrae, 2009; Orfirer & Rian, 2008). Several jurisdictions have heeded the increasing evidence in the literature describing the trauma of transition and have instituted routine mental health screening for children entering foster care (Burns et al., 2004).

While foster care providers and the child welfare system are expanding their use of mental health services for children in the foster care system, there is little indication of a systematic effort to provide mental health screenings or treatment for children living in homeless families. In fact, among the homeless providers who have initiated behavioral care that melds primary care with mental health screenings, very few target homeless children and families (Weinreb, Nicholson, Williams, & Anthes, 2007).

Overall, obtaining access to mental health services continues to be a problem because of the scarcity of providers who accept public insurance (i.e., Medicaid) as well as the increasing numbers of children who need these services. Also, it is an unfortunate reality that many Medicaid-insured children receive mental health services from social work or psychology students. If there are no protocols in place to facilitate transfer from one student therapist to another, many children in the transient situations of foster care or homelessness who are receiving mental health services have experiences like Leona's, in which every year the child client must terminate with one student therapist and transition to another. This unfortunate pattern resembles the children's past history with its series of transitions and feelings of being discarded and abandoned by adults. Of course, client-therapist relationships also may be severed when the child is moved to a new placement.

The Criminal Justice System

Like Leona, many youth in foster care also have contact with the criminal justice system. An increasing number of reports suggests that among youth, those in foster care are at higher risk for sexual exploitation (Biehal & Wade, 2000; Estes & Weiner, 2001; MISSSEY, Inc., 2009). Many foster care youth recognize that they are merely temporary residents in someone else's home and, if the CPS caseworker feels justified or if the foster care parents feel the necessity, they could be removed at a moment's notice. Although dedicated foster care parents try to promote feelings of belonging, the precariousness of the living situation is clear, and many foster youth feel a void. They have no anchor to a person or a place. Without a strong connection, older youth are vulnerable to risky behaviors. Accordingly, prevalence rates of early sexual activity, substance abuse, dropping out of school, and even criminal activity are substantially higher among foster care youth than among other youth (Geenen & Powers, 2006; McMillen, Auslander, Elze, White, & Thompson, 2003; Pilowsky & Wu, 2006; Reilly, 2003). In fact, other Western countries as well as the United States have described this link between sexual exploitation and the feelings of connection that foster care children crave (Nixon, Tutty, Downe, Gorkoff, & Ursel, 2002).

Nola Brantley of MISSSEY, an agency in Oakland, California, that works with sexually exploited youth, describes the three-stage process by which vulnerable youth are lured by sexual predators as "the pimp game" (Brantley, 2008). It begins with the pimp providing a constant shower of attention, compliments, and gifts. The second stage is a combination of encouraging the youth to sever all ties to friends and relatives, and cementing the pimp's role as the sole, central, and most helpful figure in the individual's life. The third and final stage is forced prostitution. Predators are well aware of the vulnerability of foster care youth, and many former foster care and group home youth fall prey to sexual exploitation and criminal activity (Dunlap & Grady, 2008). Sexually exploited youth who have been placed in foster or group homes constitute a substantial proportion of street or runaway and homeless youth (Ringwalt, Greene, & Robertson, 1988).

Like Leona, a large number of female foster care youth have become pregnant teens (Dworsky, 2009), and pregnant teens face many challenges—social, economic, and psychological. However, pregnant teens who have grown up in foster care face a special set of challenges. Many have never experienced a regular family life where they can watch and learn from strong parent figures who guide, teach, and model positive behaviors for their children (Roman & Wolfe, 1995). This problem often is compounded by the lack of a parent or caregiver on whom foster care children can rely for needed resources, a helping hand, answers to questions, or a shoulder to cry on. A study using data from more than a decade ago found that homeless youth were almost 10 times more likely to become pregnant during their teenage years than youth in the general population (Ringwalt, Greene, & Robertson, 1998); no more recent statistics could be found on the prevalence rate of teen pregnancies among homeless youth.

There are activities such as the Transitional Living Program and services funded by the Runaway and Homeless Youth Act to help with school tutoring, job and living skills, and counseling. However, funds are limited and not all youth who need these services have access to them (Child & Youth Permanency Branch, 2007; National Center for Youth Law, 2006). Most programs target older teenagers (Child & Youth Permanency Branch, 2007; Geenen & Powers, 2007; National Center for Youth Law, 2006), which is problematic since, teenagers are at the developmental stage when they are becoming less reliant on adults and testing their own abilities to make life-changing decisions. By that time, many youth have already been lured into risky sexual and criminal activities.

Dueling Systems: Mental Health and Substance Abuse with Criminal Justice and Child Welfare

Leona's situation, having a childhood foster care history and a subsequent history of adulthood mental health and substance abuse problems, is not uncommon. Traumatic childhood events such as histories of foster care and running away are highly correlated with both substance abuse and mental health problems (Bassuk, Dawson, Perloff, & Weinreb, 2001; Caton et al., 2000; Shinn et al., 1998; Zlotnick, Robertson, & Wright, 1999; Zlotnick, Tam, & Robertson, 2003, 2004). Many homeless parents have histories of adverse childhood events such as physical abuse, sexual abuse, foster care placement, and long-term episodes of running away or being "thrown" away (Bassuk et al., 1997; Herman, Susser, Struening, & Link, 1997; Koegel, Melamid, & Burnam, 1995; Piliavin, Sosin, Westerfelt, & Matsueda, 1993; Susser, Lin, Conover, & Struening, 1991; Zlotnick, Robertson, & Wright, 1999).

Motherhood is a defining role for many women, including those who struggle with substance abuse and mental health problems (Coordinating Center of the SAMHSA Women Co-Occurring Disorders and Violence Study, 2000). For some, like Leona, it may even be the motivation for seeking treatment. Yet mothers suffering from addiction are in a complicated and risky situation. They know they need treatment; however, if they admit their substance abuse and request treatment, they could be reported to CPS and lose custody of their children. Consequently, it may be safer (i.e., less chance of losing custody) to *not* seek treatment. Of course, if their substance abuse continues, someone may find out and report them to CPS (Coordinating Center of the SAMHSA Women Co-Occurring Disorders and Violence Study, 2000). Unfortunately, there is no clear resolution to this "catch-22."

Adding to the dilemma are the paucity of resources and the quality of residential programs that accept state payment or Medicaid and are designed for mothers living with their children (Substance Abuse and Mental Health Services Administration—Office of Applied Studies, 2009). One important resource is the assistance with parenting, building and developing a relationship with one's children, and other child-related needs (Grella, 1997). Another issue is that not all substance abuse treatment programs are equipped to care for residents with mental health problems such as depression. As a result, mothers like Leona who have clinical conditions that would benefit from medication are faced with a dilemma. If they accept the medication, they may be ejected from the treatment program. If they opt *not* to take medication, it is possible that the symptoms of their condition may have an impact on their participation in individual or group therapies as well as on their ability to provide care for their children.

Although many clients need services from both mental health care and substance abuse systems, the two often have different perspectives on treatment. Mental health professionals diagnose illness and decide whether to provide any one or a combination of treatments, including individualized, group, or medication therapy. In contrast, many substance abuse providers operating residential programs use the 12-step model, which centers on the individual's recovery and the time needed for the substance's physiological and psychological effects to leave the body. The idea of ingesting medication, even prescribed medication, may not be acceptable. The conflict between these two approaches and the problems thus caused for individuals with the dual diagnoses of mental health problems and substance abuse disorders has been noted for more than a decade (Drake, McLaughlin, Pepper, & Minkoff, 1991; Drake, Osher, & Wallach, 1989).

THE FUTURE

Children and families living in the cycle of homelessness have many needs and come in contact with a wide variety of systems and services, but without a coordinated and integrated infrastructure for these systems, families will continue to suffer from the fragmented and confusing maze of services. The systems, and the services emanating from them, are well positioned to institute interventions for children living in these transitional situations; however, they face obstacles. The first obstacle, often initiated by federal, state, and county funding streams, is the existing philosophy of targeting a subgroup of children according to their temporary living situation, such as homelessness or foster care, despite the increasing literature demonstrating that many children and youth vacillate between these two kinds of living situations. This approach dooms children living in a transient situation to fragmented care. It is this very approach that we need to change.

Safety Net

Ostensibly, there is a safety net of providers ready to help impoverished individuals, families, and children. Within that safety net are many agencies dedicated to providing mental health and social services to children; however, very few consider the context of transiency in either their assessments or their interventions. Of the agencies that are experienced with providing care to children living in transitional situations, most target either children in foster care or those in homeless situations, but rarely both. Consequently, if treatment has begun for a child living in one type of transient situation (e.g., homeless), it may be terminated if the child's living situation changes (e.g., to foster care).

Entering a shelter or requesting a shelter bed, being in residential substance abuse treatment, and having contact with CPS are all indicators of family instability. Optimally, the first agency that comes into contact with homeless or foster care children will conduct a needs assessment on the family and on the child's physical, mental, and social condition. Since families have frequently experienced a series of moves through relatives' and friends' homes before they arrive at a homeless shelter, assessments conducted during the first few months may reflect the trauma of instability (Grant, 1991). Consequently, another assessment will be needed after the family achieves some stability in order to gain a more valid indicator of a child's status. Safety net providers must allow for the flexibility of conducting off-site visits and working in tandem with school officials to smooth a child's entry into the classroom, since behaviors may influence their school participation and learning.

Case Management

Ideally there will be a single, dedicated case manager who understands the overwhelming problems faced by families and who is able to identify and coordinate other agencies' services to ensure that the family members are not overwhelmed and that their needs are met. The case manager can: (1) provide an in-depth assessment of the families and the individual family members; (2) discuss the results of the assessment and enlist the family members to identify their goals; (3) organize needed wraparound services; and most importantly, (4) follow up on all services. Simply giving families the names of agencies where they can obtain assistance is not sufficient. Families living in transitional situations are in crisis. They are overwhelmed and they need support with referrals and follow-up.

Helping professionals play an important and difficult role. They must be clear on their messages, attuned to changes in the families' situations and ways of functioning, dogged at ensuring follow-up with needed resources, facile at negotiating systems, and insightful about when to pull back so the families' goals are heard and understood clearly. The constant need for assessment and reassessment of the situation is a challenge for case managers, who must be thoughtful as they decide whether they should push forward or wait patiently. Helping professionals listen carefully, are cognizant of the power and privilege of their position, and remember that they are being invited into the family as a guest and not as a family member. Pushing families too quickly can jeopardize the relationship. Simply providing the family with services, without providing them the skills to obtain the services themselves, may convey the idea to parents that they are being "rescued" rather than assisted. A better approach is for helping professionals to function as a guide who provides patient encouragement, helpful information, and support, while indicating possible options and opportunities. No matter the skill of the professional, families' abilities and willingness to work with new helping professionals vary, as does the use of resources. An effective case manager will be certain to keep any promises made, recognize the families' cues of being overwhelmed or confused, and adjust their assistance accordingly. Achieving this delicate balance takes not only experience and education but also a consistent attitude of collaboration and hopefulness.

Approach

Families in transition live in constant flux, often moving from crisis to crisis. Many families have experienced this lifestyle for generations. Yet, experiencing constant crises does not make those crises easier to bear or even increase the families' ability to handle them. Instead the family members become resigned to losing friends, connections, and familiar environments. They become isolated and less willing to use services or even request them. Agencies interested in working with this population must be patient, willing to endure missed or broken appointments, and able to engage a family who is mobile. The health or social service professional must recognize the importance of a family's history and experience, which may include hesitancy to obtain assistance, distrust of service professionals, and little interest in engaging or sustaining relationships with others. Consequently, making a connection with the family will be labor-intensive and time-consuming. For transitional families, obtaining stable housing is a priority, as families are more likely to take advantage of needed services if their most fundamental needs are met.

Still, the family's hesitance to obtain services and the geographic boundaries of some service agencies are not the largest impediment to providing care for families in transition. Rather, the approach of the health professionals can be the biggest obstacle. A trauma-informed approach is essential. A health or social service professional who is interested in helping families in transition will want to consider the family's current situation and past experiences. Most children and families living in the cycle of homelessness present with multiple risk factors and histories of trauma. When experiences like these are overlooked, minimized, or ignored, mistakes are made. For example, mental health providers may diagnose the child's behavior solely on the basis of the observed behavior without knowledge that the child has just moved to the fourth shelter in two years. Health professionals may assume that a medication for asthma was ineffective, when the reality was that the medication lost effectiveness due to a lack of refrigeration (not available at all shelters) or that a new shelter introduced exposure to new allergens.

The approach incorporates the needs and welfare of at least three entities: the family, the child, and the parent or caregiver. Family preservation is the goal, and safety is the overriding concern. Achieving a balance can be difficult, especially as there is an inherent dilemma with service professionals' requests that families divulge their history while the same professionals are "mandated reporters" of suspected abuse or neglect. This context explains the reason for parents' hesitancy and their choice to omit important details. At the same time, by not revealing certain details, families may not receive important help, and so the problems perpetuate themselves or fester. Effective prevention activities and more-informed policies are needed to address this dilemma.

To promote the first goal of family preservation, the mental health of the parent is of paramount importance. Mental health problems in parents, including depression or stress (e.g., post-traumatic stress disorder, or PTSD), are risk factors not only for the parent's well-being but also for the child's. In fact, problematic parental mental health has been identified as a leading cause of behavioral problems in children (Cummings & Davies, 1994). Conversely, in foster care, a child's behavioral concerns can exacerbate existing family problems, initiate stress, and increase placement instability (Collado & Levine, 2007; Kliman, 1996). A family-centered approach, one that supports the needs of the family unit, parent and child, is vital.

Chronic homelessness has been identified as the most costly situation among homeless people (Culhane & Kuhn, 1998), and recent legislation has assembled many systems to focus interventions to address the concerns that have resulted from years of trauma after long periods of acculturation into the homeless lifestyle. Evidence suggests that there are opportunities to halt the progression of problems. Currently, homeless families constitute at least one-third of all homeless people (U.S. Department of Housing and Urban Development, 2007), and there is no indication that this percentage will decrease.

A proactive approach recognizes that, like chronically homeless individuals, families living in transition have experienced multi-system failure. Therefore, any change will require addressing these multiple systems. Unlike the current situation, which is plagued with fragmented and disjointed care, this coordinated approach invokes systems to assemble and implement services when the transition occurs rather waiting for the eventual consequences. Optimally, services begin when a family first enters a shelter or a child enters foster care. The systems and service providers have the opportunity to prevent a series of additional traumas and to make a thorough assessment and coordinate needed services.

Promote Social Connections Through Groups or Peer-to-Peer Connection

Families and children in these transitional situations are more likely to be unattached to places and people. It seems unfathomable that lack of social connections is a problem that can have such dire effects, yet studies continue to demonstrate the importance of social connections with respect to mental health, physical morbidity, and mortality. The impact of social connection begins with infants, who develop a variety of behavioral concerns when they do not have the opportunity to bond and develop a secure attachment to their mothers. Socialization is vital among preschool and grade school children who learn from their peers. Youth who have few social connections are more likely to engage in risky or illegal behaviors, drop out of school, and experience mental health problems such as depression (Slesnick, Prestopnik, Meyers, & Glassman, 2007; Taylor, Stuttaford, Broad, & Vostanis, 2007).

Parents of transitional families tend to be isolated from their own parents and other parents who have been in the same situation. Studies of homeless parents have suggested that many homeless parents were raised in foster care or homeless situations, and did not experience good parenting themselves (Roman & Wolfe, 1995). Effective parents often recall their own experiences as children, watch others' parenting practices, and perhaps read books or attend classes. Most parents living in transition have not had these advantages. Parents living in transition need programs that provide peer-to-peer parenting or groups that disseminate effective parenting strategies to help them build stable families to prevent more children growing up in these stressful circumstances.

Recognizing the harm that social isolation causes youth, many programs are being designed for foster care and homeless youth 16 and older. Although the idea is laudable, the execution is problematic. The time to begin such programs is not during the late teens but much earlier, at grade school or even at preschool levels, since developmentally, younger children are interested in their world and in gaining mastery of it, whereas older teenagers are working to achieve independence from adults.

To change the outcomes of children living in transition, we must change our approach. The existing structure of two parallel, unconnected systems in which a temporary living situation (i.e., homeless shelter) dictates the services leads to disjointed and fragmented services, with no follow-up. The result is that families' needs go unaddressed and the children's trauma and behavioral problems fester. This neglect on the part of our systems perpetuates a downward spiral of social and mental health consequences for a child that promotes an intergenerational cycle of homelessness.

The first task is to ensure that governmental funding sources are inclusive, rather than designating funds for children on the basis of temporary living situations. Next, a coordinated approach needs to be implemented in order to identify families and children early, when they first enter the system, either from homeless shelters or through foster care (with undomiciled parents). The child welfare and homeless systems need to begin communicating with each other to create a collaborative system that works with children whether they live in a homeless situation or in a foster care home. A key element that is vital to success is the involvement of a skilled case manager who will coordinate the services and maintain follow-up for a family no matter what their living situation is.

The current and new generations of transitional families and their children are doomed to perpetuate the cycle of homelessness without long-term, focused interventions. The creation of a collaborative, early intervention approach will ensure that the homeless child of today will not become the foster care child of tomorrow and a homeless adult of the future.

REFERENCES

Bassuk, E., & Rosenberg, L. (1990). Psychosocial characteristics of homeless children and children with homes. *Pediatrics, 85*(3), 257–261.

Bassuk, E. L., Buckner, J. C., Weinreb, L. F., Browne, A., Bassuk, S. S., Dawson, R., et al. (1997). Homelessness in female-headed families: Childhood and adult risk and protective factors. *American Journal of Public Health, 87*(2), 241–248.

Bassuk, E. L., Dawson, R., Perloff, J. N., & Weinreb, L. (2001). Post-traumatic stress disorder in extremely poor women: Implications for health care clinicians. *Journal of the American Medical Women's Association, 56*(2), 79–85.

Bassuk, E. L., Rubin, L., & Lauriat, A. (1986). Characteristics of sheltered homeless families. *American Journal of Public Health, 76*(9), 1097–1101.

Biehal, N., & Wade, J. (2000). Going missing from residential and foster care: Linking biographies and context. *British Journal of Support, 30*(2), 211–225.

Bolland, J. M., & McCallum, M. (2002). Touched by homelessness: An examination of hospitality for the down and out. *American Journal of Public Health, 92*(1), 116–118.

Brantley, N. (2008, June). *Teenage prostitution: Understanding commercial sexual exploitation of children.* Paper presented at the Continuing Education Conference for Mental Health, Children's Hospital & Research Center, Oakland, CA.

Breslau, N. (2009). Trauma and mental health in U.S. inner-city populations. *General Hospital Psychiatry, 31*, 501–502.

Burg, M. A. (1994). Health problems of sheltered homeless women and their dependent children. *Health and Social Work, 19*(2), 125–131.

Burns, B. J., Phillips, S. D., Wagner, H. R., Barth, R. P., Kolko, D. J., Campbell, Y., et al. (2004). Mental health need and access to mental health services by youths involved with child welfare: A national survey. *Journal of the American Academy of Child and Adolescent Psychiatry, 43*(8), 960–970.

Burt, M. R., Aron, L. Y., Douglas, T., Valente, J., Lee, E., & Iwen, B. (1999). *Homelessness: Programs and the people they serve.* Findings of the National Survey of Homeless Assistance Providers and Clients. Washington, DC: Urban Institute.

Caton, C. L. M., Hasin, D., Shrout, P. E., Opler, L. A., Hirshfield, S., Dominguez, B., et al. (2000). Risk factors for homelessness among indigent urban adults with no history of psychotic illness: A case-control study. *American Journal of Public Health, 90*(2), 258–263.

Child and Youth Permanency Branch. (2007). *Transitional Housing Program for Emancipated Foster/Probation Youth (THP-Plus).* Retrieved February 8, 2008, from http://www.childsworld.ca.gov/PG1353.htm.

Collado, C., & Levine, P. (2007). Reducing transfers of children in family foster care through onsite mental health interventions. *Child Welfare, 86*(5), 133–150.

Coordinating Center of the SAMHSA Women Co-Occurring Disorders and Violence Study. (2000). Parenting issues for women with co-occurring mental health and substance abuse disorders who have histories of trauma. Women, Co-occurring Disorders and Violence Study. Retrieved March 20, 2013, from http://www.nationaltraumaconsortium.org/documents/Parenting FactSheet.pdf.

Culhane, D. P., & Kuhn, R. (1998). Patterns and determinants of public shelter utilization among homeless adults in New York City and Philadelphia. *Journal of Policy Analysis and Management, 17*(1), 23–43.

Cummings, E. M., & Davies, P. T. (1994). Maternal depression and child development. *Journal of Child Psychology and Psychiatry, 35*(1), 73–112.

Drake, R. E., McLaughlin, P., Pepper, B., & Minkoff, K. (1991). Dual diagnosis of major mental illness and substance disorder: An overview. *New Directions for Mental Health Services, 50*(Summer), 3–12.

Drake, R. E., Osher, F. C., & Wallach, M. A. (1989). Alcohol use and abuse in schizophrenia: A prospective community study. *Journal of Nervous and Mental Disease, 177*(7), 408–414.

Dunlap, K., & Grady, B. (2008, April 21). Oakland pimps prey on youth. MercuryNews.com.

Dworsky, A. (2009). *Preventing pregnancy among youth in foster care.* Paper presented at the Congressional Roundtable with Senator Mary Landrieu.

Estes, R. J., & Weiner, N. A. (2001). *The commercial sexual exploitation of children in the U.S., Canada and Mexico.* Philadelphia: University of Pennsylvania.

Friedman, D. H. (2000). *Parenting in public.* New York: Columbia University Press.

Geenen, S., & Powers, L. E. (2006). Are we ignoring youths with disabilities in foster care? An examination of their school performance. *Social Work, 51*(3), 233–241.

——. (2007). "Tomorrow is another problem": The experiences of youth in foster care during their transition to adulthood. *Children and Youth Services Review, 29*, 1085–1101.

Grant, R. (1991). The special needs of homeless children: Early intervention at a welfare hotel *Topics in Early Childhood Special Education, 10*(4), 76–91.

Grella, C. (1997). Services for perinatal women with substance abuse and mental health disorders: The unmet need. *Journal of Psychoactive Drugs, 29*(1), 67–78.

Hausman, B., & Hammen, C. (1993). Parenting in homeless families: The double crisis. Homeless women: Economic and social issues [Special section]. *American Journal of Orthopsychiatry, 63*(3), 358–369.

Herman, D. B., Susser, E. S., Struening, E. L., & Link, B. L. (1997). Adverse childhood experiences: Are they risk factors for adult homelessness? *American Journal of Public Health, 87*(2), 249–255.

Institute of Medicine. (1988). *Homelessness, health, and human needs.* Washington, DC: National Academies Press.

Kliman, G. (1996). The personal life history book: A psychoanalytically based intervention. *Journal for the Psychoanalysis of Culture and Society, 1*(2), 159–162.

Koegel, P., Melamid, E., & Burnam, M. A. (1995). Childhood risk factors for homelessness among homeless adults. *American Journal of Public Health*, *85*(12), 1642–1649.

McCrae, J. S. (2009). Emotional and behavioral problems reported in child welfare over 3 years. *Journal of Emotional and Behavioral Disorders*, *17*(1), 17–28.

McMillen, C., Auslander, W., Elze, D., White, T., & Thompson, R. (2003). Educational experiences and aspirations of older youth in foster care. *Child Welfare*, *82*(4), 475–495.

McMillen, J. C., Zima, B. T., Scott, L. D., Auslander, W. F., Munson, M. R., Ollie, M. T., et al. (2005). Prevalence of psychiatric disorders among older youths in the foster care system. *Journal of the American Academy of Child and Adolescent Psychiatry*, *44*(1), 88–95.

MISSSEY, Inc. (2009). *Framing the issue of the commercial sexual exploitation of children*. MISSSEY (Motivating, Inspiring, Supporting, and Serving Sexually Exploited Youth), Inc.

National Center for Youth Law. (2006). *Broken promises: California's inadequate and unequal treatment of its abused and neglected children*. Oakland, CA: Author.

Nixon, K., Tutty, L., Downe, P., Gorkoff, K., & Ursel, J. (2002). The everyday occurrence: Violence in the lives of girls exploited through prostitution. *Violence Against Women*, *8*, 1016–1043.

Orfirer, K., & Rian, J. C. (2008). Mental health treatment of infants and toddlers: Creating an integrated system of care for infants and toddlers in the child welfare system. *The Source*, *18*(1), 1–6.

Park, J. M., Metraux, S., Brodbar, G., & Culhane, D. P. (2004). Child welfare involvement among children in homeless families. *Child Welfare*, *83*(5), 423–436.

Piliavin, I., Sosin, M., Westerfelt, A. H., & Matsueda, R. L. (1993). The duration of homeless careers: An exploratory study. *Social Service Review* (December), 577–598.

Pilowsky, D. J., & Wu, L.-T. (2006). Psychiatric symptoms and substance use disorders in a nationally representative sample of American adolescents involved with foster care. *Journal of Adolescent Health*, *38*(4), 351–358.

Public Law No. 104 (42 U.S.C. 5106h). (1996). *Child Abuse Prevention and Treatment Act: Definition Section 110*. 104th U.S. Congress, 2nd Session.

Rafferty, Y., & Shinn, M. (1991). The impact of homelessness on children. *American Psychologist*, *46*(11), 1170–1179.

Reilly, T. (2003). Transition from care: Status and outcomes of youth who age out of foster care. *Child Welfare, 82*(6), 727–746.

Ringwalt, C. L., Greene, J. M., & Robertson, M. J. (1998). Familial backgrounds and risk behaviors of youth with thrownaway experiences. *Journal of Adolescence, 21*, 241–252.

Roman, N. P., & Wolfe, P. B. (1995). *Web of failure: The relationship between foster care and homelessness.* Washington, DC: National Alliance to End Homelessness.

Shinn, M., Weitzman, B. C., Stojanovic, D., Knickman, J. R., Jimenez, L., Duchon, L., et al. (1998). Predictors of homelessness among families in New York City: From shelter request to housing stability. *American Journal of Public Health, 88*(11), 1651–1657.

Slesnick, N., Prestopnik, J. L., Meyers, R. J., & Glassman, M. (2007). Treatment outcome for street-living, homeless youth. *Addictive Behaviors, 32*(6), 1237–1251.

Substance Abuse and Mental Health Services Administration. Office of Applied Studies. (October 22, 2009). *The N-SSATS Report: Residential Substance Abuse Treatment Facilities Offering Residential Beds for Clients' Children.* Rockville, MD. Retrieved March 20, 2013, from http://www.samhsa.gov/data/2k9/219/219ResChildBeds2k9Web.pdf.

Susser, E. S., Lin, S. P., Conover, S. A., & Struening, E. L. (1991). Childhood antecedents of homelessness in psychiatric patients. *American Journal of Psychiatry, 148*(8), 1026–1030.

Taylor, H. C., Stuttaford, M. C., Broad, B., & Vostanis, P. (2007). Listening to service users: Young homeless people's experiences of new mental health service. *Journal of Child Health Care, 11*(3), 221–230.

Tsemberis, S., & Asmussen, S. (1999). From streets to homes: The pathways to housing consumer preference supported housing model. *Alcoholism Treatment Quarterly, 17*(1/2), 113–131.

Tsemberis, S., Gulcur, L., & Nakae, M. (2004). Housing first, consumer choice, and harm reduction for homeless individuals with a dual diagnosis. *American Journal of Public Health, 94*(4), 651–656.

U.S. Department of Housing and Urban Development. (2007). *The annual homeless assessment report to Congress (AHAR).* Washington, DC: Office of Community Planning and Development.

Weinreb, L., Nicholson, J., Williams, V., & Anthes, F. (2007). Integrating behavioral health services for the homeless mothers and children in primary care. *American Journal of Orthopsychiatry, 77*(1), 142–152.

Wolock, I & Horowitz, B. (1984). Child maltreatment as a social problem: The neglect of neglect. *American Journal of Orthopsychiatry, 54*(4), 530–543.

Wood, D., Valdez, R. B., Hayashi, T., & Shen, A. (1990). Homeless and housed families in Los Angeles: A study comparing demographic, economic, and family function characteristics. *American Journal of Public Health, 80*(9), 1049–1052.

Zima, B. T., Wells, K. B., & Freeman, H. E. (1994). Emotional and behavioral problems and severe academic delays among sheltered homeless children in Los Angeles County. *American Journal of Public Health, 84*(2), 260–264.

Zlotnick, C., Kronstadt, D., & Klee, L. (1998). Foster care children and family homelessness. *American Journal of Public Health, 88*(9), 1368–1370.

Zlotnick, C., Robertson, M. J., & Wright, M. (1999). The impact of childhood foster care and other out-of-home placement on homeless women and their children. *Child Abuse and Neglect, 23*(11), 1057–1068.

Zlotnick, C., Tam, T., & Bradley, K. (2007). Adulthood trauma, separation from one's children, and homeless mothers. *Community Mental Health Journal, 43*(1), 20–33.

Zlotnick, C., Tam, T. W., & Robertson, M. (2003). Substance use and separation of homeless mothers from their children. *Addictive Behaviors, 28*(8), 1373–1383.

——. (2004). Adverse childhood events, substance abuse, and measures of affiliation. *Addictive Behaviors, 29*(6), 1177–1181.

CONTRIBUTORS

EDITOR

CHERYL ZLOTNICK, RN, DrPH, has worked over the past 25 years as a clinical nurse specialist, program coordinator, evaluator, director, and scientist to promote the health and well-being of children and families living in homeless or transitional situations. Findings from her studies have been reported at international conferences and in professional journals.

CONTRIBUTING AUTHORS

LISA R. BERNDT, LCSW, grew up in an Air Force family, studied history at Duke University, education at Trinity University, and social work at California State University in Sacramento. She received a postgraduate diploma in narrative therapy and is a founding member of the Bay Area Partnership for Social Justice.

LUANN DEVOSS, PhD, has served as clinical director of the Center for the Vulnerable Child since 2008. She provides clinical oversight of mental health services to children who are homeless, or potentially homeless. Her specialties include severe adult mental illness, co-occurring disorders, brief strategic family therapy, infant mental health, and trauma-informed treatment.

LOU FELIPE, PhD, is a clinical psychologist with a focus on serving children, adolescents, and families from underserved and under-resourced communities. She earned her doctorate at Alliant International University, California School of Professional Psychology. Currently, she lives and works in San Francisco.

VANCE HITCHNER, PhD, is a licensed clinical psychologist who has worked at the Center for the Vulnerable Child since 1998. He received his doctorate from the Wright Institute in Berkeley, California. He directs the CATS Project, which provides home-based mental health services to dependent youth living with their parent(s).

ROSARIO MURGA-KUSNIR, MFT, is a licensed marriage and family therapist born and raised in Mexico City. She provides therapy to children and families in the SEED program at the Center for the Vulnerable Child, and also maintains a private practice as a bilingual therapist.

KATHRYN ORFIRER, PhD, directs the clinical SEED program, an infant mental health/child welfare/public health nursing collaborative. She specializes in infant mental health and best practices for infants, toddlers, and families in the dependency system. She also consults and trains on issues related to this population for a variety of professional audiences.

PEGGY PEARSON, MFT, is the director of the Family Outreach Support Clinic, a clinic designed to meet the complex medical, developmental, and mental health needs of children who have had contact with the child welfare system. She also leads an adoption support group and conducts many different continuing education trainings.

ROBERTO MACIAS SANCHEZ, MFT, a veteran with a master's degree in counseling psychology from the Wright Institute in Berkeley, California, works to improve the overall psycho-emotional development of preschool children living in homeless, foster care, or at-risk families. He also presents workshops on child-related topics.

KAREN THOMAS, LCSW, has worked with, and on behalf of, young children involved in the child welfare system since 1988, in child welfare, mental health, and research roles. She joined the staff of the Center for the Vulnerable Child in 1993. She has previously published on child welfare research topics.

ERICA TORRES, PsyD, is a bilingual/bicultural Chicana clinical psychologist and clinical supervisor in the SEED program. When providing psychological treatment for disadvantaged populations (including Latina/o individuals, families and children, and lesbian, gay, bisexual, transgender, queer, and questioning youth), she uses an attachment-based, family systems, and social justice theoretical framework.

MARGUERITE A. WRIGHT, EdD, is a senior clinical psychologist at the Center for the Vulnerable Child. She received her doctorate in human development from Harvard University. She is the author of *I'm Chocolate, You're Vanilla: Raising Healthy Black and Biracial Children in a Race-Conscious World*.

format, issues in use of, 74–76; cultural strategic plan, work groups for, 79–80; culture and power in, 66–69; current status, 80–81; desire for, 71–74; Handbook for Cultural Responsiveness and Accountability, 79; overview, 65–66; racism in, 72–74; statement of commitment, 80; Task Force for Cultural Responsiveness and Accountability, 76–80, 86, 92, 95; values, operationalization of, 69–70; white supervisor in, 70–71; women of color at, 71–72, 74–75

Center for the Vulnerable Child (CVC), relationship building in, 84–103: appreciation certificates, 87, 89; emotional intelligence, cultivation of, 99–100; fairness in life event acknowledgments, 90–91; at the individual level, 92–102; monthly staff meetings, changes to, 89; positive work environment (PWE) work group, 86, 87–92; positive work relationships, rediscovering, 85–86; power dynamics in, 87–88; reflective supervision, 97–99; relationship problems, origins of, 85–86, 88–89; within the SEED program, 93–102; self-care baskets, 91; summary, 102–103

Central America, emigration from, 127

Cervantes, W., 133

CFS (Alameda County Social Services Agency, Department of Children and Family Services), 47, 122, 165, 170

Chandler, M. J., 50

Chang, H. N., 127

change, in organizations. *See* Center for the Vulnerable Child (CVC), change in

Chapin Hall Center for Children, 9, 47

Chen, L., 49

Cheng, T., 24, 26

child abuse, 154, 178

Child Abuse and Prevention Treatment Act (Public Law No. 104), 211

Child and Youth Permanency Branch, 215

child development centers (CDCs), 140

child neglect, 129, 211–12

child-parent psychotherapy, 124, 130–32

child protective services (CPS), 46–47, 122, 165, 170, 211–12. *See also* child welfare systems

children (general): anxieties of, 126; development of, nature vs. nurture in, 154; early stimulation, 151–52; initial school experiences, 139; language as source of identity, 127; love and affection, necessity for, 150–51; negative self-images, 138; social skills development, 153–54; talking to, importance of, 151–52

children in transitional families: characteristics, 4–5, 139; child-parent psychotherapy, treatment modalities, 124, 130–32; feelings, importance of, 146; insensitivity to problems of, 144–45; listening to voices of, 45; nurturing environments for, 154; problems faced by, ix–xi; resources, access to, x. *See also* Center for the Vulnerable Child; child welfare system; foster care; infant mental health; parenting; SPARK program; transitional families

children of color, 47–48, 117

Children's Bureau, 4, 5, 9, 168, 169, 171

Children's Hospital and Research Center Oakland (CHRCO), 47, 164

child welfare systems: children from immigrant families in, 120–34; child welfare workers, 198; collaboration with, in CATS Project, 197–99; disproportionality children of color in, 47–48; disproportionality of infants in, 49; homelessness, interaction with, 211–12; presumptions of, 187; psychological research, recognition of, 52; therapeutic trust, effects on establishment of, 191–92

child with family or peers (microsystem), 10, 11, 12

Chisom, R., 72, 73

CHRCO (Children's Hospital and Research Center Oakland), 47, 164

churches, corporal discipline, role in use of, 30, 33–34, 38

Hayashi, T., 6, 210
Hays, Pamela, 66, 74, 86
Head Start programs, 140
health service professionals. *See* clinicians;
 service professionals
health status, relationship to homelessness,
 152–53
health system (exosystem), 10, 11, 12
Heffron, M. C., 100
Hemmeter, M. L., 139
Herman, D. B., 215
Hernandez Jozefowicz-Simbeni, D. M., 152
heterosexual dominance, 70
hierarchy of needs theory (Maslow), 14
Hill, R. B., 47, 48
Hinton, L., 24
Hispanics. *See* people of color
Hoefer, M., 129
Hoffman, K., 100, 121
Holland, J., 176
homeless families. *See* transitional families
homelessness: effects of, 152; extent of
 families experiencing, 220; as factor
 in foster care placements, 176; health
 status, relationship to, 152–53; homelessness–foster care cycle, 4; nutrition,
 relationship to, 149–50; resources, scarcity of, 148–49; subsequent to foster
 care, xi. *See also* children in transitional
 families
homeless shelters, 3, 205, 209–210, 210–11
Horn, I., 24, 26
Horowitz, B., 212
hospitals, racism in reporting of abuse and
 neglect, 47–48
Humphreys, K., 55
hyper-arousal, 156

IEP (individualized education planning)
 meetings, 142–43
IJzendoorn, M. H., 52
illegal immigration, 120
immigrant families, 120–34; border crossings, trauma of, 127–28; children in
 foster care, 5; lack of services for, x–xi;
 obtaining information about, 122–23;
 relationship building with, 123–25;

summary, 133–34; therapeutic process
 for, 130–32
implicit (procedural) knowledge, 100
individualized education planning (IEP)
 meetings, 142–43
infant mental health, 44–58; Bronfenbrenner's Ecological Model and, 51;
 child welfare system, disproportionality
 of children of color in, 47–48; intergenerational transmission, 51–52; SEED
 program, 47, 48–49, 50–51, 53; social
 justice, integration with, 48; social justice perspective on, 53–58; Stella Martinez's story, 44–47
infants and toddlers, 49–50, 53
Inkelas, M., 25
Institute of Medicine, 209
intergenerational patterns: of homelessness,
 222; multigenerational complex trauma,
 186–87, 194–97; in parenting, 46, 221;
 in people of color, 70; poverty as reason
 for transitional situations, ix; of trauma,
 10, 51–52, 175; in violence, 158
interventions, culturally accountable, 48
interventions (SPARK program), 141–43
involuntary child placement, 4
ISMS Conference, 77
Israel, N., 152
Ivins, B., 100, 132

Jackson, H., 25
Jackson, V., 70
Johnson, Debbie (CATS treatment case),
 195, 197
Johnson family (CATS treatment case), 189
Johnson, R. E., 6
Joseph, G. E., 139
Joseph, J., 24, 26

Kabat-Zinn, Jon, 99
Kaplan, N., 52
Kaplow, J. B., 190, 192, 196
Karen, R., 151, 155, 157
Kelley, M., 25, 26, 27, 28
Kendagor, R., 144–145
Kinniburgh, K. M., 11, 16, 196
Kinsler, P. J., 188

Rao, S., 100
Ray (Leona's friend), 206–207
Ray, N., 9
reconciliation homes, 34, 39
reflective supervision, 97–99
Regalado, M., 25, 26, 33
Reilly, T., 214
relationships: impact on child development, 33; in organizations (*see* Center
for the Vulnerable Child [CVC],
relationship building in); relationship-
based treatment, 189–91. *See also* attach-
ment, parent-child
religion, as factor in use of corporal disci-
pline, 26, 29–30, 38
removals, 172
resiliency of children experiencing trauma,
113–16
reunification of families in foster care system, 48, 123–24
Rian, J. C., 93, 122, 213
Rice, J., 24
Richards, M., 8
Richman, A., 27
Ringwalt, C. L., 4, 214
Rink, E., 114
risk factors, impact of, 10
Risko, V. J., 145
Risley, T. R., 151
Roberto (Mayra's father), 126, 129–33
Roberts, D. E., 48, 215
Robertson, M. J., 214, 215
Rog, D. J., 6
Roman, N. P., 214, 221
Rosenberg, L., 6, 152, 210
Rosner, D., 5
routines, importance of, 13
Rubin, L., 210
rules, corporal discipline and obedience
to, 30–31
Rytina, N., 129

safety issues, 15, 68, 112–13
safety net, future vision of, 217
Salovey, P., 99
Saltzman, W., 186, 197
Sameroff, A. J., 50
Sanchez, R. M., 14

Sanchez-Hueles, J., 25, 27
Sareen, H., 25
Saxe, G. N., 190, 192, 196
Scaramella, L. V., 157
scarcity of resources in homelessness,
148–49
school attendance, 18
school experiences, children's initial, 139
School of Public Health, University of
California at Berkeley, 77
school suspensions, 25, 36
schools, 33–34, 114
Schorr, E. L., 6
Schultz, D., 48
Sedlak, A., 26, 48
SEED program. *See* Services to Enhance
Early Development (SEED) program
self-awareness, 99–100
self-care baskets, 91
self-regulation, 17, 18, 194–95, 196
Seligman, S., 100
Seng, J. S., 16
service agencies, collaboration among, xi
service professionals, 14–15, 18–19, 33–34,
35–36. *See also* clinicians
Services to Enhance Early Development
(SEED) program: about, 47, 93; Bronfenbrenner's Ecological Model, use of,
51; Goodman's principles, use of, 55–58;
immigrant families, assistance to, 122–23;
infant mental health perspective, 48–49;
mission of, 55; multidisciplinary approach,
50; multigenerational advocacy, 53;
relationship building within, 93–102;
therapy, locations for, 124; transitioning
process for children in foster care, 132
sexism, 69–70
sexual abuse, 172
sexual exploitation of foster care youth,
213–14
shame, 110, 111, 190
Shapiro, V., 50, 51, 52, 95, 121
shared power (Goodman principle), 56
Shark Music, 100
Sharples, T., 154
shelters (homeless shelters), 3, 205, 209–
210, 210–11
Shen, A., 6, 210